Archaeology to Delight and Instruct

D1610511

One World Archaeology Series
Sponsored by the World Archaeological Congress
Series Editors: Joan Gero, Mark Leone, and Robin Torrence

One World Archaeology volumes contain carefully edited selections of the exemplary papers presented at the World Archaeology Congress (WAC), held every four years, and intercongress meetings. The subject matter of this series is wide-ranging, reflecting the diverse interests of WAC. WAC gives place to considerations of power and politics in framing archaeological questions and results. The organization also gives place and privilege to minorities who have often been silenced or regarded as beyond capable of making main line contributions to the field. All royalties from the series are used to help the wider work of WAC, including providing the means for less advantaged colleagues to attend WAC conferences, thereby enabling them to contribute to the development of the academic debate surrounding the study of the past. Beginning with volume 48, the One World Archaeology series will be published by Left Coast Press, Inc.

Archaeology to Delight and Instruct

Active Learning in the University Classroom

Heather Burke
Claire Smith
editors

Left Coast Press Inc.

Walnut Creek, California

Left Coast Press Inc.

LEFT COAST PRESS, INC.
1630 North Main Street, #400
Walnut Creek, CA 94596
http://www.LCoastPress.com

Library of Congress Cataloging-in-Publication Data

Archaeology to delight and instruct : active learning in the university classroom / Heather Burke, Claire Smith, editors.
    p. cm. — (One world archaeology series ; v. 49)
    Includes bibliographical references and index.
    ISBN-13: 978-1-59874-256-5 (hardcover : alk. paper)
    ISBN-13: 978-1-59874-257-2 (paperback : alk. paper)
    ISBN-10: 1-59874-256-6 (hardcover : alk. paper)
    ISBN-10: 1-59874-257-4 (paperback : alk. paper)
1. Archaeology—Study and teaching (Higher) 2. Active learning. 3. College teaching—Philosophy. 4. Archaeology—Study and teaching (Higher)—Activity programs. I. Burke, Heather, 1966- II. Smith, Claire, 1957-
    CC83.A73 2007
    930.1071—dc22

2006031669

Editoral Production: Last Word Editorial Services
Typesetting: ibid, northwest

Printed in the United States of America

♾™The paper used in this publication meets the minimum requirements of American National Standard for Information Sciences—Permanence of Paper for Printed Library Materials, ANSI/NISO Z39.48–1992.

07 08 09 10 11 5 4 3 2 1

For John Schafer and John Fisher,
teachers who delight while they instruct

CONTENTS

Lectures as Usual?
Teaching Archaeology for Fun

Claire Smith and Heather Burke

Speaking in the first century AD, the Roman author Horace argued that the purpose of literature is 'to delight and to instruct' (Pinker 2004). While this demonstrates that there has long been a link between learning and enjoyment, in archaeology at the early 21st century this link *is* being considered with renewed interest. A recognition that normal classroom teaching can alienate students from the teacher – prompting them to see themselves 'as fellow captives under the never-distant teacher's eye' (McClure 1990: 67) – has brought about a new concern with creating alternative classroom environments that encourage students not only to contribute and collaborate, but also to enjoy themselves. Recently, the idea that learning can combine serious intent with fun content has become a mainstay of the active learning movement. Active learning – in essence any instructional strategy opposed to the passive consumption of lecture material – incorporates all four modes of learning behavior (auditory, visual, kinaesthetic, and tactile) to enhance the ways in which students learn. It can include listening practices which help the students to absorb what they hear, short writing exercises in which students react to lecture material, and complex group exercises in which students apply course material to 'real life' situations and problems (Paulson and Faust 1998: 3). When students actively participate in teaching and learning, they are more likely to retain information, are better equipped to process new information and solve new problems (Jenkins 1992; McKeachie 1999), and are more likely to become emotionally engaged with the material (Coco *et al* 2001: 501). Moreover, and perhaps most importantly, they are more likely to enjoy themselves. Play is a powerful motivational tool. It is nonthreatening and memorable, and in the process of interacting with the teacher and each other, play can facilitate students' intellectual engagement with theoretical material that is otherwise difficult to access:

> Besides setting our students serious work in collaborative ways, we must challenge them to have fun in class, to entertain one another, to make each other laugh – in short to play. Play provides the student with immediate reasons to be involved and to spend genuine effort on the class's endeavours; play is a source of motivation that does not depend on the student's farsighted understanding ... if students and teachers can make games their work, they open the door to learning at the easiest possible place (McClure 1990: 67–68).

Active learning is not the one-time adoption of a card game or a debate in an otherwise passive classroom format. Rather, it is part of an overall classroom environment that aims to foster interaction between four key areas of learning behaviour: participation, imagination, exploration, and collaboration. An emphasis on participation recognizes that instruction is enhanced through students being actively involved in the learning process through activity, discussion, challenge, and engagement (and the sometimes negatively perceived corollaries: noise, movement, and change). Such engagement, however, is best motivated by stimulating students' imaginations and allowing them to create their own solutions to puzzling, ambiguous, or paradoxical problems. Through this students are able to explore their own personal values, beliefs, and attitudes, and the course material can be tied to their own lives and to contemporary social issues. Collaboration requires that students take some responsibility for their own learning and, in doing so, help to create the learning environment.

The four main types of active learning relevant to this volume are cooperative learning, collaborative learning, problem-based learning, and guided discovery (Florida State University 2002: 9, 12; Paulson and Faust 1998: 3; Mayer 2003: 287–88). Cooperative learning assigns complex tasks to groups of students and requires all group members to work together to complete the task (Paulson and Faust 1998: 4). Students have the opportunity to develop a variety of interpersonal and small-group social skills, including the ability to lead, develop trusting relationships, make decisions, resolve conflicts, and communicate effectively. Cooperative group work challenges the students to analyze phenomena, solve problems, apply theories, exercise judgment, or perform some combination of these activities. Collaborative learning places the instructor and the students on an equal footing, working together in, for example, designing assignments, choosing texts, or presenting material to the class (Paulson and Faust 1998: 4). Problem-based learning begins with a problem that has no clear-cut, absolute answer, thus reflecting the complexity of real-world situations (Florida State University 2002: 8–12). Guided discovery draws learners into a cumulative process of finding out information and 'discovering' answers for themselves, albeit through the guidance provided by the teacher. Both problem-based learning and guided discovery encourage the student to explore information resources other than the teacher, including primary documents, reference materials, the Internet, or community members, and to draw on knowledge from external subject areas in the process of learning. Regardless of which approach is followed, one of the keys to active learning is to engage students in the learning process – to make them into equal participants in the search for knowledge, rather than passive recipients of information, and to encourage them to construct and contribute to their own learning. The best way to envisage active learning in the classroom is to concentrate on the processes rather than the products of learning, although this is not a position advocated universally. Active learning redefines classroom practice from a static view in which knowledge is poured into the passive minds of student learners, to a dynamic exchange in which project-based, problem-based, and collaborative activities help students to create the learning environment as they participate in it (see Silberman 1998).

This book is our attempt to take this philosophy and apply it to the teaching of archaeology at a college or university level. In doing so, it explores ways to integrate the formal process of teaching the theoretical issues of archaeology with the potential to have fun in the university classroom. Archaeology is particularly well suited to adopting active-learning strategies. Like many other humanities-based subjects, the contemporary social issues surrounding archaeology promote critical thinking, problem solving, and oral communication, because the students' diverse voices, interpretations, and ideas can be brought to bear on the process of teaching and learning. Innovations such as the M.A.T.R.I.X. (Making Archaeology Teaching Relevant in the XXIst Century) project are dedicated to demonstrating how teaching strategies can be tied into topical areas of social relevance and the real-world problem solving that is so essential to effective active learning (www.indiana.edu/~arch/saa/matrix/).

A cyber-dimension to active learning in archaeology is also beginning to be tapped. In recent years rapid developments in multimedia technology have introduced new ways of interacting with students through the creation of on-line communities (eg virtual-museums and WebCT), stimulating the quest for knowledge through 3D reconstructions of ancient monuments, buildings, or artifacts, and catalyzing the imagination through the unique combination of delivery modes that multimedia offers (eg virtual reality interactive systems which allow users to interact with models of sites or artifacts) (Barceló *et al* 2000; Forte

1997). Technology can play an important role in ensuring that learning is the result of both cooperation and the production of new knowledge in new media for audiences beyond the four walls of the classroom, making both course content and student work more interactive. Because the practice of archaeology routinely ties to controversial contemporary ethical issues such as responsible practice, repatriation, ownership, and the politics of control, it can be used in many ways to encourage students to forge links between current, real-world scenarios and aspects of their own emerging professional lives.

ARCHAEOLOGY, THEORY, AND ACTIVE LEARNING

In seeking to integrate active learning concepts into our classrooms, we were puzzled at the lack of imaginative teaching exercises available in the archaeological literature. Although such teaching manuals exist in other disciplines (notably sociology, see for example Singleis 1998), the closest equivalent in archaeology were a number of useful manuals focusing on exercises teaching laboratory and field techniques (eg *The Archaeologist's Laboratory* [Banning, 2000]; *The Archaeology Workbook* [Daniels and David, 1982]; *The Next Archaeology Workbook* [David and Driver, 1989]; *Doing Archaeology: A Hands-On Laboratory Manual* [Rice, 1997], *Doing Historical Archaeology* [Barber, 1994], and *Exercises in Archaeological Methods* [Savage and Dinsmore, 1998]). In terms of theory, several excellent introductory textbooks, including Hodder's (1999) *The Archaeological Process*, Johnson's (1999) *Archaeological Theory*, and Gamble's (2001) *Archaeology: the Basics*, as well as Praetzellis' (2000) innovative and popular introduction to archaeological theory, *Death by Theory,* were available, but nothing which contained active, practical exercises for conveying these theoretical concepts to a class of students. We knew that a wealth of information must exist out there in other people's classrooms, but could find no venue for accessing this information, much less sharing it with others.

In part, the problem may lie with the artificial dichotomy created between 'thinking' and 'doing' that reinforces a perception of 'active learning' as something more appropriate to conveying method rather than theory. Theory is often seen as a pursuit that is divorced from 'real' life – despite the often intuitive realization that how we think about things is conditioned by the social and cultural contexts in which we come to know them. As a complex and often deeply philosophical topic that requires students to grapple with unfamiliar terms and come to grips with their own embedded attitudes toward knowledge, archaeological theory seems to be a subject that is often divorced (by both teachers and students) from ideas of fun. All teachers of archaeological theory would recognize a stereotypical barrier between thinking and doing, most often expressed through the perception that theory is an arcane body of knowledge only relevant to academics, rather than something that informs and underlies all archaeological practice (even if archaeologists themselves fail to recognize it). Part of this misperception is rooted in the challenges of reading and understanding the literature, but the value of teaching theory, of course, lies in its potential to teach students how to think critically and to understand where their received wisdom comes from. At the same time, while archaeological teachers have serious concepts to communicate, this doesn't mean that teaching theoretical concepts can't be enjoyable. In fact, we would argue that as students have more 'fun' they become more motivated, engage more effectively with the material, and increase their learning. Our premise is that, if students enjoy the learning process, they not only will stop resisting learning but will reach out intellectually to engage with the material. From our own perspective, we find also that we are better able to maintain 'freshness' in our own teaching if we ourselves enjoy it.

ORGANIZATION OF THE VOLUME

Rather than organizing the content of this volume according to a more traditional 'archaeological' format such as time period, geography, or subject matter, we have structured the volume around the range of instructional strategies offered by the contributors in their pursuit of active learning. This not only closely ties each chapter to the teaching philosophy that imbues its content, but also makes the volume more accessible for other teachers. As such, the chapters cover a gamut of active learning strategies, from role play and debating, to creative performance and critical reflection.

Each chapter focuses on a particular exercise – a specific activity designed to convey theoretical concepts to students in an interesting, innovative, or engaging way that can be adopted into existing curricula. To enhance the adoption of these activities into other classrooms, each author has contextualized their activity in terms of current theoretical debates, a discussion of its effectiveness and benefits and the immediate impact of the exercise on their classroom environment. With the exception of the final contributor (see below), each author was asked to include the following three core elements in their chapter:

- A contextual piece that explored the theoretical concepts addressed by the exercise, focusing on what the teacher aimed to achieve and how the exercise would achieve this
- The exercise, as it is presented to the students
- A reflection on the issues that arose when the exercise was taught, including suggestions on ways in which the exercise could be improved, expanded, or adapted to different situations

Although the chapters contain these common structural elements, authors were encouraged to present their exercises in their own 'voice'. These authors are all accomplished scholars and have diverse backgrounds, different research interests, and varied teaching experiences. It is thus not surprising that the outcome is a variety of chapters reflecting very different approaches to teaching, although unified by some common elements. Most obviously, all of the papers in this volume share a common academic style arising from their general Anglo-American-Australian orientation. As such, their approaches to teaching and learning arise from the particular educational styles and curricula common to institutions in these countries, most notably a relatively high degree of flexibility in curriculum design, coverage, and delivery. Universities in other parts of the world face different challenges. Those with more focused or structured class environments, for example, in which students are more accustomed to being passive, present a considerable challenge to any attempt to modify this behavior through active learning. In addition, the concerns of this volume also reflect a general understanding of what constitutes archaeological theory in the Western university system and the seminal institutions and schools of thought that helped to explicate it. The key archaeologists and schools of thought drawn upon by Burke and Smith, Higginbottom, or Leach, for example, reflect mainstream Anglophone archaeological culture, which may be less directly relevant to the learning context in other countries.

Finally, it is important to stress that these exercises are designed to be undertaken within a wider teaching context and are not intended as stand-alone or 'homework' exercises. Each arises from a specific classroom context and is embedded within the material of a larger university course. The reflection generated by each one of these activities needs to be focused by an archaeology teacher to be effective. All of these exercises can be taught at a range of instructional levels, from first-year undergraduate through to graduate/post-graduate level, with the depth being determined by the particular teaching situation.

INSTRUCTIONAL STRATEGIES

The eight key instructional strategies that underlie the contributions to this volume include role play, simulations, games, hands-on learning, narrative, creative construction, performance, and critical reflection. These are not necessarily separate and discrete methods, of course, and many exercises draw on more than one strategy in order to be effective. Some exercises target the use of alternative technologies, such as computer simulations, in the pursuit of active learning, while others combine real and hypothetical case studies to tie the theory-based learning experience to real-life situations. They all have two features in common, however: all of them employ some form of critical problem-solving and the associated opportunities for reflection and discussion which this generates in order to achieve effective learning outcomes; and all of them seek to harness the students' imaginations in order to generate excitement.

Role Play

Role play requires students to 'act out' a particular part, in collaboration with others. Role play is an excellent tool for encouraging students to take risks with new ways of behaving without fear of failure or negative consequences, and thus can be a highly effective learning technique (Hertel and Mills 2002). Like other active learning strategies, role play requires both choice and some form of empathy or personification with the problem being studied, and thus students are asked to use their problem-solving abilities to reach some form of conclusion or compromise. Role play, of course, can range from informally empathizing with another's point of view to more formal and structured panel discussions, where students impersonate different characters to role play a set of issues. As an active learning tool, panel discussions are most useful when students are asked to present their views in such a way that the entire class is included in the presentation and ensuing dialogue. Panel discussions are often linked to the more formal debating format, which provides an efficient structure for class presentations when the subject matter easily divides into opposing views or 'Pro'/'Con' considerations (Paulson and Faust 1998: 19). Such small group work allows every participant the chance to speak, share their personal views, and develop the skill of working with others. These sessions are most effective when participants have time to reflect on what they have learned or experienced, and when the facilitator draws out the key points of the activity (National Training Partnership 2005).

The use of role play to teach the key theoretical frameworks of archaeology is dealt with in three chapters: Kersel's 'The Great Debate', Burke and Smith's 'Seven Degrees of Archaeology', and Leach's 'Perspectives from a Pot'. The first two use a debate format to motivate students to engage with different views on a core subject. Kersel uses the renowned dispute over the Parthenon (or 'Elgin') Marbles to encourage her students to engage actively with the issues surrounding international repatriation. Apart from the specific issues covered by the class, students develop an awareness of the relevance of the wider processes of colonialism and nationalism to archaeological method, theory, and practice. Burke and Smith take a similar approach to get students to understand how archaeologists from different schools of thought can come up with diverse interpretations of the past, from the same material evidence. The fictionalized histories of seven stereotypical archaeologists are the vehicle for students to entertain the notion that personal histories and professional alliances may impact upon 'objective' archaeological interpretations. The idea here is that by engaging with a person, even if fictionalized, students are more likely to try to understand their approach to archaeology. Similarly, Leach's paper uses three personalities to espouse the central ideas of the key theoretical schools. As Leach points out in her chapter, 'students are particularly interested in biographical details, and relish hearing about hard-hitting debates, controversies in the field, and heated arguments that have arisen between famous archaeologists'. The use of a debating format such as is presented in these chapters is based on the premise that this structure can enliven the classroom and promote identification between the students' own backgrounds and beliefs and contemporary social issues. This approach derives from a desire to make students think about how different theoretical schools shape archaeological questions, methods of data collection, and interpretations, since each has its own critical questions, biases, assumptions, perspectives, and methodologies. Taken together, these chapters demonstrate ways of teaching archaeological theory so that it engages students' interest and motivates them to achieve in the classroom and to seek knowledge independently.

Simulations

Games, simulations, and role-plays are closely related, as all are structured to feel like real experiences. In simulation exercises, participants are asked to imagine themselves in a situation, or play a structured game or activity that enables them to experience a feeling or carry out a set of actions that might occur in another setting (Dorn 1989; Fischer 1993).

Rule-based simulations governed by software algorithms are generally used to model physical systems or environments, whereas role-based simulations are generally used to model social institutions and relations. In archaeology, rule-centered simulations created through computer technology have become a relatively common device to reconstruct past environments, provide students with access to simulated sites and landscapes, or to model the behavior of past groups of people. Recent initiatives to bring new visualization techniques to the field of archaeology have extended this potential by using both virtual and augmented reality to simulate archaeological excavation environments (see Benko *et al* 2005). Role-based simulations, on the other hand, are more usually created in the classroom in order to immerse students in a particular set of social relationships and obligations (eg Vincent and Shepherd 1998). Regardless of whether they are computer generated, research suggests that simulations as a learning tool are more effective than conventional teaching methods for conveying abstract concepts and engendering empathy (Dorn 1989).

Several of the contributions to this volume tap into the potential of simulated archaeological sites to engage students in learning. The notion of the simulated archaeological site structures both Bowman and Dean's mock dig 'The simulated excavation, an alternative to archaeological site destruction' and Orton's innovative attempt to engage students with archaeological statistics through the analysis of a simulated cemetery. Bowman and Dean's chapter, in particular, ties directly into the disparity between popular understandings of archaeology as these are encountered in public outreach programs and the real social and contextual frameworks within which archaeologists work. This chapter shows an alternative way of conceptualizing and realizing mock excavations, one that addresses the criticism that they emphasize the acquisition of artifacts rather than the process of meaningful interpretation and, as a result, reduce the activity to a treasure hunt (Dale 2001; Hawkins 1999). Embedding learning in 'authentic' activities that emphasize the contested ways in which meaning is constructed helps students to understand more fully the culture of archaeology and to learn that archaeology is less a process of discovery than it is a science of interpretation (Dale 2001; Sept 1998).

Adopting a multi-pronged approach to teaching archaeological history, theory, and method, Carman created 'The Game of Context', which simulates a specific aspect of an excavation – the analysis of stratigraphic context – in order to engage students with the notion of relative dating as an important factor shaping the early development of archaeology as a discipline. By dealing with the issues that arise within a simulated archaeological excavation, students are taught to identify the thought processes involved in classifying these objects and the inferences it is possible to draw from the information available, and to assess the validity of the basis on which such inferences are made. In addition, by concentrating on some of the concepts that are core to relative-dating techniques, such as the relationship between stylistic change and social group, this exercise promotes a deep understanding of early disciplinary developments.

The chapters by Orton and Bowman and Dean also demonstrate the value of simulated excavations as a device for teaching archaeological concepts. Orton's exercise 'Digging your own grave' is aimed at developing research skills in archaeology. In this exercise simulated datasets, with embedded patterns overlaid by random variation, are used to teach archaeologists how to use exploratory and confirmatory statistical techniques to analyze data and to demonstrate their subsequent relationship to model-building, research design, and data collection. Orton argues that the task is twofold: to convince archaeologists that they need a dialogue throughout their research with what they may well feel to be an alien discipline (statistics), and to provide archaeologists with some useful analytical tools. An important outcome is the training of archaeologists to collect adequate and relevant data, and to know when and where to look for help. The simulation exercise proposed by Bowman and Dean addresses a major problem with the teaching of simulated excavations to a public audience. By focusing on artifact recovery and rewarding the 'thrill of discovery', the simulated excavation can send a number of wrong messages, including the message that archaeology is excavation, and excavation is archaeology, that the purpose of archaeology is to recover artifacts, and that excavation can be undertaken with relatively little training or expertise. Bowman and Dean's exercise addresses these problems by assigning the same values and research goals to the simulated excavation that professional archaeologists express: the development of a research design and excavation strategies, the accumulation of data to address the research questions through laboratory analysis, tribal consultation for Indigenous[1] sites, and curation for future researchers. The great value of Bowman and Dean's chapter is the practical demonstration of how to present simulated excavations so that they are guided by professional and ethical standards. This approach instills the professional and ethical standards of the discipline, while keying into the delights of archaeological discovery.

Games

The great value of games is that they are fun. Games are something people choose to do. As such, they can be used to enhance student participation in the learning process and to bolster student confidence and creativity. While games became an important part of secondary school teaching and learning during the 1960s and 1970s (see Kirriemurr and McFarlane 2004), it has taken longer for games to be adopted at the university level, most likely due to a perception that games, necessarily, must be 'light' and devoid of intellectual rigor, or to an attitude that learning and having fun are not compatible. Over the last decade, however, there have been considerable developments in game-based learning, and in the use of competitive but enjoyable activities to achieve learning objectives (eg Amory *et al* 1999; Baranich and Currie 2004; Kirriemurr and McFarlane 2004; Russell 1999; Teed 2005). This is done through pitting students against each other, having students work as a team to overcome an obstacle or opponent, or asking them to challenge themselves in order to achieve learning goals.

A range of games has been developed to teach serious concepts in a number of disciplines. The 'Induction Game', or 'Eleusis' (see http://www.pagat.com/eights/eleusis.html), for instance, is a well-known example within the sciences that uses a card game to introduce students to the concepts of 'laws of nature' and 'the scientific method'. Other card games have been used to reinforce key concepts in chemistry (Granath and Russell 1999) and geoscience (Teed 2005), while Gauntlett (2004) has developed Theory Trading Cards to teach social theory in a more lively and accessible manner. Board games are another means for play that have been used to engage students with serious learning objectives in interesting and interactive ways. Board games have been used to teach English as a second language (http://www.teflgames.com/), to convey concepts of social inequality (Jessup 2001) and to reinforce key concepts in science (Russell 1999; Teed 2005). Other gaming devices such as bingo, crossword puzzles, crayons, game show formats, and even Lego® blocks, have been incorporated into teaching a variety of concepts from sociology to information systems (Childers 1996; Coco *et al* 2001; Freeman 2003; Grauerholz 1991; Levinson 1980; Wetcher-Hendricks and Luquet 2003).

Several of the chapters in this volume introduce fun gaming elements into the teaching of serious concepts. The card game 'Grasp, or Happy Families the Archaeological Way', outlined by Higginbottom in chapter 4, makes use of a card game to familiarize students with major themes and ideas in theoretical archaeology. This exercise is a great example of successfully marrying educational and achievement objectives: A winning hand is one where the cards held derive from a range of sets (eg people, theoretical ideas, movements, archaeological sites) but are played in order for the player to hold cards from a single theoretical theme. This exercise is a clever example of using a simple structure to motivate students to engage with complicated ideas. Higginbottom's other chapter, 'The Big Dig, theoretically speaking', uses a board game to teach the philosophies, people, and practices of archaeology. This exercise is particularly suited to the reinforcement of archaeological facts, giving life and interest to the 'rote' learning strategies of traditional teaching techniques. A third form of game is developed in Smith and Burke's exercise 'The skin game' (chapter 5). More akin to games developed in sociology that help to reveal the tacit rules that structure individual experience and that subsequently generate wider social patterns (eg Coco *et al* 2001; Groves *et al* 1996; O'Brien and Foley 1999), the skin game is a vehicle to teach students about the complexities of Indigenous social systems and to contrast the inherent elegance of such orally transmitted systems of knowledge with the often racist perceptions constructed by white colonial authorities. 'The skin game' transforms students into members of an Australian Aboriginal kinship system, instantly relating them to each and every other member of the class. By requiring them to figure out some of the complexities of these kin relationships (including who they can appropriately marry, and who socially they must avoid), 'The skin game' seeks to redress stereotypes of Aboriginal people as 'backward' or 'primitive' by allowing students to actively immerse themselves, even for only a brief moment, in some of the many layers of complexity that make up an Aboriginal kinship system.

Several scholars have perceived parallels between well-designed games and academic courses. Foreman (2003: 16), for example, argues that both aim to build and integrate knowledge in a structured continuum and require that participants actively engage with the subject matter and goals in order to succeed. Taking a similar approach, Teed (2005) likens the core features of a successful game to those of a good lesson. Successful games encourage competition and include a scorekeeping element and/or winning conditions that motivate the player to succeed; they engage the player by creating a desire to continue until the game is over; and they provide immediate rewards, through victory or points, and sometimes even descriptive feedback, which can be achieved as soon as the goals are accomplished. Teed (2005) compares this to a good lesson plan that includes the following: achievement, whereby each class is based on achievement objectives and on new understandings and skills for students to master; motivation, whereby the intrinsic interest of the topic is enhanced through creating an environment that challenges curiosity, invention, and creativity (cf Baranich and Currie 2004); and assessment, whereby grades and credits constitute the reward for the effort put into the learning, not withstanding the intrinsic reward of increased understanding and new skills.

Table 1.1 emphasizes the similarities between the two by comparing some core elements of games and active learning. While all these elements are important to one or the other, or both, the most important is arguably that of engagement, since this is the quality that will determine the amount of effort that students or players put into learning. Lepper and Cordova (1992) characterize engagement as 'intrinsic motivation', which they ascribe to four sources: challenge, curiosity, control, and fantasy. As Teed (2005) points out, the challenge for the instructor of game-based learning is to marry these two approaches so as to enhance the strengths of each, making learning fun and games useful. As part of this, it is important that games be designed so that the accomplishment of learning goals is essential to winning the game, otherwise important material is likely to be ignored (Lepper and Cordova 1992).

The chapters in this volume show that games can be adapted to a wide range of concepts. They can be used not only to teach complex ideas, but also to instill professional and ethical standards, and to give students a sense of cross-cultural engagement. Indeed, some concepts and theories are better illustrated through a well-conceived game than through more common teaching strategies. Far from trivializing the learning process, the use of games can ensure that students actively engage with complex theoretical and social concepts, often obtaining a nuanced understanding that is unlikely to be attained in any other way.

Hands-on learning

Due to its practical component, archaeology has always been viewed as well suited to instruction through hands-on activities. Closely linked to inquiry-based and participatory forms of learning, hands-on learning demands that students engage with concrete objects as part of the learning process. Hands-on techniques encourage students to apply the concepts they have been taught in a lecture or seminar and often generate questions that would not arise in a lecture environment. Hands-on learning provides 'learning by doing', helping students to acquire knowledge and skills outside of books and lectures, and is especially suited to teaching an understanding of the scientific process. In addition, hands-on activities provide a powerful antidote to boredom.

The value of hands-on learning experiences has been established at primary and secondary levels for several decades. Accomplished teachers, especially in math and science, include hands-on learning (eg Hands-on Activity Science Program 2005; Sandefur and Dance 2005; Waldron *et al* 2003), to ensure students actively engage with new concepts and disciplinary technique. However, at a university level, hands-on learning is often viewed as practically impossible, especially in the huge lecture environments of many undergraduate classes (eg Dion 1996). The value of this approach at the university level is clearly demonstrated, however, in the chapters by Diplock and Stein, Stottman, Miller, and Henderson, and Wobst, each of which takes the analysis of a particular type of artifact and uses it to create hands-on activities that promote an engagement with various kinds of archaeological interpretation.

The instructional strategy of hands-on learning is combined with role play by Diplock and Stein in their exercise on the making and decoding of rock markings. This exercise uses the generation of meanings from alternative and sometimes competing social contexts to teach students to appreciate the difficulties inherent in communicating symbolically and the limitations of subjective interpretation. As the authors point out, the practical and collaborative nature of the exercise generates an understanding of the social negotiations engaged in by the artifact producer, not only in making the artifact in the first place, but also in interpreting it within a socially meaningful context.

The archaeological analysis of everyday items is the basis of three chapters: that of Stottman, Miller, and Henderson, and those of Wobst and Zimmerman. The archaeological analysis of contemporary litter to connect students with real-world problems is the basis for the chapter by Stottman, Miller, and Henderson, 'Culture of Litterbugs'. These authors demonstrate that litter can be a valid, concrete source of archaeological data that students can easily link to the human behavior they see around them. The lesson plan is designed to mirror a typical archaeological research project, including problem formulation, selection of study area, data recovery, analysis and interpretation, the reporting of results, and the curation of artifacts. This exercise teaches students the processes that inform archaeological research in an interesting and accessible manner. Moreover, through compiling the data into a joint report and submitting it to an appropriate authority, this chapter demonstrates how anthropology and archaeology can effect social change. The chapter by Zimmerman also uses the everyday item of litter in order to engage students' interest in archaeological concepts. In the first of two exercises presented in his chapter, Zimmerman has students excavate the contents of his wastebasket, in order to learn the principles of stratigraphy, including the law of superimposition (and the difficulties surrounding its uncritical application) and what strata can tell us about relative time. In his second exercise, Zimmerman asks students to analyze the contents of his desk drawer, in order to get them to engage with the issues surrounding the establishment and application of archaeological classification systems. In this exercise, students gain a nuanced and memorable understanding of the complexity of classification and how much more difficult it is when applied to a culture from the past. One great value of this exercise is that students recognize how archaeological classification systems are formed, and are unlikely to accept these uncritically. Moreover, Zimmerman's chapter shows that if the basic ideas are taught well, students have a much stronger foundation for learning more complex notions.

In a similar vein, the familiar household item of the toilet is used by Wobst as a way of capturing student interest in a range of archaeological concepts. First, toilet paper is used to introduce students to concepts of time and its measurement. Second, public toilets are used to understand how notions of person, status, power, gender, and privacy are socially constructed. Wobst's chapter demonstrates that everyday objects can be useful learning devices precisely because, by their very ordinariness, they challenge students to analyze their own unquestioned assumptions, thereby adding an interesting and unexpected dimension to archaeological research.

Table 1.1. The core elements of games and active learning.

	Games	Active Learning
Clear Aims, Objectives	Yes	Yes
Structure	Yes	Yes
Participation	Yes	Yes
Engagement	Yes	Yes
Imagination	Yes	Yes
Curiosity	Yes	Yes
Creativity	Yes	Yes
Challenge	Yes	Yes
Control, Direction	Yes	Sometimes
Motivation	Yes	Yes
Exploration	Yes	Yes
Competition	Yes	Yes
Collaboration	Sometimes	Often
Achievement	Yes	Yes
Immediate Rewards	Yes	Sometimes
Critique	Not formally	Yes
Assessment	No	Yes

Taken together, the above chapters demonstrate that, while hands-on learning usually requires more planning, resources, and inventiveness on the part of the teacher, the rewards in terms of learning outcomes are considerable. As each chapter demonstrates, interactive, hands-on activities can have great pedagogical value through generating enthusiasm and energy about the topics being taught, which increases student motivation and knowledge retention. Hands-on activities can give a task a sense of authenticity by providing real tools, make lecture material more relevant and accessible, and promote critical thinking and problem solving. Well-conceived hands-on learning promotes student interaction, encouraging students to learn and to teach each other about abstract concepts as well as concrete processes, while at the same time having fun. Students learn through being involved in the new experience. To paraphrase Shipman (2001), through engaging in hands-on activities, students not only learn archaeological concepts but also learn to enjoy doing archaeology.

Narrative, creative construction, and performance

In recent years, there has been increasing interest in the role of narrative and storytelling in archaeological scholarship and teaching (eg Paynter 2002; Yamin 2001). Important features of this trend include the use of narrative techniques to give life to archaeological data or concepts, to convey ideas relating to multiple stakeholders and/or interpretations, and to teach skills of critical evaluation. In terms of archaeological pedagogy, one aspect of this trend is teachers encouraging their students to engage with their material more effectively and reflectively through the vehicles of story-telling, creative construction, or performance. Such strategies have direct links to the imaginative process, as students are asked to develop a creative project in order to convey any number of themes. Either individually or collaboratively, students produce a product that is an outcome of both their intellect and imagination. This approach is apparent in the various contributions to this volume by Lydon, Berg, Allen, and Renoe, each of which centralizes the place of creative expression in the process of learning, and ties this to an exploration of issues relating to social context, public archaeology, and interpretation.

While many archaeologists acknowledge the importance of the public to archaeology, few know how to communicate with the public effectively. Recognizing this, a number of chapters in this volume aim to develop students' abilities to connect with the public, and to critically evaluate public presentations of archaeology. Museums are a primary conduit between archaeologists and the public, and Lydon's chapter uses a hands-on activity to teach students how material objects are employed in the creation of interpretations of the past. Through the vehicle of a simulated museum installation, students are required to engage in basic archaeological concepts and approaches. Not only do they obtain an understanding of how archaeological knowledge is used in society, they also learn about how material objects can be used to support or subvert the agendas of different interest groups. An important outcome of this activity is that students learn to critically evaluate the authority of different arguments made about the past.

Using the motivational power of fiction to engage student interest, Berg asks her classes to write a short story based on their research into a particular region or time period. The use of fiction in this way is a fabulous technique for humanizing the past, and for making students aware of the difficulties involved in writing fiction while retaining archaeological integrity. Through focusing on a specific place and imagined social actors in their broader socio-historical context, this exercise encourages students to think about the individuals who lived (and live) in the landscapes they are describing, rather than to approach archaeology purely in terms of artifacts or environments. The diverse class presentations that emerge demonstrate to students that there are multiple ways of turning archaeological data into narratives, and that each may have its own validity. In a similar manner, Allen uses the technique of fictional scenarios to inject creativity and humor into the process of assessing student knowledge of course content. While the use of scenarios in this chapter is tied to assessment, Allen points out that this strategy can also be used in a range of other contexts, including that of initiating debates, or as a way of dealing with complex issues, as, for example, in the case studies on ethics that are discussed on the web site of the American Anthropological Association (eg www.aaanet.org/committees/ethics/managing_collections.htm). Apart from the content *per se*, Allen's chapter demonstrates that scenarios can be a powerful tool for instilling a sense of archaeology as a profession, with specific orientations, problems, ethical standards and professional values.

Renoe also uses an alternative form of creative expression – drawing – to initiate discussions about public perceptions of archaeology, address students' misconceptions about archaeologists, and discuss the make-up of the archaeological community. A disturbing outcome of her 'Draw-an-archaeologist' exercise was her realization that even though she herself, as the teacher, was female and African American, student perceptions of archaeologists were that they are overwhelming male (64%) and white (98%). Renoe makes the point that what she initially perceived as bias was actually an accurate reflection of the archaeological community according to a 1994 study undertaken by the Society for American Archaeology (Zeder 1997: 9). Linking this exercise to wider understandings of what it means to be an archaeologist, Renoe uses these figures as a platform for considering the impact upon descendant communities, such as African Americans and Native Americans, of perceptions of archaeologists as the sole arbiters and interpreters of the past.

Critical reflection

Having students keep a journal or regular log entries (on paper or computer, in or out of class) requires them to engage in brief critical reflections or analyses of each entry and the issues that it raises. One of the underlying principles of active learning is that it should encompass assessment as well as instruction, and journals or other vehicles for long-term critical reflection are a key means of encouraging student self-assessment.

Rubertone's chapter demonstrates clearly that these kinds of assessment practices help to showcase students' development and focus on the process of learning, not just on the graded paper or outcome. Her exercise, centered around a cumulative scrapbook that students are asked to compile throughout the duration of her course, challenges students to unpack their preconditioned assumptions about the past and allows them to explore controversial yet fundamental issues about death that cannot be reduced to a single essay topic or set of exam questions. Such practices have been discussed elsewhere as particularly effective tools for promoting a critical process of engagement with the past, since new ideas can emerge from the self-reflexivity inherent in the process and help students to understand the ways in which their own experiences and backgrounds inform and shape understandings about the past and its role in the present (Hamilakis 2004: 297).

The final chapter, by Anne Pyburn, exemplifies the philosophy that underpins this volume. Pyburn's chapter stands alone in that it is the only one not to offer a discrete activity. Instead, she draws upon a range of creative instructional strategies from her own teaching career as she guides the reader through a series of exercises, in the process providing insight into the lived experience of teaching archaeology to delight and instruct. Written in a style that is simultaneously charming and elegant, it serves as an apposite end-paper to this volume.

TEACHING ARCHAEOLOGY TO DELIGHT AND INSTRUCT

It is the application of theory to the analysis of material culture that transforms a treasure hunt or adventure outing into archaeology. Theory is central to the archaeological endeavor. Nevertheless, a persistent problem that has dogged the teaching of archaeological theory is the perception that it is too difficult, too arcane, or too boring. The chapters in this volume show that this is a fallacy. In fact, without theory, archaeology *is* boring. Theory makes minutiae explicable and takes the specific to the general, and the general to the specific, allowing us to understand the processes that shape human behaviors. But teaching theory in interesting ways is a challenge, one that involves a rethinking of pedagogy. Acknowledging that students learn best by engaging in inquiry necessitates a change from didactic or lecture-oriented science instruction to an interactive approach. Drawing upon a wide range of active learning strategies, the creators of these exercises demonstrate the manifold value of teaching archaeology to delight and instruct.

While archaeologists routinely use active learning strategies to teach field and laboratory methods, the use of such techniques to teach theoretical concepts in archaeology may challenge conventional notions of academic propriety. For some teachers, active learning may appear too much like entertainment and not serious enough to convey complex ideas. We hope that the chapters in this book demonstrate quite the opposite. Learning is fundamentally a social process, rather than something that occurs within the head of the student (cf Dale 2002: 1). Active learning can be used to foster critical reflection, and numerous studies have demonstrated that students learn better when they actively engage in the production of knowledge, rather than accept being passive recipients (Davis 1993; McKeachie 1999). The chapters presented here demonstrate that active learning strategies achieve much more than simply ensuring that students enjoy their university experience. Through actively engaging with the concepts being taught, students are motivated to seek knowledge and gain command of the subject. In the process, they increase their ability to think critically, become better scholars, and are better prepared for learning situations encountered outside the classroom.

Good teaching takes place on two levels: in terms of those concepts and ideas that we, as lecturers, see as important to teach and thus the identifiable learning outcomes we want students to achieve because of this; and those things that emerge unexpectedly from a course – what the students teach us. It's this latter aspect that can change a course from year to year and that helps to make the classroom active – it is never the same because the student body, their diversity of backgrounds, and the combination of personalities and opinions they represent is always changing. To tap into this potential and help people discover that something can be fun is an achievement in itself. In our view, the best teaching delights while it instructs and should always be more than 'lectures as usual'.

ACKNOWLEDGMENTS

We thank Jane Balme, Wendy Beck, and other colleagues with whom we have discussed teaching methods over the years, including many of the contributors to this volume. In addition, we would like to thank Gary Jackson and Justine O'Sullivan for productive and insightful discussions. Mitch Allen's and Joan Gero's support and enthusiasm have been essential to the completion of this project.

NOTE

1. Following the increasing practice of Indigenous authors (eg Craven 1999; Smith 1999), we use a capital 'I' for Indigenous, to indicate the sovereignty of Indigenous peoples. The line of thought is British, Australian, Greek etc ... Indigenous.

REFERENCES AND FURTHER READING

Amory, A, Naicker, K, Vincent, J and Adams, C (1999) 'The use of computer games as an educational tool: Identification of appropriate game types and elements', *British Journal of Educational Technology* 30(4), 311–321

Banning, EB (2000) *The Archaeologist's Laboratory. The Analysis of Archaeological Data,* New York: Plenum/Kluwer

Barber, R (1994) *Doing Historical Archaeology. Exercises Using Oral, Documentary and Material Evidence,* New York: Prentice Hall

Barceló, JA, Forte, M and Sanders, DH (2000) *Virtual Reality in Archaeology,* Oxford: ArcheoPress, Oxford (British Archaeological Reports, International Series #843)

Benko, H, Ishak, E and Feiner, S (2005) *Collaborative Visualization of an Archaeological Excavation,* Available on-line at: www1.cs.columbia.edu/graphics/projects/ArcheoVis/index.html, accessed 19 March 2005

Baranich, K and Currie, C (2004) 'Using games to teach, motivate and engage', September/October *Come. Play!* 6–9, Available on-line at: www.stc.org/intercom/PDFs/2004/20040910_06–09.pdf, accessed 19 March 2005

Childers, CD (1996) 'Using crossword puzzles as an aid to studying socio-logical concepts', *Teaching Sociology* 24, 231–235

Coco, A, Woodward, I, Shaw, K, Cody, A, Lupton, G and Peake, A (2001) 'Bingo for beginners: A game strategy for facilitating active learning', *Teaching Sociology* 29(4), 492–503

Craven, R (1999) *Teaching Aboriginal Studies*, Sydney: Allen and Unwin

Dale, J (2001) 'Situating archaeology education: The relevance of socio-cultural theory in developing public archaeology programs', Available on-line at: http://www.educ.sfu.ca/archaeology/theorypaper.html, accessed 19 March 2005

Daniels, S and David, N (1982) *The Archaeology Workbook*, Philadelphia: University of Pennsylvania Press

David, N and Driver, J (1989) *The Next Archaeology Workbook*, Philadelphia: University of Pennsylvania Press

Davis, B (1993) *Tools for Teaching*, San Francisco: Jossey-Bass

Dion, L (1996) 'But I teach a large class...', *About Teaching, a Newsletter of the Center for Teaching Effectiveness* 50, Available on-line at: http://www.udel.edu/pbl/cte/spr96–bisc2.html, accessed 19 March 2005

Dorn, DS (1989) 'Simulation games: One more tool on the pedagogical shelf', *Teaching Sociology* 17, 10–18

Fischer, MW (1993) *American History Simulations*, Huntington Beach, CA: Teacher Created Materials Inc.

Florida State University (2002) *Instruction at FSU: A Guide to Teaching and Learning Practice*, Available on-line at: http://online.fsu.edu/learningresources/handbook/instructionatfsu/, Chapter 8, accessed 6 August 2005

Foreman, J (2003) 'Next generation. Educational technology versus the lecture', *Educause Review* July/August, 12–22, available on-line at http://serc.carleton.edu/resources/1686.html, accessed 4 March 2005

Forte, M (ed) (1997) *Virtual Archaeology: Great Discoveries Brought to Life Through Virtual Reality*, London: Thames and Hudson

Freeman, L (2003) 'Innovative classroom practices. Simulation and role playing with LEGO® blocks', *Journal of Information Systems Education* 14(2), 137–144

Gamble, C (2001) *Archaeology. The Basics*, London: Routledge

Grauerholz, E (1991) 'This is Jeopardy! How to make preparation for examinations fun and challenging', *Teaching Sociology* 19, 495–497

Granath, PL and Russell, JV (1999) 'Using games to teach chemistry. 1. The Old Prof Card Game', *Journal of Chemical Education* 76, 485, Available on-line at: http://jchemed.chem.wisc.edu/Journal/Issues/1999/Apr/abs485.htm, accessed 4 March 2005

Griffiths, Y and Ursik, K (2004) 'Using active learning to shift the habits of learning in health care education', *The Internet Journal of Allied Health Sciences and Practice* 2(2), Available on-line at: http://ijahsp.nova.edu/

articles/Vol2num2/Griffiths%20-%20Active.htm, accessed 19 March 2005

Groves, J, Warren, C and Witschger, J (1996) 'Reversal of fortune: A simulation game for teaching inequality in the classroom', *Teaching Sociology* 24, 364–371

Gauntlett, D (2004) 'Theory Trading Cards', available on-line at: www.theory.org.uk/david/theorycards.htm, accessed 19 March 2005

Hands-on Activity Science Program (2005), available on-line at: http://www.dcs.edu/HASP/HASPwhat.html, accessed 19 March 2005

Hamilakis, Y (2004) 'Archaeology and the politics of pedagogy', *World Archaeology* 36(2), 287–309

Hawkins, N (1999) 'Precollegiate excavations: Archaeologists make the difference', *SAA Bulletin* 17(1), 15–17

Hertel, JP and Mills, BJ (2002) *Using Simulations to Promote Learning in Higher Education: An Introduction.* Herndon, VA: Stylus Publishing

Hodder, I (1999) *The Archaeological Process: An Introduction*, Oxford: Blackwell

Jenkins, A (1992) 'Active learning in structured lectures', in Gibbs, G and Jenkins, A (eds), *Teaching Large Classes in Higher Education*, London: Kogan Page

Jessup, M (2001) 'Sociopoly: Life on the boardwalk', *Teaching Sociology* 29(1), 102–109

Johnson, M (1999) *Archaeological Theory*, Oxford: Blackwell

Kennedy, H (2003) 'Computer games, ideology and play', available on-line at: http://ludology.org/calendar_event.php?eid=20030411074613393, accessed 4 March 2005

Kirriemurr, J and McFarlane, A (2004) 'Literature review in games and learning', National Endowment for Science Technology and the Arts (NESTA) Futurelab series, report no 8. Bristol: NESTA Futurelab, available on-line at: http://www.nestafuturelab.org/research/lit_reviews.htm#lr08, accessed 19 March 2005

Lepper, MR and Cordova, DI (1992) 'A desire to be taught: Instructional consequences of intrinsic motivation', *Motivation and Emotion* 16(3), 187–208

Levinson, RM (1980) 'The soap opera game: A teaching aid for sociology of the family', *Teaching Sociology* 7, 181–190

Mayer, RE (2003) *Learning and Instruction*, Upper Saddle River: Pearson Education, Inc

McClure, M (1990) 'Collaborative learning: Teacher's game or students' game?', *English Journal* 79(2), 66–68

McKeachie, WJ (1999) *Teaching Tips: Strategies, Research and Theory for College and University Teachers*, Boston: Houghton Mifflin

National Training Partnership (2005) *Active Learning Strategies*, Available on-line at: http://www2.edc.org/NTP/trainingdesign_activelearning strategies.htm, accessed 19 March 2005

O'Brien, E and Foley, L (1999) 'The dating game: An exercise illustrating the concepts of homogamy, heterogamy, hyperogamy and hypogamy', *Teaching Sociology* 27(2), 145–149

Paynter, R (2002) 'Time in the Valley', *Current Anthropology* 43(4), 85–102

Paulson, DR and Faust, JL (1998) 'Active learning for the college classroom', *Journal on Excellence in College Teaching* 9(2), 3–24, Available on line at www.calstatela.edu/dept/chem/chem2/Active/, accessed 19 March 2005

Pinker, S (2004) *The Best American Science and Nature Writing 2004*, New York: Houghton Mifflin

Praetzellis, A (2000) *Death by Theory*, Walnut Creek, CA: AltaMira Press

Rice, P (1997) *Doing Archaeology. A Hands-On Laboratory Manual*, Palo Alto: Mayfield Publishing Company

Russell, JV (1999) 'Using games to teach chemistry 2: CHeMoVEr board game', *Journal of Chemical Education* 76: 487

Sandefur, J and Dance, R (2005) 'Hands-on activities for algebra at college', Available on-line at: http://www.georgetown.edu/projects/handsonmath/, accessed 19 March 2005

Savage, H and Dinsmore, E (1998) *Exercises in Archaeological Methods and Techniques. Partial Curriculum for Anthro 156–103: Digging Up the Past! Approaches to Archaeology,* Available on-line at: www.archaeology.asu.edu/Jordan/Archlabs.pdf, accessed 19 March 2005

Sept, J (1998) 'Engaging students in prehistoric problem-solving: The development of investigating Olduvai-archaeology of human origins CD-ROM', Available on-line at: http://old.ihets.org/learntech/distance_ed/fdpapers/1998/33.html, accessed 19 March 2005

Shipman, HL (2001) 'Hands-on science, 680 hands at a time', *Journal of College Science Teaching* Feb, Available on-line at: wwwlb.aub.edu.lb/~websmec/hands-on_science.htm, accessed 19 March 2005

Silberman, M (1998) *Active Learning. 101 Strategies to Teach Any Subject,* Boston: Allyn and Bacon

Singleis, T (ed) (1998) *Teaching About Culture, Ethnicity, and Diversity: Exercises and Planned Activities*, Thousand Oaks, CA: Sage

Smith, LT (1999) *Decolonising Methodologies: Research and Indigenous Peoples*, second edition, London: Zed Books

Teed, R (2005) 'Starting point. Teaching entry level geoscience. Game-based learning', Available on-line at: http://serc.carleton.edu/introgeo/games/index.html, accessed 4 March 2005

Vincent, A and Shepherd, J (1998) 'Experiences in teaching Middle East politics via Internet-based role-play simulations', *Journal of Interactive Media in Education* 98(11), Available on-line at: www-jime.open.ac.uk/98/11/Vincent-98-11.pdf, accessed 19 March 2005

Waldron, I, Pohlschroder, M and Poethig, S (2003) 'Hands-on activities for teaching biology to high school or middle school students', Available on-line at: http://www.bio.upenn.edu/faculty/waldron/labs/, accessed 19 March 2005

Wetcher-Hendricks, D and Luquet, W (2003) 'Teaching stratification with crayons', *Teaching Sociology* 31(3), 345–351

Yamin, R (2001) 'Alternative narratives: Respectability at New York's Five Points', in Mayne, A and Murray, T (eds), *The Archaeology of Urban Landscapes. Explorations in Slumland*, Cambridge: Cambridge University Press

Zeder, M (1997) *The American Archaeologist: A Profile*, Walnut Creek, CA: AltaMira Press

Part I

Role Play

2

Seven Degrees of Archaeology, or Diverse Ways of Interpreting the Past

Heather Burke and Claire Smith

Theory is central to the archaeological process. It helps us understand why we do what we do, and gives insight into the processes that shape human behaviors. Without theory, archaeology is not archaeology. Because of its centrality to the intellectual endeavor that is archaeology, however, the use and misuse of theory has been an area of heated debate (eg Binford 1968, 1989; Hodder 1989; Praetzellis 2000; Trigger 1995; Wylie 1982). While it may be tempting to dismiss this as politically motivated polemic, the space of contention such debate occupies has the potential to bring into focus many of our underlying assumptions about human behavior, and the ways in which archaeologists connect this with archaeological material. The debates between Binford and Bordes, for example, (see Binford 1973; Bordes 1973) over whether variations in Mousterian stone tool assemblages were due to ethnic differences or were simply a reflection of different activities not only engaged a contemporary audience, but are still thought-provoking 30 years later. Similarly, the debates between Binford (1988, 1989) and Hodder (1985, 1991) over the merits of processual versus postprocessual archaeology still provide exciting and pertinent grist for the archaeological mill. It is not only the issues themselves that are interesting, but also the different opinions that archaeologists bring to the material and how this affects their interpretations of past human behavior.

The exercise we outline in this paper arose from our desire to encourage third-year undergraduate archaeology students to engage with the complexities of alternative ways of explaining variability in archaeological interpretations of the past, particularly in terms of the different theoretical schools of thought that have been central to the growth of the discipline. It is situated in our jointly taught course: 'ARCH3301: Archaeological Theory and Method', and in 2004 Smith (with ongoing discussion and assistance from Burke) taught this exercise as part of the course 'ANTH V3820x: Theory and Method in Archaeology' at Columbia University, New York. The Seven Degrees of Archaeology exercise keys into an ongoing seminar format that covers major historical developments in archaeological thought since the 19th century, the major players in archaeological theory and method over the past 150 years, and the relationships between a practitioner's theoretical perspective and subsequent data recognition and analysis. This exercise comes toward the end of the course, after students have presented their major seminars and completed most of the assigned readings and assessment pieces. Other aspects of active learning in 'Archaeological Theory and Method' have been discussed separately in Smith and Burke (2005).

As a third-year core course, 'Archaeological Theory and Method' is a compulsory course for all Bachelor of Archaeology majors at Flinders University, and is therefore not one in which students are necessarily enrolled by choice. This situation typically brings to the fore prejudices about the relevance of theory to contemporary practice, most often expressed through the perception that theory is an arcane body of knowledge only relevant to academics, rather than being something that informs and underlies all archaeological practice (even if the archaeologists themselves fail to recognize it). In Australia – a country known for its frankness – students sometimes express this as a view that 'theory is shit'. Part of this misperception is rooted in the challenges of reading and understanding the literature, which normally requires that students come to grips with a raft of unfamiliar terms and many difficult philosophical concepts. The value of the course lies in its potential to teach students how to think critically and to understand where their received wisdom comes from. In part our goal throughout the course is to help them understand this bigger picture by thinking of the discipline of archaeology itself as a multifaceted dataset that includes archaeological papers, careers, and thought patterns.

PREPARING THE EXERCISE

The materials for this exercise are:

- An outline of the seven major characters representing seven major schools of thought (Handout 3)
- Images of a collection of artifacts (we use a variety of real artifacts), along with the imaginary site plans and notes that contextualize the finds (Handouts 1 and 2)

- Any accoutrements that will enhance the group's presentation of their character (we encourage our students to dress up for their roles).

APPROXIMATE LENGTH OF EXERCISE ·

This exercise takes at least one two- to three-hour session (at Columbia all the upper-level classes are one-and-a-half to two hours), although it is much better if broken down into smaller components and conducted across several weeks of class.

THE EXERCISE

Students are assigned to small groups (4–6 members, but this varies with the size of the class), each of which is allocated one of the Seven Degrees of Archaeology characters (Handout 3). Each group is given a copy of the project brief (Handout 1), the field notes and sketch plans (Handout 2), and the list of characters (Handout 3), as well as images of a collection of artifacts. The brief, notes, and sketch plans are all imaginary, although the collection of artifacts we customarily use is real and drawn from a disparate array of real sites. In their groups the students are asked to generate an interpretation of the site and the objects that is consistent with their assigned school of thought and then to select one member of their team to present their interpretation in front of the class. We structure these presentations as a debate, with all seven characters sitting as a panel of distinguished experts, and with one of us to facilitate the debate and often with other members of the class contributing. At the end of the class we ask the students to vote on which presentation they thought was most convincing and then give a small prize to that group.

REFLECTIONS ON THE EXERCISE

For the Seven Degrees of Archaeology exercise, students are asked, as a group, to take on a single, fictitious (and in many ways stereotypical) character who typifies some of the characteristics of a particular school of thought, and to bring their understanding of this particular body of archaeological knowledge to bear on the interpretation of an equally fictitious collection of artifacts. In essence, the students are asked to both take on the stereotype we provide, and then use the stereotype to analyze a batch of data (the site report, field notes, plans, and artifact collection) in a theoretically stereotypical way. There are seven different characters, each one derived from a different school of thought, all of whom have some personal and/or professional links with each other. The exercise role plays each of these characters against the others in asking them to interpret the same collection of artifacts.

Role play is a well-accepted means of encouraging students to 'act out' a particular part, and in the process to gain a better idea of the concepts and theories being discussed in class. Role play activities range from the simple, such as telling a story 'in character', to the complex, such as when a specific situation is acted out. Role play activities have been a significant breakthrough in many fields, but particularly in language learning (eg Al-Saadat and Afifi 1997). Since role play involves students in researching and presenting the views of another person, it can provide them with a greater understanding of their own society, as well as enhanced cross-cultural understanding (cf Burges 1992). In the teaching of archaeology, role play is regularly used to give 'life' to situations that are contested (see Kersel, this volume), a context that is nowhere more appropriate than to the teaching of archaeological theory. In regard to our own teaching of archaeological theory and method, we hope that by asking students to engage not only with the nuances of a particular school of thought, but also with the competing interpretations of other schools, they would gain an understanding of the ways in which different paradigms both articulate and diverge, and obtain some sense of how alternative interpretations might key into different sources of data. By linking the characters in various ways, we also hope that students will recognize some of the personal undercurrents that might surface in their character's attitude and in the ways in which the characters might relate to each other.

This exercise worked well in terms of class enjoyment and participation, particularly as many of the students were more inventive than we predicted – even to the extent of 'discovering' new information that aided them in their interpretations (of which, needless to say, their opponents remained unaware). Unfortunately, in our initial trial, it did not achieve the depth of interpretation we had hoped for, in part due to the length of time the exercise took. To counter this, we moved from first running it as part of a larger three-hour class, to allocating it a class by itself, to spreading it across two classes to give students adequate time to prepare. Recently we have run it as increments across several classes, giving students the opportunity to build up their persona and interpretation gradually. This also gives them time to decide how their character will look and behave and to plan their habits and dress accordingly. The structure of the exercise lends itself well to small group work across several weeks as part of ongoing larger classes by splitting it into its major components, such as:

Week 1: An outline of each character's school of thought and its major approaches/intellectual tools. What are the fundamental organizing principles that explain how this school of thought approaches data and interpretation?

Week 2: An outline of the particular terminology associated with each school of thought and some of its major practitioners and seminal studies.

Week 3: Adapting these principles into a list of 'rules' to guide each character's approach to the archaeological analysis of material remains (both 'dos' and 'do nots'). For example, what does this school of thought recognize as data? What aspects of human behavior are they most interested in? What types/range of artifacts do they concentrate on in order to do this? What do they tend to steer away from? In this way each type of analysis can be given a few simple rules that might produce different results.

Week 4: Construction of each character's persona – what would they be like? How would they think and behave? How would they relate to the other characters?

Week 5: Detailed preparation of each interpretation.

Week 6: Presentation of each interpretation as part of the panel of experts.

We chose to assign the characters based on the topics the students had already presented for their major seminars, on the assumption that they would be likely to know more about this particular school of thought than any other. If given sufficient time to prepare, however, it would also work well if students were assigned a relatively unfamiliar school of thought that would require them to read more widely. This would work particularly well if using this exercise in a graduate class. Class discussion of the complexities inherent in trying to define any school of thought or to construct any historical trajectory for a discipline would work well as a complement to this exercise. Surprisingly, while we expected (and hoped) that the students would criticize the stereotypical nature of some of the Seven Degrees characters, this has yet to eventuate – perhaps a pointer that there is much more to learn about archaeological theory and method than a single semester's class can convey. Having presented students with stereotypical characters, there is a responsibility to make them aware that often people's views change over time, and that it is harsh to hold someone accountable for views they published twenty years ago. We do make an effort to encourage students to question the link between writer and text and to understand archaeological theories, and the people associated with them, as products of a particular time, place, and social milieu.

One potential criticism is that there is not enough information in the Seven Degrees of Archaeology exercise to get the students sufficiently involved and to enable them to do a provocative job. Other teachers we are aware of who use a similar approach employ detailed sets of real data (such as actual site reports) in order to engage the students' analytical abilities. The structure of the Seven Degrees exercise could be applied to any data set – either real or imagined. We chose to use a fictitious site simply because we enjoyed the creative process of 'making it all up' and the freedom this allowed us to bring in many different types of artifacts and contexts. We don't necessarily always use the same collection of artifacts from year to year, but do always keep the same site and characters. The more detailed background data we provide to the students to contextualize the plans and artifacts shown here draw upon the range of finds and site types excavated in numerous real archaeological sites of the Middle East, and thus is not so fictitious as to provide an unrealistic picture of past human behavior. The students can also access this literature to provide comparisons for their own analyses.

DISCUSSION

So, what do students learn from this exercise? They learn that theory is central to the practice of archaeology, and that each theoretical school uses common terms and procedures. They learn that often the procedures that are used are the same, even when the theoretical orientation is different, and that theoretical differences emerge most clearly at the point of interpretation. They learn that the choice of a particular framework is largely dependent upon which factors the individual archaeologist considers to be more important in terms of explaining change, and that there can be an element of political choice inherent in such decisions. They learn that archaeologists live within social networks and career structures and that how individuals are positioned within these networks will impact upon their interpretations, as well as whom they choose to support or criticize. They learn that archaeological explanations are not value-free and that different people approaching the same materials can come up with wildly diverging interpretations. Having recognized this, they are in a better position to question why some interpretations are accepted while others are overlooked, and to question the bases of their own interpretations and the consequences they may have. While these issues have been much debated in the archaeological literature (eg Kohl 1993; Leone *et al* 1987; Tilley 1989), the Seven Degrees of

Archaeology exercise teaches these concepts to students in such a way that the ideas are both created and challenged in a process of active learning.

All archaeologists use some framework to explain variability or change in human behavior, and this usually comes with a common set of procedures and terms. The choice of a particular framework is largely dependent upon which factors the individual archaeologist considers to be more important in terms of explaining change, though there is an element of political choice inherent in such decisions. The paradox for teachers of archaeological theory and method is that while this area is full of 'hot' debate, it is also one with which students are reluctant to engage. The challenge for us as teachers of archaeological theory and method is to use the intrinsic appeal of archaeological personalities as a basis for engaging with major theoretical and methodological developments in the field.

ACKNOWLEDGMENTS

We apologize to anyone whom we have affronted in this text. We thank Gary Jackson, who tolerated, and even encouraged, our rabid cackling late one night at the end of semester when we thought up this exercise. Mark Leone kindly commented on an earlier draft of this chapter, Paul Shackel discussed his use of a similar exercise with us, and Matthew Johnson gave us his help in refining the Seven Degrees of Archaeology exercise. Finally, we thank the students who shared (and will share) this course with us.

REFERENCES AND FURTHER READING

Al-Saadat, A and Afifi, E (1997) 'Role-playing for inhibited students in paternal communities', *English Teaching Forum Online* 35(3), 43, Available on-line at: http://exchanges.state.gov/forum/vols/vol35/no3/p43.htm, accessed 1 October 2004

Binford, LR (1968) 'Archaeological perspectives'. In Binford, SR and Binford, LR (eds) *New Perspectives in Archaeology*, Chicago: Aldine, pp. 5–39.

Binford, LR (1973) 'Interassemblage variability – the Mousterian and the "functional" argument', in Renfrew, C (ed), *The Explanation of Culture Change. Models in Prehistory,* London: Duckworth

Binford, LR (1989) 'Science to seance, or processual to "post-processual" archaeology', in Binford, LR (ed), *Debating Archaeology,* San Diego: Academic Press

Binford, LR and Stone, N (1988) 'Archaeology and theory: reply to Ian Hodder', *Man n.s* 23, 374–376

Bordes, F (1973) 'On the chronology and contemporaneity of different Palaeolithic cultures in France', in Renfrew, C (ed), *The Explanation of Culture Change. Models in Prehistory,* London: Duckworth

Burges, P (1992) 'Improvisational acting and language learning', *English Teaching Forum* 30(4), 20–23

Gamble, C (2001) *Archaeology. The Basics,* London: Routledge.

Hodder, I (1985) 'Post-processual archaeology', in Schiffer, M (ed), *Advances in Archaeological Method and Theory* 8, New York: Academic Press

Hodder, I (1989) 'Post-modernism, post-structuralism and post-processualism', in Hodder, I (ed), *The Meaning of Things,* London: Unwin Hyman

Hodder, I (1991) 'Postprocessual archaeology and the current debate', in Preucel, RW (ed), *Processual and Postprocessual Archaeologies*, Center for Archaeological Investigations, Occasional Paper No. 10, Carbondale: Southern Illinois University Press

Johnson, M (2000) *Archaeological Theory*, Oxford: Blackwell

Kohl, P (1993) 'Symbolic cognitive archaeology: a new loss of innocence', *Dialectical Anthropology* 9, 105–117

Leone, MP, Potter PB Jr and Shackel, PA (1987) 'Toward a critical archaeology', *Current Anthropology* 28(3), 283–302

Mackenzie, I (ed) (1994) *Archaeological Theory: Progress or Posture?* Avebury: Aldershot

Praetzellis, A (2000) *Death by Theory. A Tale of Mystery and Archaeological Theory*, Walnut Creek, CA: AltaMira Press

Preucel, R and Hodder, I (eds) (1996) *Contemporary Archaeology in Theory: A Reader*, Oxford: Blackwell Publishers

Renfrew, C and Bahn, P (1994) *Archaeology Theories, Methods, and Practice*, London: Thames and Hudson Ltd

Smith, C and Burke, H (2005) 'Becoming Binford: fun ways of teaching archaeological theory and method', *Public Archaeology* 4(1), 35–49

Tilley, Christopher (1989) 'Discourse and power: the genre of the Cambridge inaugural lecture', in Miller, D, Rowlands, M and Tilley, C (eds), *Domination and Resistance*, London: Unwin Hyman

Trigger, B (1995) *A History of Archaeological Thought,* Cambridge: Cambridge University Press

Wylie, A (1982) 'Epistemological issues raised by a structuralist archaeology', in Hodder, I (ed), *Symbolic and Structural Archaeology,* Cambridge: Cambridge University Press

HANDOUT 1

SEVEN DEGREES OF ARCHAEOLOGY

In a recent clean-out of their storage facilities (Depot Q, at the back of the complex, behind the chemical toilets), staff at the National Museum of Archaeology unexpectedly came across seven crates of a previously unknown archaeological collection. No one is quite sure of how this material got to be there, nor of exactly where it came from, although local janitorial lore has it that this is part of the Tell Machus collection, previously thought to be lost to the world since the untimely death of Dr. Clever Smirk, renowned field archaeologist and specialist in Middle Eastern antiquities. It has obviously been in the depot for a long time, but nobody currently working in the museum has any knowledge of it. When the collection was unpacked it was obvious that the crates contained a unique collection of highly important and valuable artifacts, but unfortunately there was no documentation inside the crates and most of the paper labels had been eaten by mice. Because the artifacts are potentially of great importance, the museum wishes to display them in their new $1.3 billion, state-of-the-art (but as yet unnamed) gallery and interpret them to the public.

Three months ago one of the junior undersecretaries to the Personal Assistant of the Associate Curator found a few stray pages from an archaeological field notebook in the lower drawer of an obscure filing cabinet which obviously hadn't been opened for decades. The pages were sandwiched in between a folder of receipts and an old *National Geographic* magazine, and had obviously been torn out of a larger notebook. The last page contained the last will and testament of Dr. Clever Smirk, who worked for over 40 years in the Middle East although he was also known to have moonlighted in Central America (he had a holiday house in Yucatan). Sadly for the archaeological community, Dr. Smirk disappeared during his last field season in the Middle East, where he had been working for the last several years on the site of Tell Machus, a 4th–8th millennium BC site near present-day Jordan. The results of Smirk's earliest work at Tell Machus were published by the Museum as an interim report, but considerable secrecy surrounded all of Smirk's subsequent field seasons at the site. For the past 15 years he had been working on a great synthesis of all of his published work, which he claimed would set out his controversial theories about the origins of religion, although it is not known precisely how Tell Machus may have fitted into this scheme. The whereabouts of his field notes and data have long been speculated upon (at least one world-famous archaeologist has built their career on arguing that Smirk, in fact, had no data and was so desperate to prove his idiosyncratic theories on religion that he was offering a reward to the first worker who could uncover incontrovertible proof). The Museum is very excited because, based on the sketch map and the notes, not to mention the last will and testament, it looks like this may well be part of his archival record, although it is unfortunate that no further pages could be found. To further complicate matters, the finds from the first field seasons at Tell Machus never returned from the Middle East. All of the material had been stored in a specially constructed civic building in a nearby village, but unfortunately, not long after Dr. Smirk disappeared, there was a minor coup and this building was razed to the ground. None of the finds from the earlier field seasons are known to have survived and if they had, it is unlikely that the authorities would now let them leave the country. As a result, and if the Depot Q artifacts are indeed from Tell Machus, they will be one of the world's most important archaeological collections.

In an attempt to decide just what they have in their possession and to determine the right way to interpret the collection, the Museum has convened an international workshop and invited you to be one of seven key participants. The Museum has asked each participant and their research team to provide an interpretation of what the artifacts might be and what the collection might represent, so that they can make the best decision about how to present it to the public. The workshop is intended to be a forum for all seven participants to argue the relative merits of their interpretation. There will be considerable prestige attached to being chosen as the patron and interpreter of the collection (not to mention being the author of the many high-quality, glossy publications which the Museum is sure to fund) and it is highly likely that the museum will name the gallery after their new expert. Because these objects are intended for museum display, the Museum's Board of Directors requires three levels of information from you, in order to present the best possible display:

- What these artifacts are
- What these artifacts signify (ie what they were used for, how, and why)
- What life was like at this site in the past (ie how people used these artifacts and lived their day-to-day life at the site)

Like all museums, they really just want you to tell them a good story.

HANDOUT 2

FIELD NOTES RECOVERED FROM THE NATIONAL MUSEUM FILING CABINET

The pages contain a rough, hand-drawn map of a site, which the Head Curator, Herman A. Pilfer, believes to be part of Tell Machus, and this partial (although almost illegible) account of Smirk's work there:

> …many ceramics are elaborately decorated, often imitating textile patterns. There is a great variety of imported materials, most notably the thin beaten gold which is similar in appearance to that mined from Kush, and very finely worked amber beads which I am used to associating with Anatolian burial sites. These materials are found in much larger quantities than comparable sites such as Tell Mi and Tell Athon. The subterranean chambers have yet to be fully excavated but initial indications from Structure F suggest that they may have played a role in complex burial rites. No human remains have been found in the three chambers excavated at Structure B, but the high-quality stonework found in the rear 'sanctuaries' of these chambers is highly suggestive of a ritual purpose. Two of the chambers in Structure B interconnect and it is possible that the third is also adjoining, though we will not be able to establish this until next field season.
>
> Figurines and effigy vessels are numerous, but even ordinary household objects are highly decorated. The abundance of figurines and effigy vessels in household contexts may reflect increased ritual activity, as might the higher quantities of items brought in as trade from elsewhere, although we have discovered no centralized ritual locales. The purpose of the subterranean chambers is as yet tentative, but once we have fully excavated all three known examples from Structures B, C, and F, we will be able to contrast them with the purposes of the above-ground shrines to illuminate the contrasts between above-ground and below-ground activities. I am confident that this will put paid once and for all to Dr. Highhorse's unfounded speculation that the shrines are in fact ordinary domestic features!

Fig 2.1. Tell Machus sketch plans.

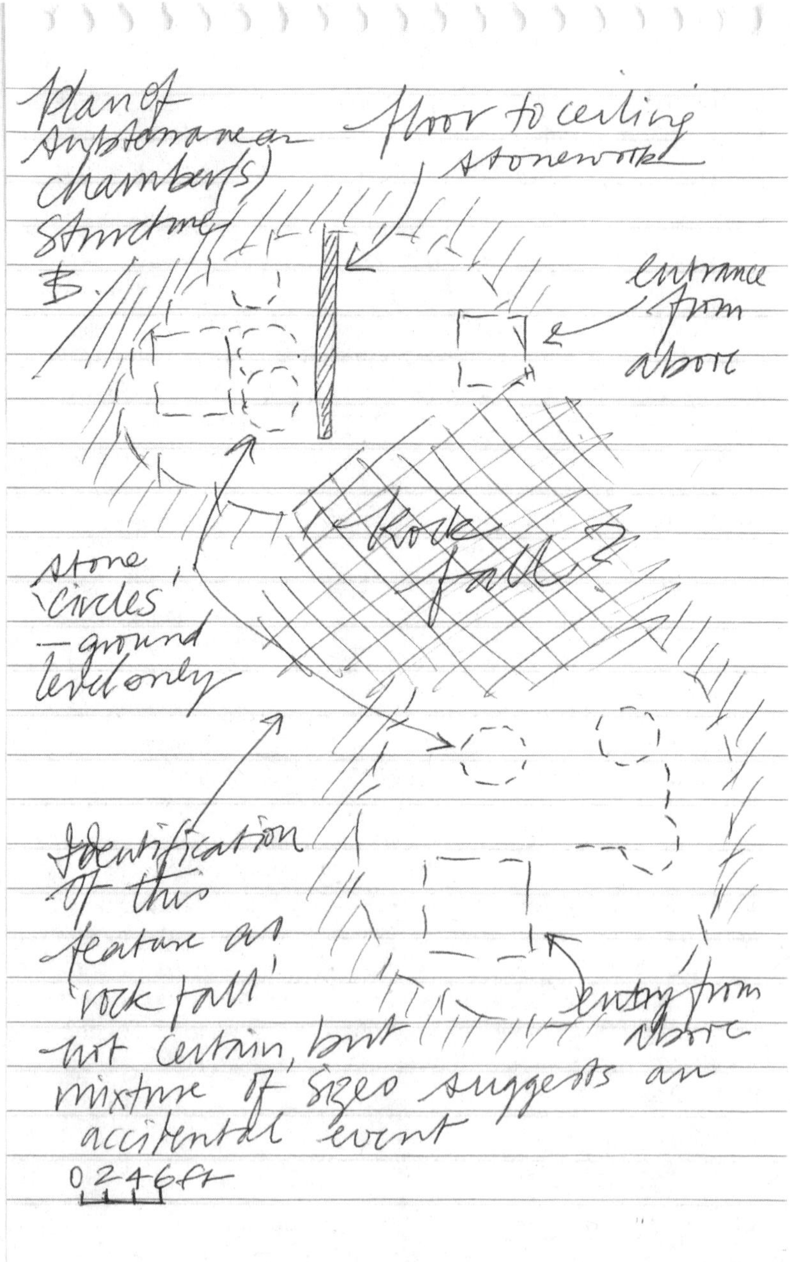

Fig 2.1. (continued) Tell Machus sketch plans.

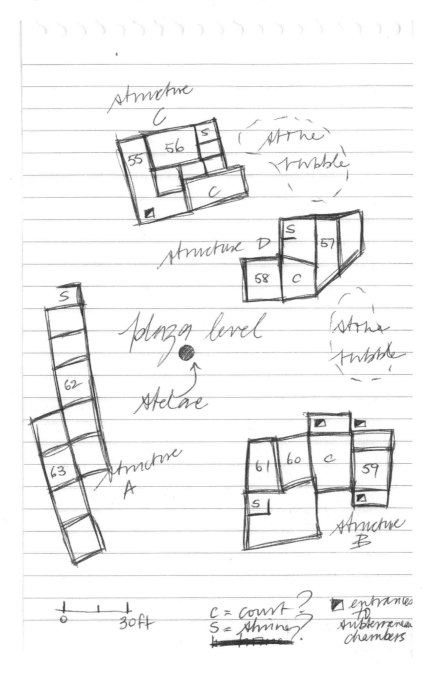

HANDOUT 3

THE CHARACTERS

1. CULTURE HISTORIAN

Your name is Sir Mortimer Potts. You graduated from Fisher House, Cambridge in 1922.

You undertook a groundbreaking study into the migration of Assyrians to Anatolia around 2,500 BC, as interpreted through changing pottery types in the region. This produced the fundamental culture history for this part of the world. You did not ever undertake a higher degree, but in 1955 you were awarded an honorary Doctor of Letters as a result of your many years of meticulous research.

Now, you are planning to excavate the tomb of an ancient pharaoh. You hope to provide the British Museum with a new collection of rare artifacts – and wouldn't be surprised if they named a gallery after you.

You believe in facts, that at the end of the day it's the raw data that count. You believe that cultural change is the result of external influences on societies, such as invasion, migration, and diffusion.

You are disappointed that Cambridge archaeology has not produced any new insights since 1942.

You read Greek and Latin.

The book by your bed is *War and Peace*.

Your friends, who are also 105, say that you 'invented' archaeology. You were one of the first people to dig in squares and put artifacts into sequences. The retrieval and classificatory systems you invented are now the basis of archaeological method.

2. POST-PROCESSUAL ARCHAEOLOGIST

Your name is Dr. Sebastian Wiley. Nephew of the renowned archaeologist, Sir Richard Cherrington, you are a graduate of Cambridge. In 1981 you finished your PhD, in which you interpreted clefts in rock shelters as depictions of female genitalia in Upper Palaeolithic rock art. Remember, you are from Cambridge.*

You were trained as a processual archaeologist, but have become heartily sick of being told 'the environment made them do it'. Instead, you are interested in how power works within societies.

You don't believe in truth. Truth is a word often deployed by old farts at those awful Cambridge dinners, when they want to justify their indolent existence. You believe that everyone will interpret things in different ways – and that which story is believed will depend on how powerful you are. You understand about power. You also understand that everything is political – especially the fact that it took you so long to get a job. Several weeks, actually. In the end, the only place that would employ you was Cambridge. You are deeply angry about the iniquity of your current situation.

Because of this you have recently become interested in the archaeology of the working classes (and you studiously check out your new theories each week with your cleaner – who would be *really* interested if only she spoke better English).

The book by your bed is *Star Trek: The Complete Encyclopedia.*

You read French, naturally, and you would be more at home discussing *habitus* with Bourdieu or Foucault than having a pie and chips down at the pub.

At a conference in Greece awhile back you tried speaking French to Teresa Tolstoy, but all she said was 'Nick off, rich boy'. You think she is gay.

Your big contribution to archaeology is making people aware of the political uses of the past in the present.

*This can be interpreted in many ways. The particular interpretation you make is up to you – and we would like to assure you that it is correct.

3. PROCESSUAL ARCHAEOLOGIST

Your name is Professor Rep Sample. You graduated from the University of Michigan in 1965 with a PhD focusing on the settlement systems of New Mexico. You were most definitely a radical in your time – and you still wear the hippie gear occasionally to prove it.

You believe in science. You believe that with the right scientific methods, you can answer most questions and can find the closest thing there is to archaeological truth.

Because of your years of seasoned experience, you understand the relationship between man and the environment. You are particularly interested in how cultural processes work, and how change in one part of a system can influence other parts.

You have had a succession of wives and partners. Your current partner, Fleur, who was your graduate student until last week, has been very understanding about your high blood pressure.

The book by your bed is the classic Western, *Lone Star.*

You speak French fluently, but keep this secret.

Your big contribution to archaeology has been making people do things in a scientific and systematic way.

4. STRUCTURALIST ARCHAEOLOGIST

Your name is Professor Pierre Chauvin. You graduated from the Sorbonne in 1962. Your doctoral thesis was a semiotic analysis of the rock art of Altamira, bringing to light the contrasting contributions of men and women to the establishment of past hierarchies and social orders. You were not surprised to discover that males have always had the biggest motifs. One of your graduate students once had the temerity to suggest that, statistically speaking, it was actually the females who had the biggest motifs. She no longer studies under you.

Your mentor, the great linguist Professor U. P. Himself once told you that 'the proper study of man is mind'. You believe that 'Culture' is first and foremost a system of classification and that all social and cultural phenomena are intimately related, and in fact can be distilled to a few simple underlying principles.

Your current book, *The Prehistoric Mind of Man*, has lots of nice images. Critics say that you see things only in black and white, but this in unfair because your book is full of color pictures. The blurb beneath your jacket photo (incidentally, a very flattering shot taken of you in the mid-1970s, which you insist the publishers still use), praises you as 'single-handedly inventing the only genuinely new paradigm to be developed in the last forty years'.

You scorn the environmental determinism of processualists and once, in a heated debate at WAC–1.5 (the 1.5th World Archaeological Congress in Timbuktu), you threw a chair at Rep Sample's head, shouting 'Everything he says is lies!' The only people you hate more than processualists are post-structuralists (but that's okay because lots of people hate post-structuralists).

The book by your bed is *Le Nom de la Rose*, by your personal friend Umberto Eco.

Your first language is French but you speak Italian, English, and a little Polish.

5. FEMINIST ARCHAEOLOGIST

Your name is Dr. Susan G. Hunter. When you graduated from the University of Michigan in 1977, you were the first woman to graduate in anthropology in 13 years. That was a tough school.

You were trained as a processual archaeologist, and your PhD was on the cultural ecology of the !San. As a student you started to wonder where women fit into the picture. You couldn't quite bring yourself to believe that men made *all* the artifacts and *all* the rock paintings.

As the only female student of your year, young and naïve, you had an affair with Rep Sample. This did not turn out well – but it gave you valuable critical insights into his work.

Your first book, *Woman The Huntress*, was a best seller (archaeologically speaking) – and you got a $7.50 royalty check that year.

You believe in the importance of finding gender in the archaeological record – even if you have to strain the interpretation of the data occasionally.

You're not a lesbian, though lots of your friends are.

The book by your bed is the Mills and Boone classic, *Destined for Love*. When challenged about this, you defend yourself on the grounds that this is an exercise in post-modern irony.

Your big contribution to archaeology is interpreting material culture in terms of gendered relationships, and in putting women into the stories of the past.

6. MARXIST ARCHAEOLOGIST

Your name is Dr. Teresa Tolstoy. You graduated from the University of California, Berkeley in 1986. Your doctoral thesis had words like 'dialectical materialism' and 'alienation' in it. You are a very good speller.

Your father was a butcher. You believe that class conflict is inevitable and that this is the basis of the archaeological record. You see change as generated internally within societies.

Your seminal paper, 'Rank inequality: The problems of interpreting culture change in Anatolia', was a re-interpretation of Sir Mortimor Potts' classic 1932 study. Your paper was published in the *International Journal of Marxist Archaeology*.

You believe that there is no substitute for reading Marx himself, which you have done, at great length. You have even sat in his chair at the British Library.

You see yourself as a champion of the working classes. At least you come from the working classes. You feel an allegiance to feminists, who also have had to engage in a struggle against bourgeois forces in academia, even though feminists are perverse enough to believe that they can pursue their ideas outside of a Marxist framework.

You don't like upper-class boys from Cambridge who think they do working class archaeology.

The book by your bed is the draft that you are co-authoring with Dr. Susan Hunter, *How to Succeed in Archaeology Without a Penis.*

You speak English, but learned German in order to read Marx in the original.

7. POST-STRUCTURALIST ARCHAEOLOGIST

Your name is Dr. Toby W. Torso. You graduated from the University of Wales, Lampeter, in 1990. Your doctoral thesis integrated Derrida's ideas of the body with structuration theory. This produced a novel.

Your current research is into the generative capacity of the sign according to the socially and historically situated nature of social interactions. However, you are also interested in the application of literary and dramatic theory to the analysis of material culture.

People say that you use jargon to mystify, to create a language of exclusion in which the outsider is made to feel small. This hurts you.

In a recent critical review of your latest book, *Difficult Points to Grasp: The Phallocentric Nature of !San Weaponry from the Museum of the Netherlands Collection*, Professor Rep Sample commented that 'the only structure he could perceive in post-structuralism is the requirement to write page upon page of citations from Foucault, Lacan or Schopenhauer in support of the simplest statements'. You want to hurt him.

You are gay, but dabbled with heterosexuality as a young person — and are still trying to live down the memory of this.

Your latest research interest is queer theory. You religiously attend every TAG (Theoretical Archaeology Group) conference and you regularly publish in the *Cambridge Archaeological Review* and the cutting-edge journal, *Latest Bandwagon in Archaeology.*

The book by your bed is *American Psycho.*

Your first language is English but you are more at home speaking jargon.

Your big contribution to archaeology is … still to come.

The Great Debate: Archaeology, Repatriation, and Nationalism

Morag M. Kersel

Who owns the past? The answer to this question is a hotly debated subject around the world. There are those who believe that all artifacts belong in the country of origin, and those who believe that artifacts acquired legally and long held in museums and collections far from their countries of origin should remain in their present locations. A significant number of objects have been returned in response to international pressure, legal strategies, and public awareness campaigns. The repatriation of Egyptian Pharaoh Ramses I from the Michael C. Carlos Museum at Emory University, Atlanta, Georgia, was a coup for Dr. Zahi Hawass, Director General of Egypt's Supreme Council of Antiquities, in his ceaseless crusade to have all antiquities of national importance repatriated to Egypt (El Aref 2003). Other notable repatriations include many Native American ritual objects and human remains from US institutions (Fforde *et al* 2002); the return of the Lydian Hoard to Turkey from the Metropolitan Museum in New York (Kaye and Main 1995); and the recent wrangling between Italy and Ethiopia over the Axum obelisk (*BBC News* 2004).

The marble statuary removed from the Athens Acropolis by Lord Elgin in the early part of the 19th century is perhaps the best-known example of a claim for cultural property repatriation. Before removing them to England, Elgin had acquired permission of the Turkish government, then the occupying power in Greece. But the details of this permission and the authority of the Ottoman government to give such consent are questionable. Discussion over the return of the Marbles to Greece has been ongoing since Lord Byron appealed to the masses in his lament over the Marbles, referring to them as 'the last poor plunder from a bleeding land' (Byron's Canto the Second). The dispute intensified in the political arena after Greece submitted a formal request to the

Council of Ministers of Culture of UNESCO in 1982. The controversy between England and Greece over the Marbles has spurred academics and politicians around the globe to consider broader questions about competing claims that nations have on art and artifacts and the manner in which they should be displayed. There is a growing movement to repatriate cultural property that was looted or carted off by those on the grand tour, crusading archaeologists and scientists, and military missions.

The debate over the repatriation of the marble statuary from the Parthenon in Greece remains one of the most visible, emotionally charged debates in cultural property protection. On a basic level, the dispute is one country vs. another with no apparent middle ground. Even the standard names for the Marbles – Elgin and Parthenon – reveal the underlying biases of the speaker. However, the debate is far more complicated because there is more at stake than national identity and pride; there are the potential economic benefits of owning the Marbles. The legendary Marbles attract tourists wherever they reside. With tourists come revenues and whoever holds the Marbles is the economic victor.

Bringing this debate into the classroom challenges students to think about issues of ownership, cultural property protection, representations, and nationalism and archaeology. Originally, this exercise was conducted as part of an introduction to archaeology survey class. The textbook for the class was Colin Renfrew and Paul Bahn's *Archaeology, Theories, Methods and Practice* (2000) and various supplemental readings. This assignment was used as an introduction to the topics covered in the final chapter (14) of Renfrew and Bahn, 'Whose Past? Archaeology and the Public', a detailed discussion of the issues associated with destruction, interpretation, ownership, and access to the past. By this point in the class, students were familiar with the methods, theory, and practice of archaeology and this exercise provided them with insights on how the public intersects with archaeology and how we are all affected by the past in our daily lives.

As a vehicle for introducing concepts of nationalism, repatriation, colonialism, and cultural property protection, this exercise is a good way to engage students in a class discussion. The debate over the Marbles is sometimes covered in current newspapers, articles, and television reports and so it is one that students may vaguely know about but have not intellectually considered. As an introductory exercise in classes on ethics in archaeology, nationalism, and archaeology or museum practice, students are able to consider the relevance of the debate to their own lives by thinking through the issues of cultural property presentation through museum display, archaeological enquiry, and the rights of indigenous populations.

PREPARING THE EXERCISE

The materials for the exercise are:

- An outline of the current debate over the Marbles, from both the Greek and British perspectives
- Slide show of the Marbles and background in the debate
- Images of the Marbles *in situ* and in the British Museum, a plan of original location of the Marbles on the Parthenon, and a breakdown of where the various fragments of the Marbles now reside.

APPROXIMATE LENGTH OF EXERCISE

This exercise usually takes about a single one-hour class period. In the previous class, I hand out the supplementary reading packet, which includes the assignment, a list of relevant readings, and a note assigning each student to the side of either Greece or Britain. At the beginning of the class, I give a brief (10–15 min) background on the case, illustrated with images.

THE EXERCISE

Question for debate: The marble statuary removed to Britain by Lord Elgin in the 19th century from the Parthenon in Athens Greece should be returned to the country of origin. Why or why not?

The students are asked to defend their assigned country's position based on the readings. Reading lists that include material relevant to both sides of the debate are supplied with the expectation that they will develop arguments to counter the opposing country's claim. Readings are designed to encourage students to think about the greater issues of nationalism, colonialism, repatriation, and cultural property protection in the context of this single issue. The exercise is structured as a debate and each side is given a set amount of time to present their country's argument for keeping the Marbles. Once each side has presented their position, the debate is then open for class discussion where we consider the various arguments and add any salient points that have not already been covered. I act as the moderator and facilitator if discussion wanes or the debate verges toward acrimony. Near the end of the class, I ask the students, regardless of their assigned positions, to cast their votes on whether the Marbles should be repatriated to Greece. The outcome is often very interesting.

The Mission

In each reading packet there is a yellow Post It© assigning each person a side for the great debate: those supporting the Greek claim for the repatriation of the Marbles and those supporting the British position to keep the Marbles. When the students are completing the assigned readings or surfing the web for relevant sites, they should be formulating the defense of their position. I use these questions to guide their reading:

- What are the Marbles? Why do Britain and Greece want them?
- List the arguments for the return of the Marbles to Greece or for keeping them in Britain. Discuss briefly the motives of those people involved.
- What role have the Marbles played in the construction of British and Greek national identities? What are the main historical and political factors influencing the construction of those identities?
- List the issues surrounding the restitution of cultural property in a global context. Discuss the Marbles with regard to disputes of ownership and representation.
- Despite the position you were assigned, what is your opinion on whether the Marbles should be returned?
- What effect (if any) do international legislation and institutions (UNESCO, ICOMOS, ICOM) concerning cultural property have on this case? (See UNESCO web site on legal protection of cultural heritage www.unesco.org/culture/legalprotection/ and see the Hellenic Ministry of Culture web site for appeals to UNESCO www.culture.gr/6/68/682/).

Background

I use this background, illustrated with slides, in the brief introduction to the debate. On the acropolis (high city) of Athens there sits a group of buildings, one of which – the Parthenon – is dedicated to the patron goddess of the city, Athena Parthenos. Built between 447 and 438 BC, the monuments were commissioned by Pericles after victories over the Persians to convey the political and military supremacy of Athens (Hamilakis 1999: 305). The buildings on the Acropolis have a long and checkered history of opulence, glory, and destruction. In the past, the Parthenon served as a mosque, a church, and a military arsenal. Marble statuary from the various structures were used for target practice, crushed for mortar, and reused by the local populace for hearthstones and building blocks.

At the end of the 18th century, Lord Elgin, a diplomat posted to Turkey, was in the process of building a mansion for himself and his new bride in his native Scotland. Emulating classical buildings was all the rage in Britain, so Elgin sought permission from the Ottoman occupiers of Greece to take casts and copies of the statuary and architectural elements of the Parthenon. It is here that the details of the story become confusing:

- Did Elgin ask for permission to actually remove statuary or just to make copies and casts?
- Did he bribe Ottoman officials to receive greater leeway in removing pieces?
- Did he remove statuary still *in situ* on the Parthenon or only those he found on the ground?
- Was he greedy, corrupt, and unscrupulous or did he have the best interests of the Marbles at heart?

The original permission from the Ottoman government has been lost, but scholars have pieced together archival evidence indicating that Elgin never had permission to take away pieces of statuary (see Rudenstine 2000; Stewart 2001). However, Elgin was not the only person poking around in the rubble of the Parthenon. Napoleon's men, on direct orders from the General, and a contingent of Germans, were all very interested in acquiring pieces for their national museums. In 1804 on his journey back to England, Elgin was seized by Napoleon's forces. Elgin languished in a French jail for over two years, losing his nose to a disfiguring disease because he would not concede the ownership of the Marbles to Napoleon. Eventually Elgin returned to England, penniless, noseless and wifeless, with no recourse but to find a buyer for the Marbles.

In 1816 after a lengthy parliamentary debate and public outcry the Marbles were acquired by the British Museum – at taxpayer expense – through an act of Parliament. However, the vote was not unanimous, as some 30 members felt that Elgin had removed the statuary without the proper authority. This parliamentary debate with its dissentions began the great debate over where the Marbles should reside.

The majority of the Marbles are now housed at the British Museum in London, where visitors can enjoy them at eye level in the Duveen gallery, not visible against the backdrop of the Athenian sky as the original artisans intended. Earlier in the 20th century, Duveen commissioned cleaning of the Marbles with wire brushes in order to make them whiter and more appealing to the public. Reports of this treatment and the Marbles themselves were hidden away for some years to avoid embarrassing comments on the stewardship of the Marbles (St Clair 1999).

In theory, repatriation should be easy. Cultural property is, for most legal purposes, like other property: the owner can recover it, subject to the possible rights of good faith purchasers (Merryman 1985). In many analyses of this case, the legal issues come down to two positions: (1) First, the Marbles were wrongfully taken by Lord Elgin and have never legally or morally belonged to Britain, or (2) Elgin had the proper authority as granted to him by the Ottoman government to remove the Marbles and Greece has waited too long to file a formal claim in the courts.

One of the purposes of this exercise is to move beyond the legal positions in the case to the underlying motivating factors behind England and Greece wanting the Marbles. The objective of a class debate on the topic is to clarify, outline, and articulate the position of each claimant and then to decide which country (if either) has the most compelling argument.

Arguments

Greece (Why?)

1. The Marbles were constructed for a specific structure in Athens and they belong in that context.
2. In Athens the Marbles will be exhibited within sight of the Parthenon, providing visitors with a complete view of the temple and sculpture.
3. The Marbles represent Greek cultural and historical significance. They symbolize the pinnacle of Greek Classical civilization.
4. The Greeks were the victims of foreign occupation during the period when the Marbles were taken to England. The legality of the removal is highly contentious.

Britain (Why not?)

1. The Marbles were removed on the basis of legally obtained permission from the governing authority of the period.
2. The act of repatriation may start a chain reaction in other countries demanding the return of their cultural property. The

educational role of the museum would be very limited if everything in the museum had to be repatriated to the country of origin.

3. By removing the Marbles from their location in Athens, they were saved from other foreign invaders, pollution, and the ravages of time.

4. The Marbles have become an integral part of the British cultural heritage.

The Role of Devil's Advocate

If the debate lags you may want to take on the role of devil's advocate, asking each side to consider their less altruistic motives for wanting to 'own' the Marbles. As devil's advocate you may also want to bring up the issues surrounding the economics of the Marbles and the paths of least resistance – doing what is easiest and leaving them in England. The following can be used to guide the debate in directions other than those of nationalism, legal issues, and cultural patrimony.

Why do Britain and Greece really want the Marbles?

Greece:

- Is Greece requesting the Marbles under the pretext of nationalism, when perhaps their immediate motives are of an economic nature? In the years immediately preceding the Olympics, there was an increased effort on behalf of repatriation, as event organizers sought to capitalize on greater tourism due to the Games.
- The new museum at the base of the Acropolis to house the repatriated Marbles would not be free to the public, thus generating income and revenue for the tourist industry. Presently, the new museum is embroiled in various legal battles over the destruction of archaeological resources during its construction.

Britain:

- The British Museum regularly rents out the gallery space in which the Marbles are housed for private functions and receptions, thus gaining monetary benefit from the Marbles. The Duveen Gallery is a coveted backdrop for corporate events, showcasing the glory days of the British Empire and alluding to the birthplace of democracy.

- The Marbles have resided in the British Museum for almost 200 years and form an integral part of the museum's collection. Their location in London makes them easily accessible for scholarly study.
- The Marbles were acquired through an act of Parliament; it will take another act to return them to Greece.
- The Marbles have become enmeshed in British culture over nearly two centuries, inspiring architecture, artistic undertakings, and literary endeavors.

REFLECTIONS ON THE EXERCISE

This exercise was a huge hit with the students. They enjoyed the lively exchange over the issues and were very engaged for the entire hour class. Be forewarned, most students will side with Greece, following their intuitive sense that both the British and the Ottoman governments wronged them. In order to play devil's advocate, it may be best for the instructor to be armed with arguments supporting the British contention that, had they not been taken, the Marbles would probably not still be in Greece at this stage – either taken by some other government, private individuals, or very possibly destroyed through exposure to pollution and/or environmental degradation. Illustrating this point through examples of other instances of monuments and artifacts being repatriated to their countries of origin, only to be destroyed or resold on the market (see the case of the Nok and Ife statues in Benin, Willett 2000), is highly effective. Be prepared with suggestions for compromise: Can high-quality replicas be manufactured so that even the discerning museum visitor will be unable to tell the difference? Alternatively, Greece and Britain could work out a situation where long-term loans of cultural material would allow the Marbles to reside in Greece on a part-time basis. In some instances, the debate had a tendency to dwell in the emotional. It is a poignant topic for both sides, and at times it was difficult to bring the discussion back to the relevant laws and arguments that are germane to the various standpoints.

DISCUSSION

What do the students get out of the exercise? They learn that there are usually more than two sides to an argument and that not all issues are black and white. They learn that the underlying motives for a particular position may not be clear or directly related to the issue at hand. They learn that the issues of colonialism and nationalism are relevant to the current practice of archaeology and should be taken into consideration when discussing methodology, theory, and practice. The inherent biases and preconceived notions of individuals are also present in national agendas, heritage policy formulation, and legal precedents, and, as archaeologists, students should always question the motivating factors in both sides of an argument. The debate of who owns the past has been much discussed (Gathercole and Lowenthal 1990; Kohl and Fawcett 1996; Rowan and Baram 2004; Trigger 1984) and cannot be resolved in a single class period. However, considering this topic can bring to the forefront often-overlooked aspects of the ramifications of archaeological practice.

SUPPLEMENTAL READING ASSIGNMENT FOR THE GREAT DEBATE

Hamilakis, Y (1999) 'Stories from exile: Fragments from the cultural biography of the Parthenon (or "Elgin") marbles', *World Archaeology* 31(2), 303–320

Handler, R (1991) 'Who owns the past? History, cultural property and the logic of possessive individualism', in Williams, B (ed), *The Politics of Culture*, Washington D.C.: The Smithsonian Institution

Kersel, M (2004) 'The politics of playing fair. Or who's losing their marbles?', in Rowan, Y and Baram, U (eds) *Marketing Heritage: Archaeology and the Consumption of the Past*, Walnut Creek CA: AltaMira Press

Rudenstine, D (2000) 'Did Elgin cheat at marbles?', *The Nation* May 29, 43–51

Stewart, WG (2001) 'The Marbles: Elgin or Parthenon? IAL Annual Lecture, December 2000', *Art, Antiquity and Law* 6(1), 37–56

Trigger, B (1984) 'Alternative archaeologies: nationalist, colonialist, imperialist', *Man, n.s* 19(3), 355–370

RELEVANT WEBSITES

British Museum's Collection: www.thebritishmuseum.ac.uk/gr/debate.html
Campaign to Return the Parthenon Marbles: www.parthenon2004.com/
The Parthenon Marbles: www.uk.digiserve.com/mentor/marbles/
The Parthenon Marbles Virtual Museum: www.parthenonas.com/
Restitution of the Parthenon Marbles: www.culture.gr/6/68/682/
UNESCO Cultural Heritage and Legal Protection: http://portal.unesco.org/culture/en/ev.php-URL_ID=2187&URL_DO=DO_TOPIC&URL_SECTION=201.html
www.unesco.org/culture/legalprotection/
Website dedicated to the return of the Parthenon (Elgin) Marbles: www.museum-security.org/elginmarbles.html

REFERENCES AND FURTHER READING

BBC News (2004) 'Deadlock over the Axum obelisk', *BBC News Online*, World Edition, accessed 14 September 2004

El Aref, N (2003) 'Recovering heritage', *Al-Ahram Online* Issue 637, May 8–14

Fforde, C, Hubert, J and Turnbull, P (eds) (2002) *The Dead and Their Possessions: Repatriations in Principle, Policy and Practice*, London: Routledge

Gathercole, P and Lowenthal, D (1990) *The Politics of the Past*, London: Routledge

Greenfield, J (1996) *The Return of Cultural Treasures*, Second Edition, Cambridge: Cambridge University Press

Hamilakis, Y (1999) 'Stories from exile: Fragments from the cultural biography of the Parthenon (or "Elgin") marbles', *World Archaeology* 31(2), 303–20

Hamilakis, Y and Yalouri, E (1996) 'Antiquities as symbolic capital in modern Greek society', *Antiquity* 70, 117–29

Handler, R (1991) 'Who owns the past? History, cultural property and the logic of possessive individualism', in Williams, B (ed), *The Politics of Culture*, Washington D.C: The Smithsonian Institution

Hitchens, C (1997) *The Elgin Marbles: Should They Be Returned to Greece?* London: Verso

Kaye, L and Main, C (1995) 'The saga of the Lydian hoard antiquities: From Uşak to New York and back again and some related observations on the law of cultural repatriation', in Tubb, KW (ed), *Antiquities Trade or Betrayed: Legal, Ethical and Conservation Issues*, London: Archetype

Kohl, P and Fawcett, C (eds) (1996) *Nationalism, Politics and the Practice of Archaeology*, Cambridge: Cambridge University Press

McBryde, I (ed) (1985) *Who Owns the Past?*, New York: Oxford University Press

Merryman, JH (1985) 'Thinking about the Elgin marbles', *Michigan Law Review* 83, 1880–1923

Rowan, Y and Baram, U (eds) (2004) *Marketing Heritage: Archaeology and the Consumption of the Past*, Walnut Creek, CA: AltaMira Press

Rudenstine, D (2000) 'Did Elgin cheat at marbles?', *The Nation* May 29, 43–51

St Clair, W (1998) *Lord Elgin and the Marbles*, Third edition, London: Oxford University Press

St Clair, W (1999) 'The Elgin marbles: questions of stewardship and accountability', *International Journal of Cultural Property* 8(2), 391–521

Stewart, WG (2001) 'The Marbles: Elgin or Parthenon? IAL Annual Lecture, December 2000', *Art, Antiquity and Law* 6(1), 37–56

Trigger, B (1984) 'Alternative archaeologies: nationalist, colonialist, imperialist', *Man, n.s* 19(3), 355–70

Tubb, KW (ed) (1995) *Antiquities Trade or Betrayed: Legal, Ethical and Conservation Issues*, London: Archetype

Vrettos, T (1997) *The Elgin Affair: the Abduction of Antiquity's Greatest Treasures and the Passions It Aroused*, New York: Arcade Publishers

Willett, F (2000) 'Restitution or re-circulation: Benin, Ife and Nok', *Journal of Museum Ethnography* 12, 125–32

Yalouri, E (2001) *The Acropolis: Global Fame, Local Claim*, New York: Berg Books

Part II

Games

Grasp, or Happy Families, the Archaeological Way

Gail Higginbottom

> *'Learning that is fun appears to be more effective.'*
> —Lepper and Cordova, 1992, in Amory *et al* 1999: 311

WHY THIS GAME?

'Grasp' is a strategy game that involves logic, memory, and visualization. It brings students together and can be used as either an informal or formal cooperative activity. 'Grasp' itself was developed as a response to how theoretical archaeology is often taught at many universities today: a semester module frequently focusing upon more recent philosophies with lots of new information that remains unintegrated. The information presented frequently has no historical or philosophical context, often due to a lack of time in single modulated subjects. Such modules rarely contain a firm background in the previous history or philosophies connecting to the more recent developments, and often fail to connect these developments at a more in-depth level than contrasting, for example, processualism with post-processualism. The result is that the information presented to students is often free-floating and, apart from their own project work, students easily forget what is taught to them. Further, rather than seeing it as a part of a firm grounding in archaeology, students see it as an option, with the consequence that they can ignore it as not being part of 'real' archaeology. These modules are often not taught before the second year of a degree.

This is the situation into which many contract lecturers enter; having no control over the way the degree is structured, they are unable to involve students in theory and theorizing from the students' first year. I have two main strategies to deal with this situation. One, which I mention in Chapter 6, is to teach a year of theory within its historical context, firmly connecting thought with time and place and the influence upon archaeology at specific times by particular people. With such an opportunity for in-depth learning, students feel more confident due to the firmer grounding they have acquired. In this situation students can delight in the new intellectual knowledge and understanding they have obtained and feel a sense of significant achievement. Hand in hand with this, in the second strategy, is the enjoyment of learning from a different angle: game playing.

WHY GAMES AT ALL?

There are ways of learning that can center on fascinating archaeology students within a non-rigid environment and encouraging self-paced and self-engaged personal development. Using cooperative student activities as learning devices is more beneficial than using activities that do not involve group engagement. When performing cooperative activities, students appear more motivated and are more capable of successful critical thinking (Wenzel 2000: 293A). Game playing is a form of cooperative activity even though it involves competing against one another to achieve a similar goal. Wenzel, in his review of learning devices, concluded that, when performing cooperative activities, students appeared more motivated, were more capable of successful critical thinking, proposed more new ideas and solutions when presented with problems, and transferred more of what they learned in prior situations to new problems (Wenzel 2000: 293A).

Games appear to inherently motivate people by stimulating curiosity and are goal oriented because they can be innately challenging (Thomas and Macredie 1994). By containing elements of fantasy, novelty, and complexity, games are also fun (Amory et al 1999). However, certain games are more appealing to students in an educational context than others (Amory 1999: 312). Of the various games tested by Amory, including 3-D adventure, strategy, and simulation, first- and second-year university students reported that the adventure and strategy games contained better entertainment and educational aspects (Amory et al 1999: 316–317). Ultimately, they preferred stimulating games that required the use of logic, memory, visualization, and problem-solving (Amory et al 1999: 318). This implies that games that involve as many of these four qualities as possible should do well in gaining students' attention and improving their learning experience.

GRASP

'Grasp' helps students gain an understanding of the big picture of major themes or theories in theoretical archaeology, and enables them to connect the myriad threads they are expected to know individually and together. As well, it helps them to retain more knowledge than might otherwise be possible. Similar to Burke and Smith's game, 'Seven Degrees of Archaeology', students see that archaeologists use theoretical frameworks to explain the phenomena they wish to study, be that change, social structure, or belief systems. 'Grasp' is a card game that can be incorporated halfway through a one-semester module, once students have some knowledge 'under their belt'. It can be used at mid-semester and end of semester as part of the continuous assessment format or just as part of a dynamic learning environment from mid-semester onward. For year-long subjects, it would be best to incorporate 'Grasp' about a quarter of the way into the course.

Game Overview

'Grasp', or as I like to call it 'Happy Families, the Archaeological Way', is a simple card game. Basically, a pack of 49 or 98 cards is made up of several discrete sets or suits that can be put together in a number of ways. The individual sets could be, for example, people, theoretical ideas, movements, archaeological sites or finds, and anthropological or archaeological studies, and each set will need to contain a minimum of seven cards. This would mean that a pack of 49 cards could have seven sets of seven cards each and a pack of 98 cards could have seven sets of 14 cards each. Although the total number of cards in the pack is up to you, you will need a minimum number of seven sets, as this equals the number of cards in the hand that gains the maximum number of points. The aim is to create a hand that contains cards that can be united under the same theoretical archaeological theme, but each card must be from a different set or suit. The winning flush would be a hand in which all of the cards belong to the same theoretical theme (such as post-structuralism, or evolutionary theory). An example might be combining a person card, a theoretical umbrella card (like structuralism or culture-history), theoretical or methodological notion card (like middle-range theory, stratigraphy or cultural heritage, see Figures 4.1, 4.2, and 4.3), archaeological site card, key quote or catch phrase card (Figure 4.4), experimental or study card and a definitive publication card. Another idea might be associating known recognizable historical symbols or architectural technical features learned during the course on a notion card (see Figure 4.5). Some cards could be less specific, where quote or idea stands on its own without a reference and the students have to work out its most appropriate group (Figure 4.6). You could play it so that the winner must have the theoretical umbrella card in order to hold a winning hand, or perhaps allocate more points to that kind of winning hand,

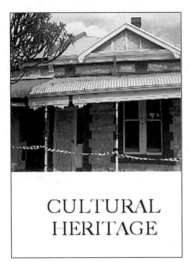

Figure 4.1. A notion card with a representative picture and title. The house was built in approximately 1925 in Adelaide, Australia (photograph by Gail Higginbottom).

Figure 4.2. A notion card with a representative picture, title, and description. This card has a more fun design and shows that hand-drawn pictures can be just as effective (picture by Padric McGee and used with permission).

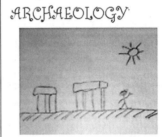

Figure 4.3. A notion card with a representative picture and title. This picture shows students on a field trip to Avebury, England, walking down a possible processional way. Students enjoy seeing pictures from a fieldtrip they were involved in, so if you have any put in a couple (photograph by Gail Higginbottom).

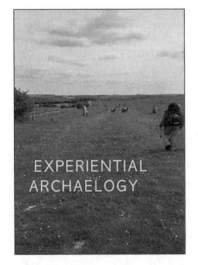

"There is
nothing outside
the text"

Derrida, 1976, 158.

Figure 4.4. A key catchphrase card. This shows that cards can be very simply laid out and do not have to take much work.

Interpreting Architectural
Form

What can form tell us about the way
people thought about their world?
What can you tell us about the
sigificance of any items in this
picture?

Figure 4.5. A notion card with a representative picture and title. This is a photograph of Salisbury Cathedral. This photograph highlights architectural design that may contain either symbolic or/and technical information in its detail with which the students may have become familiar through a course studying historical documentation of architectural features (photograph of cathedral by Gail Higginbottom).

Thinking
through the
body

Figure 4.6. An example of a quote card that is disconnected from its source and thus is more challenging for the student (photograph of students at Stonehenge by Gail Higginbottom).

QUESTION CARD
✳✳✳✳✳✳✳✳

Who said ....?

For the subjective idealism of scientistic archaeology we substitute a view of the discipline as an hermeneutically informed dialectical science of the past and present unremittingly embracing and attempting to understand the polyvalent qualities of the socially constructed world in which we live.

Or what does it mean?!!!!

Figure 4.7. An idea for a question card for advanced students (Who said this? or What does it mean?). The quote comes from M. Shanks and C. Tilley, 1992, *Reconstructing Archaeology: Theory and Practice*, page 243.

and lesser combinations of points for other hands (eg no theoretical umbrella card, or allow the use of wild cards). Students will be aware of what items should be drawn together as the card game should be enmeshed with their lecture topics, tutorials/seminars, and reading materials, remembering that the game is meant to help students draw together the myriad threads they encounter.

As a practical example of playing, I might be dealt cards with the following words or pictures: Darwin, Hodder, a gothic picture of a laboratory (as a possible view that some post-processualists may have of the scientific method), an illustration of V. Gordon Childe's timetable of cultural groups, a Neo-marxist article or book title, the word 'post-structuralism', and a picture of rock art at Nämforsen, Lillforshällan, northern Sweden. I might choose to keep the cards 'post-structuralism' and 'the cave paintings of Nämforsen' and continue my search for cards that might connect with these. For the latter, it might include the name or a picture of Christopher Tilley. Naturally, I will discard the remainder of my hand upside-down in the center. I will then ask the dealer for the replacement number of cards. Once everyone has been given the opportunity to discard unwanted cards and reorganize their hands, the entire process begins again.

When the allotted time is reached for playing the game, the person with the most points wins the game from that group. Or, if you are using it as part of your marking scheme, you could allocate a small percentage such as 2% of their overall grade per class session if you do it many times, or 5% each time, offering it at mid-term and the end of term. As the game has an element of chance, it would be unfair to weight the activity too heavily.

PREPARING THE EXERCISE

You will need to make up a certain number of packs of cards yourself depending on the size of the class – one pack will be sufficient for five people. The cards can be mainly black-and-white text and could be printed on labels to attach to pre-bought cards (or 'card', as the art shops call it) that are the same size or a little bit bigger. As we are using the cards for educational purposes only, you can obtain main pictures from the web as long as they are acknowledged or cited appropriately, according to the web site used. Alternatively, for those wishing a professional look, there are web sites that sell blank cards and downloadable software for creating personalized photo playing cards and educational card games. Some sites go so far as to 'create free educational worksheets such as flashcards, game boards, and quizzes to print directly from your browser', such as www.educationalpress.org/educationalpress/.

APPROXIMATE LENGTH OF EXERCISE

The game can be played instead of a lecture or tutorial or for an allotted time within it; the outcome of it can be assessed as part of students' continuous assessment. For instance, the game could be played in class twice a month for 30 minutes during a two-hour lecture slot (as a break) or for half an hour in a tutorial time, thus consistently reinforcing students' own knowledge while having fun with their peers. Naturally, the students can play in their own time for as long as they like.

HOW TO PLAY STEP BY STEP

1. Shuffle the cards.
2. Beginning with the person to their left, the dealer gives each player one card at a time until everyone has a total of seven cards. The cards, or 'hands', must remain concealed from the other players.
3. As the game progresses, players must organize their hands into archaeological theories, *not* sets or suits. The aim is to complete a 'full-house' composed of one card from each set that is connected to the same theoretical archaeological theme.

4. Each player decides which cards they want to keep and which cards they want to discard in the middle of the table. The pile of cards this creates is called 'Tappable Knowledge'. Each player may only put cards down when it is their turn.

5. The first person to start is the one to the left of the dealer.

6. The turn: each player places their rejected cards face-down in the middle of the table and tells the dealer how many they want from the pack (which must equal the number thrown out).

7. This is repeated for each person until everyone has had a turn.

8. Repeat steps 1–7 until the cards the dealer holds run out. Then the dealer must pick up the discarded 'Tappable knowledge' cards, reshuffle them, and use these as above.

9. Repeat steps 1–8 until someone declares herself or himself to be 'out' when they obtain their 'winning' card and the game stops.

10. The first person to gain a confirmed theoretical grouping of five or seven cards wins. Such a grouping can be a made up of either five or seven cards as long as each card comes from a different set accumulated during the course of the game (see example above).

11. The basic idea is that if a player aims to collect a winning hand of seven cards, they will get more points than a player who only aims for a five-card win. This means that each player needs to balance his or her possible outcomes and strategies. If the teaching instructor, as final arbitrator, does not confirm the hand as a winning hand, the person does not win any points and the game begins again with a new dealer. The number of points gained per win can be left up to the course designer.

CONSIDERATIONS ON USING THE GAME

The advantage of this game is that it has a simple structure for its basic creation but the actual card content and the playing of this game can be as complicated as one would wish to make it. Thus it can be molded to suit the appropriate course and year level. From the start of the course students can be advised to complete a weekly compulsory reading associated with lectures and tutorials and the cards can be based upon this. Thus, for more advanced students who are reading original philosophical texts, the more obscure yet still key quotes that they would have read for themselves can be included. For example, you might like to create 'Questions cards', like that found in Figure 4.7, that might ask 'Who said this?' or 'What does this mean?', where students can't pick up or perhaps keep that card unless they can address the question. If they can answer the question they may keep the card; if not, they must throw it away and get another. Other ideas for cards are treatise titles, specific excavations or finds mentioned in the texts, but not the lectures, and so forth. At this level the percentage grades awarded for the game could be increased.

It could be argued, however, that assessing the game would take away the fun. 'Grasp' might be a good game to play in the last class of the entire course – as both a roundup of the key concepts/ideas and also a fun way to say goodbye to the class and the things they've learned. Indeed there are studies that have revealed, for younger students at least, that students offered an extrinsic reward for finding the correct answer were less effective at problem-solving and less confident (Lepper and Cordova 1992). As mentioned in the context section above, assessment is not necessary and the game could simply be used as part of a vibrant learning environment. It should be left up to the individual to decide how they would like to apply it.

Arbitration of the game is rather tricky. The teaching instructor should be the final arbitrator for these games, but of course, people who are creative players (and thinkers) will be able to make cases for why certain cards should be placed together. If you don't want a game with flexibility, you can control this by offering very stereotyped options of theories and their associations; but for more creativity and fun, the more you offer on the detail of a topic, and the more flexible you are with possible combinations, the more lively the games will be! In these situations students can be encouraged to debate among each other as to whether their final hands are a winner. If there is final agreement between all parties playing at the same game that an individual has a winning hand, then it is so. If not, the instructor should be called over to hear the debates and make the final decision. Explanations should be offered as to the reasons behind the instructor's arbitration.

FINAL REFLECTIONS

A very important consideration is not to present these more interactive and fun forms of teaching as part of an apology for teaching theory. If the course is presented as essential learning without apology, then students respond accordingly. A more positive approach to theory can be attained by not having that obligatory lecture on why your course on theory is important. Rather, the points in this lecture that may have focused upon the importance of theory *per se* should become apparent when you discuss what the course is about (its aims and desired outcomes) and as the course unfolds. University students choose to learn, they want to know (whether to increase their knowledge or to become professionals), and it is our responsibility to assist them. Adding an element of fun is one of these ways.

ACKNOWLEDGMENTS

I would like to thank Heather Burke and Claire Smith for their support throughout the production of this chapter. The comments from the anonymous referees were extremely helpful and enabled the clarification of many points. Naturally, any errors remaining are my own.

SUGGESTED READINGS FOR HISTORY OF CARD GAMES:

http://www.unifr.ch/psycho/pgp/boardgames/abstractsFinal.html. Board Games in Academia IV, International Colloquium, April 17–21, 2001 in Fribourg, Switzerland

Short list of websites for games used in teaching:

http://edweb.sdsu.edu/courses/edtec670/Cardboard/CardTOC.html. A site put together by Ed Tech Dept, San Diego State University. This site is just for card games, many of which you can adapt for your subject and age group. If you click on EDTECH670 there are game ideas and debates in using games in education.

http://edweb.sdsu.edu/courses/edtec670/Cardboard/Cardboard Cognition.html. This is the home page of the above address that has a link to an age game matrix to help you choose a game for your level of students. Particularly excellent is *Battle of Dark Age Britain* by Michael McKean, designed to educate the players about the political and military environment of Dark Age (sixth century) Britain by allowing them to construct or reconstruct the political and military conflicts between Saxon, Welsh, and Irish kings.

http://serc.carleton.edu/introgeo/games/index.html. A major site on games-based learning.

Short list of websites for pictures that can be used in 'Grasp':

Many archaeology departments have their excavation journals or reports on-line.

www.educationindex.com/archeol/. An archaeological resource mainly for pictures (eg LITHICS – net)

www.canterburytrust.co.uk/schools/galindex.htm

REFERENCES AND FURTHER READING

Amory, A, Naicker, K, Vincent, J and Adams C (1999) 'The use of computer games as an educational tool: Identification of appropriate game types and elements', *British Journal of Educational Technology* 30(4), 311–321

Bransford, JD, Franks, JJ, Vye, NJ and Sherwood, RD (1979) 'New approaches to instruction: Because wisdom can't be told', in Vosniadou, S and Ortony, A (eds), *Similarity and Analogical Reasoning*, Cambridge: Cambridge University Press

Derrida, J (1976) *Of Grammatology*, trans. Gayatri Spivak, Baltimore: Johns Hopkins University Press

Shanks, M and Tilley, C (1992) *Reconstructing Archaeology: Theory and Practice*, Oxford: Polity Press

Sugar, S (1998) *Games That Teach: Experiential Activities for Reinforcing Learning*, San Francisco: Jossey-Bass/Pfeiffer

Lepper, MR and Cordova, DI (1992) 'A desire to be taught: Instructional consequences of intrinsic motivation', *Motivation and Emotion* 16(3), 187–208

Schwartzman, R (1997) 'Gaming serves as a model for improving learning', *Education* 118(1), 9

Thomas, P and Macredie, R (1994) 'Games and the design of human-computer interfaces', *Educational Technology* 31, 134–142

Wenzel, T (2000) 'Cooperative student activities as learning devices', *Analytical Chemistry* 72, 293A–296A

5

The Skin Game:
Teaching to Redress
Stereotypes of Indigenous People

Claire Smith and Heather Burke

Stereotypes are powerful and omnipresent facets of our contemporary lives. They inform our actions and understandings of the world, help us manuever our way through human diversity, and are an integral part of how we judge others. The stereotypes from our cultural backgrounds act as a kind of shorthand that help us to make sense of difference, influence our interactions with others, and shape our actions throughout each day, whether we are consciously aware of this or not. Once in place, stereotypes have a life of their own. Predicting other people's opinions and actions, they can stand in the way of meaningful human exchange (Kunda and Thagard 1996). Stereotypes are grossly simplified and usually negative portrayals of human complexity and are often tied to racist beliefs, practices, and institutions that negatively discriminate against people based on their perceived or ascribed race (American Psychological Association 2002). For the people being stereotyped, they are insidious, difficult to engage with, almost impossible to redress. As Kunda and Thagard (1996) point out, the traits associated with stereotypes – even in the face of alternative information – become the dominant feature of how people are viewed and thus fail to recognize the diversity within groups. This is especially so if there is motivation to confirm the stereotype (Kunda and Sinclair 1999). More sobering still is the finding that even those who consciously hold egalitarian beliefs have shown unconscious endorsement of stereotypes about groups (American Psychological Association 2002: 22; Greenwald amd Banaji 1995).

Although all facets of social identity – ethnicity, age, gender, sexuality, occupation, class, status – are open to stereotyping, the effects of stereotyping are perhaps most apparent when dealing with ethnic identity and gender. Negative gender stereotyping has been challenged successfully over the last few decades (eg Gero 1988; Meskell 1999; Moser

1993), but the fight against negative ethnic stereotypes has been less successful. While both men and women can be the victims of gender stereotyping, the assault on gender stereotyping was led by middle-class, female intellectuals (eg de Beauvoir 1989 [1953]; Greer 1972; Heilbrun 1988). For ethnic stereotyping, however, the battle has to be fought on a multitude of intersecting fronts, and often without the critical mass of middle-class intellectuals from those groups. The socioeconomic status of different ethnic groups comes into play here, with a lack of individual achievement being related to social disadvantage (Reid 2002). As de Beauvoir points out, it is difficult for economically and politically dominated peoples anywhere to rebel against the status quo (Gerassi 1976). Even when there is action at a legislative level, such as with antidiscrimination or hate crime laws, the fight against racial and ethnic stereotyping also has to battle the lingering effects that harm in ways that cannot be attributed to unintentional discrimination (see Cunningham et al 2002: 3).

One way of redressing negative stereotypes is through education (American Psychological Association 2002). The teaching exercise that is the focus of this paper concentrates on the representation and understanding of one particular ethnic group, Australian Aboriginal people from the communities of Barunga and Wugularr in the Northern Territory, Australia (Figure 5.1), where we have worked for over 16 years (eg Smith 2004). One common stereotype, often applied to Indigenous people as a whole, misrepresents them as 'simple', 'primitive', 'backward', and, in some sense, unintelligent. A closely related stereotype of the 'noble savage' depicts Indigenous people as timeless, unchanging, and uncivilized (Aboriginal and Torres Strait Islander Commission 1998). These stereotypes arose during the early colonial era, emerging from the inability of European colonists to understand the structures of Indigenous cultures. The British colonization of Australia, for example, was based on the concept of terra nullius – land without people – that derived from the notion that people who did not till the earth, or have a tradition of buying and selling land, must also lack a system of land ownership (Reynolds 1987). Unable to understand the Indigenous system of communal ownership of land, based on inalienable inherited rights, the British colonists argued that the land was unowned, and therefore free to be claimed by Britain.

Along with lacking rights to land, early colonists also assumed that Indigenous societies lacked complex laws and social organization, and so never engaged with the complexities of Indigenous society. Colonial settlers, immured in a mindset that privileged the material over the spiritual and only recognized achievement that had a material dimension, were unable to understand or convey the spiritual and social complexity

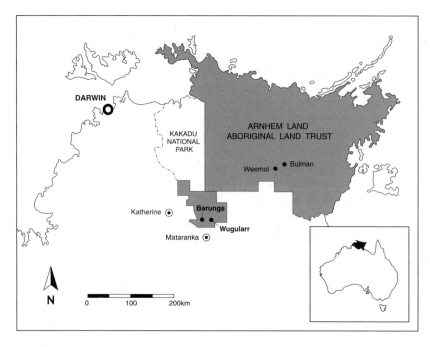

Figure 5.1. Map of Barunga-Wugularr.

of Indigenous cultures, even on those occasions where they recognized its existence. Indigenous peoples in places like the Northwest of the United States were deemed to be more sophisticated than those in other places, simply because their more sedentary lifestyles, and greater use of material objects, could be understood and conveyed in terms that were familiar to settler peoples. The majority of Indigenous people, however, were relegated to categories such as 'simple' or 'backward', and it was assumed their cultures would die out, or at best be integrated, in the face of superior European cultures. The irony is that Europeans were judging cultural complexity purely on the basis of material goods – and that the cultural, social, and intellectual complexity of Indigenous Australian groups far exceeded that of European cultures, either then or now.

Colonial encounters with a cultural 'other' were theorized as both wonderful and strange, worthy of scholarly attention. Anthropologists and archaeologists were essential conduits between the bastions of European civilization and exotic colonial worlds and, as such, had a critical role in the process of colonial stereotyping. This role is clear in the titles of books such as Bronislaw Malinowski's (1987[1929]) *The Sexual*

Life of Savages or Daisy Bates' (1938) *The Passing of the Aborigines,* but also is apparent in the inherited discourse of colonialism, in words such as 'prehistory', which creates an artificial opposition between Indigenous and European history, or 'myth', which implies invention rather than reality (cf Craven 1999; Mihesuah 1999). Emerging from a colonial desire to conquer unknown worlds, the discipline of archaeology concentrated on the analysis of artifacts that were the material proof of a nation's conquests, establishing what Said (1978) refers to as the 'positional superiority' of the colonizers. The collections established by the colonizers represented the paradox of unknowable, yet known, worlds; each display a symbol of the European ability to navigate the uncharted worlds of the colonial exotic. Integral to this process was an appropriation and stereotyping of Indigenous cultures, emerging from research and representation conducted through a cultural lens that could view only tiny facets of complex and sophisticated cultures in action.

While these stereotypes shaped the colonial imagination, the reality was very different. Indigenous Australians, the primary focus of this chapter, have occupied the mainland and islands of Australia for at least the past 50,000 years (Mulvaney and Kamminga 1999). During this time they have developed subtle and complex social systems and their own unique solutions to the range of climates and environments offered by the Australian continent. The achievements of these first Australians include what were probably the earliest planned sea voyages by people anywhere in the world; the earliest examples of deliberate human burials as part of spiritual/religious ceremonies; some of the earliest rock art and items of personal adornment; and the first boomerangs, ground-edge axes, and grindstones (see Mulvaney and Kamminga 1999). In keeping with these remarkable achievements, Indigenous Australian cultures were highly dynamic and adaptable. For thousands of years Indigenous Australians maintained complex social relationships with each other and trading relationships with Melanesian and Indonesian traders long before the first British colonists landed at Sydney Cove. An ability to adjust to change was characteristic of Indigenous Australian social systems, manifested in a flexibility that fine-tuned core social structures to suit the challenges of new circumstances. This intellectual and physical adaptability enabled Indigenous Australians to find the resilience and strength to survive extended contact with the British colonizers.

Given the roles of their predecessors in the establishment and ratification of colonial stereotypes, and that we all inherit both the benefits and challenges of our disciplines, it seems reasonable to expect contemporary anthropologists and archaeologists to assist in the process of redressing colonial stereotypes. Indeed, this has been a focus of recent archaeological and anthropological research as well as Indigenous scholarship. Archaeologists working with Indigenous peoples in the area of cultural tourism have worked to undermine notions of extinction and political absence (eg Beck *et al* 2005). Anthropologists have delineated some of the complexities of Indigenous knowledge systems, especially in terms of the relationships between art and social structures (eg Morphy 1991) and the processes through which Indigenous peoples interact with their environments (eg Ucko and Layton 1999; Hirsch and O'Hanlon 1995). Moreover, much recent Indigenous scholarship has addressed the general issue of stereotypes of Indigenous peoples, for example Devon Mihesuah's (1999) *American Indians. Stereotypes and Realties*, Rhondda Craven's (1999) *Teaching Aboriginal Studies*, and the Aboriginal and Torres Strait Islander Commission's (1998) *As a Matter of Fact: Answering the Myths and Misconceptions about Indigenous Australians*, while other Indigenous scholarship has focused on particular case studies (eg Rosenblum and Travis 1999; Spindel 2000) or decolonising methodologies (eg L. Smith 1999).

For the archaeologist or anthropologist who wishes to address colonial stereotypes in their teaching, there are two principal problems. The first is to identify both the overt and covert ways in which these stereotypes inform our theories, methods, and practice. Many imbue our works in subtle ways, and identifying stereotypes relating to ethnic identity necessarily involves teasing out those stereotypes that relate to gender, class, and other categories of social being. This is no easy task, and one that is beyond the scope of this chapter. The second challenge is to convey the complex configurations of another culture in a manner that will be understood – and remembered – by students. The exercise in this paper speaks to this second challenge.

THE BARUNGA-WUGULARR KINSHIP SYSTEM

The Barunga-Wugularr communities host several different language groups. The kinship system we focus on here is particular to one of these language groups – Dalabon. Indigenous Australians have always led sophisticated and culturally rich lives. Their societies are founded on relationships between individuals, their kin, and their lands, all of which involve very specific rights, obligations, and rules of behavior. Manuevering through the complexities of these rules and relationships is integral to the lives of Indigenous Australians.

The social and cultural complexity of Indigenous Australian societies is perhaps most clearly understood in terms of kinship systems. In Barunga-Wugularr, one of the fundamental principles of society is that the entire world is structured into two complementary halves – the Dhuwa and Yirritja moieties (see Figure 5.2). This system of classification and relationships arose during the Dreaming, when ancestral beings assigned everything in the world – people, animals, plants, places – to moieties and, where appropriate, also to a skin group. Everything – the land, the animals, the plants, the people – belongs to one or the other moiety. Each moiety is associated with particular physical characteristics: Yirritja is also associated with light colors (white, yellow) and the concept of 'long'; Dhuwa is associated with dark colors (black, red) and the concept of 'short'. Thus, yellow ochre and a long-necked turtle are both Yirritja, but red ochre and a short-necked turtle are both Dhuwa. Because each moiety represents only one half of existence, however, the two must be joined for the world to be complete. Balancing this relationship maintains order in the universe, and structures the social relationships between people, between people and animals, and between people and the land.

One of the ways in which this relationship is expressed is through the marriage system. The basic rules of marriage are that people should marry across moieties (ie a Dhuwa person should marry a Yirritja person), and that a child's moiety will always be the opposite of her mother's and thus the moieties will alternate between generations. In this way, the relationships between child and mother and between husband and wife are elegantly balanced. Other rules for marriage, however, are far more complex than this. The Dalabon social system, for example, is broken into sixteen social divisions, called subsections by anthropologists and 'skin' by Aboriginal people, since it is something that people are born with and cannot be changed. Skin is inherited from the mother. For Dalabon people, the skin system is arranged in two circles, each of eight groups (Figure 5.3). For example, within one circle of eight skin groups a mother whose skin is Gotjan will have children whose skin is Beling (if they are female) or Balang (if they are male). The children of the daughter whose skin is Beling will be Bangirn (female) or Bangardi (male). Galijan, the daughter of Bangirn, is herself the mother of Gotjan and thus the cycle continues. A separate circle exists which provides comparable inherited links between the other eight skin groups of mothers and children.

These two circles of skin relationships are joined in two principal ways: through marriage and through a reciprocal relationship between 'owners' and 'custodians' of cultural knowledge. In marriage, there are only two skin group categories from which a partner can be selected. Both of these choices come from the opposite moiety (uniting Dhuwa and Yirritja) and from the opposite skin group circle (minimizing the possibility of incest within the mother's line). One consequence is that men or women from the other skin groups for each sex – that is, three-quarters of the population of the opposite sex – are prohibited as marriage partners. These very strict marriage rules serve to regulate social interactions, cementing kinship relationships and acting as a taboo against marriage between biologically close relations, even in those areas where population numbers are low.

A second way in which moieties are united is through the ownership and responsibility for land, enacted via a reciprocal relationship between 'owners', called *gidjan*, and 'custodians', called *junggayi*. This relationship involves reciprocal rights and responsibilities, since all people are owners for some tracts of land and ceremonies, and custodians for others. Yirritja people will be the 'workers' in ceremonies that are owned by Dhuwa people and Dhuwa people will be the workers in ceremonies that are owned by Yirritja people. This is fine-honed at the level of skin group. In ceremonies, for example, the first preference will be for men of Wamut skin group to paint designs on men of Gojok skin group and *vice versa*. This preferred ceremonial partner is called *bunji*, and applies to both genders (but only within genders). Thus, Wamutjan and Gammanj are *bunji* to Bangirn and Gotjan, because they are all women, but not to Bangardi and Gojok, who are men. If people of the correct skin group are not available, other members of that moiety are called in. This builds in flexibility, combining preference and back-up, ensuring that ceremonies and land can be cared for properly. In the end, all Dhuwa people are custodians for all Yirritja people and land, and all Yirritja people are custodians for all Dhuwa people and land. Thus the fundamental social division of moiety is an important means by which people from Barunga-Wugularr conceive of the world around them.

Since the complexity of this kinship system is so strikingly at odds with perceptions of Indigenous cultures as 'simple' or 'primitive', we decided to focus on teaching the kinship system as a way of challenging these stereotypes. While we have tried a number of approaches, we have found that the exercise outlined in this chapter conveys our ideas most effectively. We have taught this exercise at various levels of complexity to undergraduate students in their 1st, 2nd and 3rd years of enrollment, although the degree of detail necessarily varies according to both the level of the students' prior knowledge and the size of the class.

PREPARING THE EXERCISE

The materials for this exercise must be prepared by the teacher. They are:

1. Name tags (one per student). These represent each of the skin groups from the two skin circles and are both gendered and

color-coded to identify moiety. We have done this exercise with groups ranging from 20 to 100 students. However, to ensure a good class dynamic, make sure you have at least one person representing each skin group. Odd numbers of students simply become 2nd or 3rd wives, husbands, sisters or brothers, and so forth.

2. Overheads, outlining each social exchange to preface each stage of the exercise. Note that many of these overheads are designed to be overlaid on top of each other. In other words, each successive overhead builds upon the previous set of relationships, so that knowledge of the complexity of the system is built up gradually.

3. A large bag of small, individually wrapped, light-colored chocolates or lollies (candy).

4. A large bag of small, individually wrapped, dark-colored chocolates or lollies (candy).

APPROXIMATE LENGTH OF EXERCISE

This exercise takes at least an hour, and is better conducted across a two-hour seminar to allow for proper discussion. We have also run this exercise in segments across a weekly seminar, focusing on a new stage each week.

THE EXERCISE

Stage One

1. Ask students to call out from the audience (or work out in buzz groups of three or four) some words they associate with 'Aboriginal' or 'Indigenous'.

2. Write these words on the board.

3. Discuss the issues that these words raise in terms of the preconceived ideas that already exist in the class about Indigenous people.

Stage Two

1. Hand out the name tags. Make sure that people receive tags for their correct gender.

2. Show Overhead 1 (Figure 5.2), moieties. Introduce the Dalabon concept of dividing all aspects of the world into complementary halves, highlighting the association between the Yirritja moiety and light colors and the Dhuwa moiety and dark colors.

3. Ask the students to take a moment to work out which moiety they belong to and therefore which color lollies they are entitled to.

4. Ask people to take three lollies each, according to their moiety. This means that Yirritja people will take three light-colored lollies and Dhuwa people will take three dark-colored lollies (ask people to refrain from eating their lollies until the end of the exercise).

5. Show Overhead 2 (Figure 5.3), the two circles of skin/kinship relationships, and explain the basic patterning.

6. Place Overhead 3 (Figure 5.4), first-choice husbands and wives and ceremonial partners ('bunjis'), on top of Overhead 2 (Figure 5.3). The arrows show the kinship relationships for the first and best choice marriage relationships in each skin group – ie who, ideally, each person should marry and, according to this system, who has ceremonial obligations to whom.

7. Ask people to use the overhead to identify their first-choice husband or wife. Tell men to identify and write down the skin name of their first-choice wife and women to identify and write down the skin name of their first-choice husband.

8. Direct people to find their first-choice spouse and to exchange one lolly with them. Note that some people may find more than one spouse, but try and make sure that everyone finds at least one first-choice marriage partner (note, this is where your careful forethought beforehand with the nametags will pay off).

9. Make it clear at this stage that, under the rules of Dalabon society, men will be able to take more than one wife, but women will only be able to take one husband (this may require some rearranging). To allow the new social relationships to sink in, ask the students to stay standing or sitting beside their partners.

10. Ask people to tell you the colors of the lollies they now hold. They should have given away at least one lolly of their own moiety and received at least one lolly from the other moiety in return. Point out to students that this is one way in which they can make a mental check on the correctness of their choice: because the idea behind marriage partners is to join moieties, it is easy to check whether they are trying to exchange a lolly with the correct person.

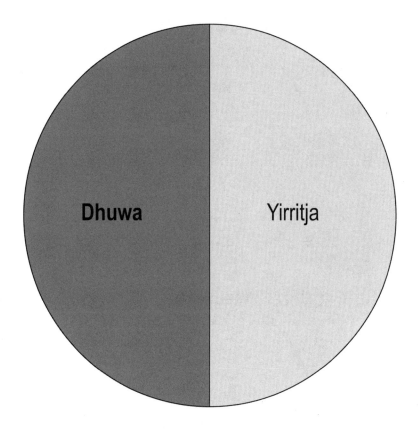

Figure 5.2. Overhead 1: Moieties for Dalabon people.

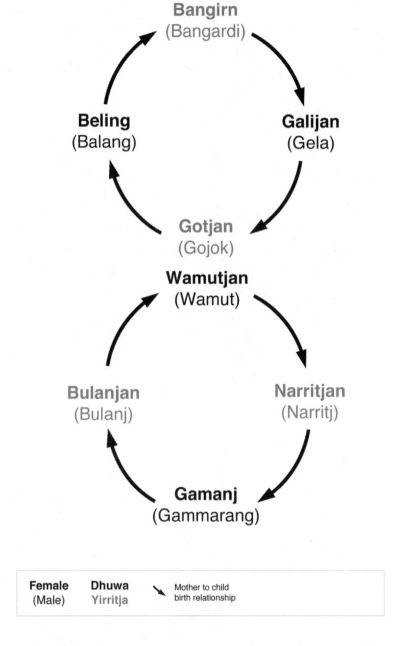

Figure 5.3. Overhead 2: The two circles of skin/kinship relationships derived from birth relationships between mothers and children.

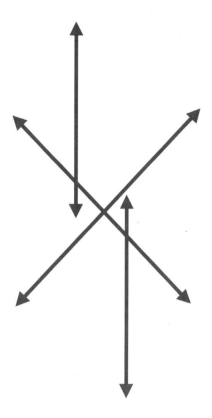

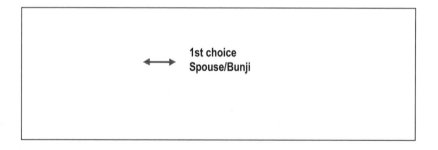

Figure 5.4. Overhead 3: First-choice husbands, wives, and 'bunjis'.

11. Point out that men who have acquired more than one wife should have exchanged a lolly with each one. Once they have run out of lollies they have also run out of their capacity to support more wives.

12. Students may eat their lollies now.

The points on which we reflect at this time are:

- The essential interconnectedness of Dhuwa and Yirritja
- The notion of marriage being one means to unite moieties (or bring them 'in company')
- The concept of having multiple partners, with an emphasis on gender differences (eg a man can have three wives at the same time, but a wife can't have three husbands, other than sequentially)
- The relationship between having multiple partners and social status

For upper-level classes, this stage can be taken further by asking people to identify and locate their second-choice marriage partners (Figure 5.5 Overhead 4: Second choice marriage partners), thus engaging more deeply with the complexity of the social structure.

Stage Three

Ask people to take three lollies each, according to their moiety. Yirritja people will take three light-colored lollies and Dhuwa people will take three dark-colored lollies (again, remind people that they can't eat their lollies until the end of the exercise).

1. Return to Overhead 2 (Figure 5.3), the kinship relationships between mothers and children.

2. Ask men to identify and write down the skin name of their mother and women to identify and write down the skin name of their son.

3. Direct the men to find one mother and the women to find one son and exchange one lolly with them. Note that there will in all likelihood be more than one possible candidate, but that they should choose one and then stay standing or sitting beside them.

4. Ask people to check the colors of the lollies they now hold. They should have given away at least one color lolly of their own

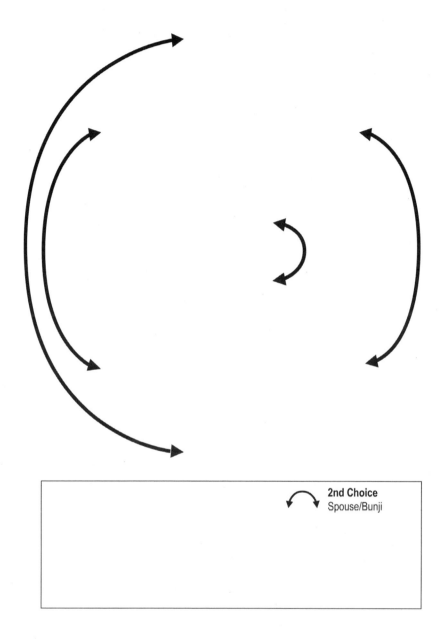

Figure 5.5. Overhead 4: Second-choice marriage partners and 'bunjis'.

moiety and received at least one color lolly of the other moiety in return.

5. Students may eat their lollies now.

The points on which we reflect at this time are:

- The essential interconnectedness of Dhuwa and Yirritja
- That mothers and sons will always have opposite moieties
- That skin is inherited through the mother, not the father
- That people have social obligations according to their classificatory (skin) relationships, not just their biological relationships, so all skin 'sons' have kinship relationships with their skin 'mothers'
- The similarities and differences between classificatory and biological relationships.

Stage Four

Ask people to take three lollies each, according to their moiety. Yirritja people will take three light-colored lollies and Dhuwa people will take three dark-colored lollies (once more, ask people to refrain from eating their lollies until the end).

1. Return to Overhead 2 (Figure 5.3), the kinship relationships between mothers and children.
2. Ask women to identify and write down the skin name of their brother and men to identify and write down the skin name of their sister.
3. Direct women to find one brother and men to find one sister and exchange a lolly with them. They should stay standing or sitting beside them.
4. Ask people to check the colors of the lollies they now hold. Unlike the previous stages, students should make sure that they have *not* received a lolly from the opposite moiety. Because moiety is inherited from the mother, and in opposition to her, sisters and brothers will always be of the same moiety.
5. At this stage, make sure that students are still standing or sitting with their brother or sister.
6. Ask the students if they are older than 12 years.

7. Point out that, although they are standing close to their brother or sister, these are actually avoidance relationships in adult life. In other words, after the age of 12 brothers and sisters will not spend time together.
8. Tell them to step away from their brother or sister.
9. Explain that one consequence of this particular skin relationship is that the brother is responsible for the sister's behavior and that she in her turn is expected to obey him. Because this is an avoidance relationship, she is also expected to walk five or six paces behind him, if they go anywhere together.
10. Students may eat their lollies now.

The points on which we reflect at this time are:

- That brothers and sisters inherit the same moiety.
- That social relationships are structured by both gender and power.
- The existence of avoidance relationships, and that they cover all facets of interaction with that person.
- Incest taboos.
- The details of brother/sister avoidance. After puberty brothers and sisters keep a physical distance from each other at all times. This structures how closely they can sit or walk near each other.
- Gender relationships in this society. Barunga-Wugularr society has greater gender segregation than Anglo-European societies, and in some respects, women have more autonomy.
- That people have social obligations according to classificatory relationships, not just biological relationships and that people in avoidance relationships still have social responsibilities to each other.
- The similarities and differences between classificatory and biological relationships, especially in terms of kinship and reciprocity.

For upper-level classes, this stage can be taken further by asking people to identify other avoidance relationships, such as mother-in-law/son-in-law (see Figure 5.6 Overhead 5: Avoidance relationships between mothers-in-law/sons-in-law, or 'poison cousins'), thus engaging more deeply with the complexity of the social structure.

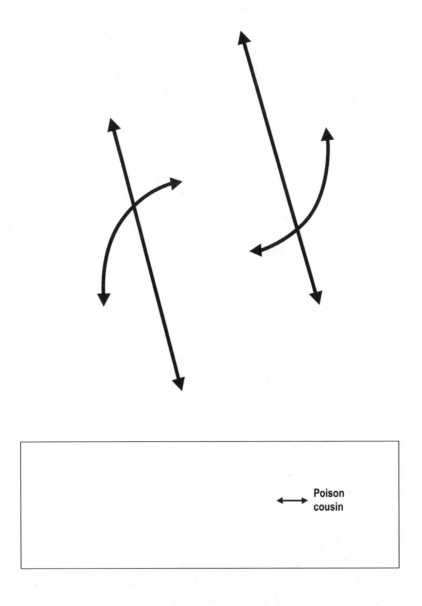

Figure 5.6. Overhead 5: Avoidance relationships between mothers-in-law/sons-in-law (also known as 'poison cousins').

Stage Five

The final stage of this exercise is to discuss the archaeological implications of what we have learned. The class discusses the difficulty of finding this level of social complexity archaeologically, and suggests the kinds of material evidence that are most likely to be useful to archaeologists in this respect. This is done specifically in terms of the Barunga-Wugularr communities, and then addressed more generally. What material correlates would any social system of this complexity be likely to have?

Even though the joining of moieties is the dominant structuring principle of Barunga-Wugularr society, it is very difficult to identify the concept of moiety archaeologically, much less recognize more complex levels of cultural interaction. At its simplest, the notion of joining moieties is most easily recognized through rock art, in the combination of light colors with dark colors. This is complicated, however, when other rules come into play. For example, the light background of a rock surface may be enough to indicate Yirritja moiety, or the knowledge that a painting is made on Dhuwa land may mean that the joining of moieties can be achieved through depicting a painting solely in a Yirritja color. Given the wide range of ways in which it can be coded into Aboriginal material culture, many of which can appear to be conflicting, it is virtually impossible to distinguish moiety archaeologically. The point to be taken by the class is that social complexity does not necessarily mean material complexity – and that material complexity itself needs to be rethought, both anthropologically and archaeologically. Our final point is that archaeology is all about people, and we reinforce this with an image of Barunga-Wugularr community members, usually the family members of senior traditional owner, Phyllis Wiynjorroc (Figure 5.7).

REFLECTIONS ON THE EXERCISE

This exercise arose from a longstanding desire to counter aspects of injurious stereotypes that often still underpin students' perceptions of Indigenous peoples. Europeans tended to judge as sophisticated only those societies that valued and produced an elaborate material culture, especially those grounded in forms that mirrored European achievements. This 'palaces and pyramids' approach assumed that Indigenous societies, having produced no such monuments of this kind, must be 'backwards' or 'primitive'. This exercise demonstrates to students that in fact the opposite is the case: the human intellect and energy that Europeans invested in building sophisticated and elegant material edifices was used by Indigenous peoples to build sophisticated and elegant social and intellectual structures. The core challenge is to convey this complexity in

Figure 5.7. Phyllis Wiynjorroc and great-granddaughter Georgina (photograph by Heather Burke).

such a way that students can begin to grasp the depth and breadth of knowledge that underlies Indigenous peoples' every daily interaction, and structures every facet of their social and material worlds. The success of this exercise is due in part to it being designed so that students need to engage with some of these complexities in one particular Indigenous culture in order to fulfill the requirements of the exercise. In order to enhance the impact of our teaching, we do our best to make this exercise 'fun'. As each student searches for their potential partner/mother/child, they become an active learner – living one aspect of a different life and learning through the experience.

Sometimes, there is confusion, especially if there is a large class. Although we control this confusion as best we can, we actually see it as an integral part of the learning process. In some ways, it is to be encouraged, because it highlights the complexity of the Dalabon social system and forces students to think about the nuances of who relates to whom and how. One of the most effective points we make is that all of these relationships (and many, many more) are held inside peoples' heads, not written down. This leads to reflections on the stereotypes associated with social systems based on the oral transmission of knowledge versus those based on the transmission of knowledge through written means. Within the academy oral histories are perceived as emotional, subjective, and changeable, while written histories are depicted as detached, objective, and reliable, and archaeologists normally privilege written histories over oral ones (eg the Hindmarsh Island Bridge controversy, see Bell 1998). This exercise challenges these stereotypes.

DISCUSSION

There are many lessons that can be interwoven into students' experience of the skin game. As archaeologists we are often called upon to draw inferences between the technological or other material by-products of a group of people and the ideational structures that gave meaning to those artifacts. The skin game shows just how difficult a task this is, even with detailed ethnographic knowledge of the culture in question. Beyond any individual lesson, we hope that students will develop their critical abilities and extend these to analyzing and critiquing their own underlying assumptions and knowledge systems. As Ouzman (2005) points out, making explicit the systems of thought that are embedded in people, places, and objects can help to overturn stereotypes that remove Indigenous peoples from both the present and from the arena of sociopolitical action. We hope our students will engage with this outside the classroom, as well as within it. We hope they will use the critical skills acquired during our classes to question other stereotypes, such as those relating to age, gender, sexuality, or occupation, and to lead lives that seek to understand difference, rather than condemn it.

ACKNOWLEDGMENTS

We thank the Barunga-Wugularr community for giving us 'skin' and teaching us about kinship and the sophistication of Aboriginal societies. The original diagrams came from discussions between Daisy Borduk and Claire Smith, at 'Jacko's camp' at Barunga, refined through extended discussions with Glen Wesan and confirmatory discussions with Jimmy Wesan, Phyllis Wiynjorroc, and Peter Manabaru. Andrew Warner and Stephanie Ford gave important feedback on the design of these educational materials. Finally, we thank the students who have played, and will play, the skin game.

REFERENCES AND FURTHER READING

Aboriginal and Torres Strait Islander Commission (1998) *As a Matter of Fact. Answering the Myths and Misconceptions about Indigenous Australians,* Available on-line at: www.atsic.gov.au/News_Room/As_a_Matter_of_Fact/default.asp, accessed 19 March 2005

Adams, PC (1998) 'Teaching and learning with SimCity 2000', *Journal of Geography* 97(2), 47–55

American Psychological Association (2002) *Guidelines on Multicultural Education, Training, Research, Practice, and Organizational Change for Psychologists,* Washington, D.C.: American Psychological Association, Available on-line at: http://www.soemadison.wisc.edu/cp/documents/APAMCCompetencies.pdf, accessed 5 August 2005

Bates, D (1938) *The Passing of the Aborigines. A Lifetime Spent Among the Natives of Australia,* London: John Murray

Beauvoir, Simone de (1989 [1953]) *The Second Sex,* New York: Vintage Books

Beck, W, Murphy, D, Perkins, C, Perkins, T, with Smith, A and Somerville, M (2005) 'Aboriginal ecotourism and archaeology in coastal NSW, Australia: Yarrawarra place stories project', in Smith, C and Wobst, HM (eds), *Indigenous Archaeologies. Decolonizing Theory and Practice,* London: Routledge

Bell, D (1998) *Ngarrindjeri Wurruwarrin: A world that is, was, and will be,* Melbourne: Spinifex Press

Bordewich, FM (1996) *Killing the White Man's Indian: Reinventing Native Americans at the End of the 20th Century,* New York: Doubleday

Brown, MF (2003) *Who Owns Native Culture?* Cambridge, MA: Harvard University Press

Butler, J (1990) *Gender Trouble: Feminism and the Subversion of Identity,* New York: Routledge

Craven, R (1999) *Teaching Aboriginal Studies,* Sydney: Allen and Unwin

Cunningham, CD, Loury, GC and Skrentny, JD (2002) 'Passing strict scrutiny: Using social science to design affirmative action programs', *Georgetown Law Journal* 90, 835–882 (April 2002), Available on-line at: http://law.gsu.edu/Equality/PSS-TOC.html, accessed 6 August 2005

Gerassi, J (1976) Interview with Simone de Beauvoir. The Second Sex Twenty Five Years later, Available on-line at: http://www.marxists.org/reference/subject/philosophy/works/fr/debeauvoir-1976.htm, accessed 6 August 2005

Gero, JM (1988) 'Gender bias in archaeology: Here, then and now', in Roser, SV (ed), *Feminism Within Science and Health Care Professions: Overcoming Resistance,* New York: Pergamon Press

Greenwald, AG and Banaji, MR (1995) 'Implicit social cognition: Attitudes, self esteem, and stereotypes', *Psychological Review* 102, 4–27

Greer, G (1972) *The Female Eunuch,* New York: Bantam Books

Heilbrun, C (1988) *Writing a Woman's Life,* New York: Ballantine Books

Hirsch, E and O'Hanlon, M (eds) (1995) *The Anthropology of Landscape: Perspectives on Place and Space,* Oxford: Clarendon Press

Indigenous Law Resources (2005) *Regional Report of Inquiry into Underlying Issues in Western Australia – 18.9 Racial and Colonial Stereotypes and Images,* Available on-line at: www.austlii.edu.au/au/other/

IndigLRes/rciadic/regional/wa_underlying/248.html, accessed 19 March 2005

Kunda, Z and Thagard, P (1996) 'Forming impressions from stereotypes, traits, and behaviors: A parallel-constraint-satisfaction theory', *Psychological Review* 103, 284–308

Kunda, Z and Sinclair, L (1999) 'Motivated reasoning with stereotypes: Activation, application, and inhibition', *Psychological Inquiry* 10, 12–22

Malinowski, B (1987 [1929]) *The Sexual Life of Savages*, Boston: Beacon Press

Meskell, L (1999) *Archaeologies of Social Life. Age, Sex, Class, Etcetera in Ancient Egypt*, Oxford: Blackwell

Mihesuah, D (1999) *American Indians. Stereotypes and Realities*, Atlanta, GA: Clarity Press Inc.

Morphy, H (1991) *Ancestral Connections: Art and an Aboriginal System of Knowledge,* Chicago: Chicago University Press

Moser, S (1993) 'Gender stereotyping in pictorial reconstructions of human origins', in du Cros, H and Smith, L (eds), *Women in Archaeology: A Feminist Critique. Proceeding of the Women and Archaeology Congress,* pp 75–92. Occasional publication, Canberra: Department of Archaeology and Anthropology, Research School of Pacific Studies, Australian National University

Mulvaney, DJ and Kamminga, J (1999) *Prehistory of Australia,* Washington DC: Smithsonian Institution

Ouzman, S (2005) 'Silencing and sharing southern African indigenous and embedded knowledge', in Smith, C and Wobst, HM (eds), *Indigenous Archaeologies. Decolonizing Theory and Practice*, London: Routledge

Reid, PT (2002) 'Multicultural psychology: Bringing together gender and ethnicity', *Cultural Diversity & Ethnic Minority Psychology* 8, 103–114

Reynolds, H (1987) *The Law of the Land,* Melbourne: Penguin

Rosenblum, KE and Travis, T-M (1999) *The Meaning of Difference: American Construction of Race, Sex and Gender, Social Class and Sexual Orientation*, New York: McGraw Hill

Said, EW (1978) *Orientalism*, New York: Vintage Books

Smith, C (2004) *Country, Kin and Culture. Survival of an Australian Aboriginal Community,* Adelaide: Wakefield Press

Smith, L (1999) *Decolonizing Methodologies: Research and Indigenous Peoples*, Dunedin: University of Otago Press

Smithsonian Institution (2005) 'Native Americans: Stereotypes and realities', Available on-line at: www.si.edu/resource/faq/nmai/naster.htm, accessed 19 March 2005

Spindel, C (2000) *Dancing at Halftime: Sports and the Controversy Over American Indian Mascots*, New York: New York University Press

Ucko, P and Layton, R (eds) (1999) *The Archaeology and Anthropology of Landscape. Shaping Your Landscape*, London: Routledge

The Big Dig: Theoretically Speaking

Gail Higginbottom

THOUGHTS ON TEACHING THEORY AS THEORY

The idea of separating theory and practice in teaching is considered by many to be inappropriate (qv Pluciennik 2001: 24). Instead, it is seen as necessary to completely incorporate theory into the context of any methodological program, whether this be theoretical notions developed in the past or those spontaneously realized or considered in the present by students themselves. In such a program, recent or hands-on case studies are the vehicles for experiencing and reflecting upon the methods students use and the impact these methods have on a project, on those around them, and on their own thinking. Indeed, Pluciennik emphasizes that 'it is now more educationally productive for students to engage and develop their own theoretical preoccupations through thoughtful practice and reflection upon that practice, rather than merely present them with "theory" in the lecture theatre' (Pluciennik 2001: 24).

While agreeing with much Pluciennik writes, I would ask, if students are only provided with the opportunity to contemplate theoretical notions developed by themselves via recent or hands-on case study, will students really develop a comprehensive and in-depth understanding of the extent to which theory can develop and where theory can take us? As well, there is the old concern of 'reinventing the wheel'. If I were a student in this circumstance, how much depth will my reflexive or lateral thought have if I am only talking about things that I have done in practice in my own subject area? For, regardless of the level of my thoughtfulness, how can I put myself outside of my own archaeological practice if I do not learn about the pervading influences upon another's? Further, even if some past theories are used to investigate recent or current case studies, it is unlikely that students will come to any real understanding of theories or methodologies. What will be their depth of understanding of archaeological methodology if they do not know the various influences or critiques behind Childe's, Binford's, or Tilley's methods that are influencing how archaeology is practiced today? Ultimately, it is not possible for students to really understand theoretical notions that have already been developed if they do not know something of the original philosophies and the history of the philosophies that lay behind them. To address these issues, theory should also be taught *as theory against the background of its historical context*. Further, teaching 'theory as theory' without this context will result in students applying theoretical notions, by now third-hand, to their archaeological practice without informed considerations of how original theories underpin the assumptions that influence all methodologies.

Deep learning, then, is necessarily dependent upon understanding the systems and schemes within philosophical debates. The board game 'The Big Dig: theoretically speaking' is designed to encourage and allow students to develop an understanding of philosophical notions and their place in the past, present, and future in an engaging and amusing way.

THE CONTEXT OF THE EXERCISE

'The Big Dig: theoretically speaking' was initially devised to create an enjoyable interactive classroom experience. The main aim of 'The Big Dig' is for students to become competent in the recall and understanding of influential and challenging theoretical notions of the past and present as part of a wider educational program. 'The Big Dig', as it is presented here, is a tool that is applicable to any individual theoretical topic or to an entire course, but is easily applied to the study of the history of archaeological thought and practice and the philosophies that influenced them. It can also be used to explore specific methodological approaches of possible future case studies and the possible theoretical notions that could underpin them, although this requires more thought.

There are an optional number of levels of complexity in 'The Big Dig' that can be dependent upon the intellectual capacity and the year level of the students involved and the time allowed for the exercise. It is a game that can be used to assess students formally and informally, or just as a learning experience. It is possible for a class to play together if split up into teams – in which case the game could either be set up within a virtual learning environment or played with cards only – or they can play in small groups of two to six, each with their own game.

This game is a trivial pursuit or quiz-night type of game usually constructed with a board, dice, and game cards. The board and cards can be developed by the students themselves or by the teacher. If developed by the students as part of the class, the former becomes integral to the learning process, as the students will need to research primary and secondary resources for designing the questions and answers, with at least 50% of the questions coming from primary sources. All questions and correct answers must be fully referenced on a separate sheet that is given to the lecturer for assessment. The question/answer cards do not need to be assessed (see below). By creating questions, the students engage with theoretical notions more genuinely than they might do otherwise and come to a more thorough understanding of specific points. Musing upon a single issue and then trying to make the question appropriate deepens their comprehension and appreciation. Making up interesting questions, along with the alternative answers, with the other group members adds a very playful and enjoyable element to the learning process. Here is an example of a list of questions and alternative answers that could be produced on a card:

Which of the following most neatly encapsulates the essential difference between the philosophy of Husserl and that of Merleau-Ponty?

1. Husserl holds that all proof has an objective point of origin in the ego (self), whereas Merleau-Ponty believes that we achieve objectivity by means of a direct and primitive contact with the world (adaptation of Max van Manen 2002).
2. Husserl's earlier phenomenology is based upon transcendental meditation, whereas M-P's phenomenology is existential, dependent upon outer-body experiences (cannibalizing of Max van Manen 2002).
3. For Husserl the fundamental relation of a person to the world is that of the content of an *individual mind* to the world of objects, events, and states of affairs as *represented* by that content, whereas for M-P it is essentially *physical*, a matter of direct and primitive contact with the world (Dreyfus 1991:52 in van Manen 2002).
4. For Husserl, the body is indivisible from the external world, as well as internally. For M-P, 'things' exist as separate entities from the human body.

Much of this creative process will therefore be stimulating emotionally and intellectually. Making a working game that is fun to play will be a very gratifying experience.

PREPARING THE EXERCISE

The board and cards

The board needs to have about 100 'stepping stones', each a different color, matching the color of a card group, which itself represents a theme (for example all red cards will cover the theme of linguistics, all orange will cover the theme of evolutionary theory). The themes selected for the cards may be broad or narrow depending on the course/assessment aims. Themes might include processualism, functionalism, Binford, ethics, and so forth. Even community chest-type cards, like those found in Monopoly, can be used. Community chest cards offer flexibility and fun, as well as an element of chance, in the game. Each community chest card contains an instruction to be followed, such as special movements around the board. These cards sit in a pile on the board and can be picked up by a person landing on a community chest 'stepping stone'. You could call it something suitably silly like 'Indiana Jones and the Temple of Knowledge'. An example of a community chest card might be: "Have you heard of Binford? Prove this to your colleagues by explaining one idea or action of his to the tune of *Mama Mia*. If successful, go forward 5 paces."

On each colored card is a question with multiple-choice answers (such as the example given above) and the fun part is often making up the wrong answers, which can be very amusing. If you are making up the cards and board yourself, I would suggest that you type the questions, optional answers, and the real answer, print them out on address labels and stick them onto pre-made colored cards (this is usually called 'card' in art shops) that are the same size or a little bigger. You should format the labels so that the question is at the top, with all the 'optional answers' below it and the real correct answer on a separate label, the idea being that both of these labels are attached to the same card with the question on one side and the real answer on the other. For rapidly distinguishing which side of the card is which, place a large colored dot on the top right-hand corner of the side with the question.

The simplest and most classic style of board is that used for chess or checkers, with 10 rows across by 10 rows down or more. Using such a format, each person travels neatly around the board by moving across each row, having started from a corner position. Adopting such a layout makes it possible to add additional levels of play, such as a 'scare tactic' using the 'snakes' or 'chutes' from the 'Snakes and Ladders' rules, for example. So, if someone gets a very easy or fundamental question wrong, for example, then their counter will have to move down the snake to an earlier position on the board.

Other ideas for a board might include a map of the world or of a particular country with pathways across it along which the stepping stones would lie. You could even use a map of an elaborate ancient or modern site. With this type of board format as a base, you could make sure that every time someone stops at a particular geographical location, they have to answer a question relating to that location – this could be either a fun question or a complex archaeological one. For instance, if the board is based on ancient Egypt, a player may have to pass by the Sphinx and answer her riddle or, more aptly, answer a question that relates to a particularly renowned dig that has been covered in lectures or in class readings. The ideas are quite endless.

THE EXERCISE

To play the game roll the dice, make your move, and answer the question on the matching colored card. A player other than the one who threw the dice must pick up the card and read out the question and possible responses. The person in play gives their response and the card holder, along with another, confirms the answer. If the answer is correct, the player is able to throw the dice again (up to a maximum of two throws). First around the board 'wins'!

Options

If using for assessment when students design the game

All members of the same group are allocated the same grade for their board/card design including presentation, the degree of difficulty implicit in the range of correct and incorrect answers on the cards, their creativity, and the degree of contribution by each member. In relation to the creation of answers, you will need to assess whether they have tried to make the answer difficult to guess, by not just including one right answer and several obviously incorrect ones. Naturally some funny or silly responses scattered throughout the pack are acceptable.

Each individual is responsible for one theme and must do the research and create a minimum of 20 questions (cards) for that theme. A helpful reading list for the theme should be constructed by the teacher/coordinator. Students are marked on accuracy and the effort required to produce the questions/correct answers. If not fully referenced – no mark. Further, it is suggested that each question and answer must come from a different text. For those who want firmer evidence of individual work coming from the actual texts themselves, you can always ask for their notes as well. These will not be marked but can be a guide to genuine research conduct. In total, the piece would probably carry about 40–50% of the weight of a semester's assessment loading.

If using for assessment when the teacher designs the game for others to play and the playing is assessed

Students are told what they must read to find the answers for the game. All play the same game. This can be as a board game or as an on-line game done in class. Various virtual learning environments (VLE) can be set up to do the marking of the latter. For the board games in class, place about six people in each group and give the students a mark sheet to keep score of the correct answers. A player other than the one who threw the dice must pick up the card and read out the question and possible responses. The person in play gives their response and the card holder, along with another, confirms the answer.

Using 'The Big Dig' for assessment in such a fashion means that there will be two levels to 'doing well': through grading the students' scores, and by grading their progress around the board. The first around the board in each group is awarded a small prize and/or 'The Big Dig' certificate.

Playing for fun, learning and laughter only!

This will be similar to the second option above, but without assessment. Alternatively, you could get the students to swap the games they make as a group and play them in an extended class.

The assessment date for this game will need to come later in the course/module but can be developed over the course of the semester or even year. Before telling the students anything, show a picture of an ancient/medieval and mysterious-looking board game as a backdrop. Discussing games in general, with examples of ancient games discovered archaeologically or that we have some archaeological evidence for, is always good fun – eg the Roman game *Felix Sex* or explanations of the origin of games like snakes and ladders (Moksha Patamu – the Hindu game of morality) or the Royal game of Ur (see Figure 6.1). Alternatively, you can have an entire lecture on ancient or traditional games. There are references provided below with which you can begin your research for such a lecture. You can begin by explaining that, using this ancient or traditional art of instruction, the class will be designing and/or playing the game 'The Big Dig'.

When explaining how to make a game, give them examples of board styles, card types, possible themes, questions and answers. All the

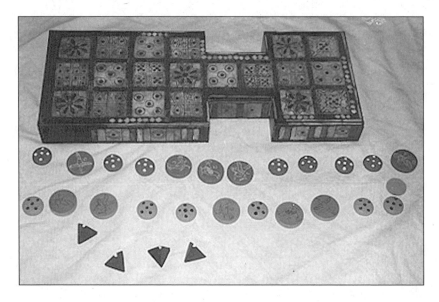

Figure 6.1. This is a replica of a game found in a royal tomb at Ur, Sumeria, dated around 2600 BC. According to James Masters this makes it one of the oldest game boards in existence. The original is on display at the British Museum. For a discussion of the importance of material cultural and games in society, the history and use of games is extremely useful. This picture was used with permission from James Masters and his website can be found at www.tradgames.org.uk.

information in the paragraphs contained under 'Preparing the Exercise' onward is explained here, as well as how to play. If the making of the game is to be assessed, then the information under the heading 'The Exercise' will also need to be explained.

APPROXIMATE LENGTH OF EXERCISE

If you are playing this game in a class, it will take a double lesson, regardless of whether you are using a board or VLE in a computer cluster. If using the latter, try to book the room/computers for an extra couple of hours so that students can play on if they want to. Naturally, if you are assessing them on any level for their participation, such as the provision of correct answers or win/loss of the game, they can play as a group anytime on a computer cluster without a teacher's supervision.

REFLECTIONS ON THE EXERCISE

This game is very adaptive. The best thing about it is that you do not have to use a board, as it can be drawn on the ground or on the sidewalk with chalk, or played just using cards. When you do not use the assessment angle above, it allows for culturally responsive teaching. Remembering, too, that not all universities reflect the culture of the students concerned, it may also give the students the opportunity to express some of their own esthetic cultural values in the creation of either the game rules or the board and cards.

The main concern might be with fair assessment, making sure that each person gets the mark they deserve in a group project. In the UK, I came across the validation survey format where each student had to send an email to the instructor stating the amount of work the others contributed, expressed as a predetermined mark along a very simple range. This mark can be used as a guide to your own initial grading.

A variant of this game is to make it narrower in concept and include more detail, basing both game and research upon a very specific theme. This allows for much more detailed research to be carried out and a greater amount of knowledge about a single area to be understood and learned. In this manner, learning such detail can be made a more enjoyable experience. It would not be considered as a replacement for the writing of a research essay or a research report, as the creation of these has quite different learning aims and outcomes. The 'Big Dig: theoretically speaking' will allow students and teachers to have some fun together, and students should become more confident in working with source material and ultimately take greater pleasure in matters theoretical.

ACKNOWLEDGMENTS

I warmly thank Heather Burke and Claire Smith for their support in the production of this chapter. I would also like to thank the anonymous referees for their comments; these enabled the clarification of many points. Naturally, errors remaining are my own.

REFERENCES

On phenomenology

Dreyfus, H (1991) *Being-in-the-World: A Commentary on Division I of Heidegger's Being and Time*, Cambridge, MA: MIT Press.

van Manen, M (2002) http://www.phenomenologyonline.com/inquiry/
1.html, http://www.phenomenologyonline.com/inquiry/4.html

On teaching

Gibbs, G and Jenkins, A (1994) *Teaching Large Classes in Higher Education:
How to Maintain Quality with Reduced Resources*, London: Kogan Page

Hamilakis, Y (in press) 'Learn history!: Antiquity, national narrative and
history in Greek educational textbooks', in Brown, KS and Hamilakis, Y
(eds), *The Usable Past: Greek Metahistories*, Lanham, MD: Rowman and
Littlefield

Holtorf, C (2001) 'Fieldwork theory: towards archaeological ways of see-
ing', in Rainbird, P and Hamilakis, Y (eds), *Interrogating Pedagogies.
Archaeology in Higher Education*, Oxford: British Archaeological Reports
S948

Pluciennik, M (2001) 'Theory as praxis', in Rainbird, P and Hamilakis, Y
(eds), *Interrogating Pedagogies. Archaeology in Higher Education*, Oxford: British Archaeological Reports S948

Websites (for pictures and information about the history of games)

http://nabataea.net/games1.html

www.tradgames.org.uk/index.html

www.personal.psu.edu/users/w/x/wxk116/roma/tesserae.html

www.gamesmuseum.uwaterloo.ca

www.shikanda.net/ancient_models/gen3/mankala/notesmankala.htm. This
is a section of the web pages of Wim M.J. van Binsbergen, who is the
Professor of the Foundations of Intercultural Philosophy, and Senior
Researcher at the Philosophical Faculty, Erasmus University Rotterdam,
African Studies Centre, Leiden, the Netherlands

www.gamesmuseum.uwaterloo.ca/Archive/Hillbom/. This is a paper by
Niklas Hillbom (Department of Classical Studies, University of Lund,
Sweden) entitled 'Minoan and eastern Mediterranean games and game
boards: A history of research', originally from Opuscula Atheniensia,
25–26, 2000–2001, Pages 53–65 (no part of this paper can be reproduced without permission). This has a very good bibliography.

Selected written references for ancient or traditional games

This list attempts to contain references from a number of cultures. They are starting points. Some of these, like Bell and Finkel, or Petrie, will be quite familiar to anthropologists, historians, or archaeologists working in games research or material culture. I am, however, indebted to Wim van Binsbergen's games reference list which I found very helpful. It is located within his personal web pages above.

Austin, RG (1940) 'Greek board games', *Antiquity* 14, 257–271

Bell, RC (1960) *Board and Table Games from Many Civilizations*, Tome I, London: Oxford University Press

Bell, RC (1969) *Board and Table Games from Many Civilizations*, Tome II, London: Oxford University Press

Bell, RC (1979) *Board and Table Games from Many Civilizations*, New York: Dover

Culin, S (1975[1907]) *Games of the North American Indians*, New York: Dover

Dundes, A (1964) 'On game morphology: A study of the structure of non-verbal folklore', *New York Folklore Quarterly* 20, 276–88

Eagle, V (1995) 'On some newly described mancala games from Yunnan province, China, and the definition of a genus in the family of mancala games', in de Voogt, AJ (ed), *New Approaches to Board Games Research: Asian Origins and Future Perspectives*, Leiden: International Institute for Asian Studies

Finkel, I (1995) 'Notes on two Tibetan dice games', *Board games research* 2447

Hamilton, C (1962) 'Notes on the newly found bau petroglyphs and the Masai game "ngeshui"', *Journal of the East African Natural History Society* 24(1), 50–52

Harrington, A (1990) 'Hnefatafl: The Viking game of strategy', *Northways*, Winter 1990 (there are quite a few web pages devoted to how one should play this game)

Lee, J (1982) 'Early Bronze Age game stones from Bab edh-Dhra, Jordan', *Journal of the British School of Archaeology in Jerusalem* 14, 171–174

Murray, HJR (1978) *A History of Boardgames Other Than Chess*, New York: Hacker

Meggitt, M (1958) 'Two Australian Aboriginal games and a problem of diffusion', *Mankind (Official Journal of the Anthropological Societies of Australia)* 5(5), 191–194

Pennick, N (1992) *Secret Games of the Gods: Ancient Ritual Systems in Board-Games*, York Beach, ME: Red Wheel/Weiser

Petrie, Flinders (1927) *Objects of Daily Use*, London: British School of Archaeology 42

Some games or books to obtain for fun

Caesar & Cleopatra Board Game, Rio Grande Games

Farnsworth, JT (2003) *Colonial Games, Pastimes and Diversions for the Genteel and Commoner*, New York: Iuniverse Inc

Finkel, I and Sweet, S (1997) *Ancient Board Games: Everything You Need to Play the Games: Book and Game Pieces*, New York: Harry N Abrams Inc

Fisher, A and Loxton, H (1997) *Secrets of the Maze: An Interactive Guide to the World's Most Amazing Mazes*, London: Thames and Hudson

De Voogt, AJ (1997) *Mancala Board Games*, London: British Museum Press

Part III

Simulations

The Game of Context: Teaching the History of Archaeology Without Foregone Conclusions

John Carman

Recent informal surveys among the staff of departments of archaeology in British universities have demonstrated the generally held belief that introducing students to the historical development of the discipline is useful and enlightening. Very few courses in archaeology fail to contain at least a few sessions on the history of archaeology from its antiquarian beginnings to the mid-20th century, when ideas and practices became more immediately relevant for current practitioners. Developments post-1960 or thereabouts are usually referred to as 'theory' rather than 'history', and valued accordingly (Hodder 1986; Johnson 1999; various chapters this volume). The value of teaching the deeper history of the field can, however, be measured in the creation of a sense of archaeological professionalism, especially the idea that the community of archaeologists represents a specific institution to which one can formally belong. It also delivers a sense of that community and its continuity to new entrants to the field.

The problem with teaching the history of any field, however, is that the outcomes are already known: The very fact that it is being taught in a reasonably structured way imparts the idea that there is a body of agreed material to be shared. The notion that things may not have turned out as they did, and that key ideas and principles all have their origins in particular sets of circumstances rather than being inevitable and obvious, can be difficult to get across. The pattern of teaching also tends to be common. It is usually a rather 'static' lecture-based approach with appropriate supporting readings, often of secondary materials – most often histories of the discipline written by archaeologists themselves – rather than the primary literature of the period under study or broader studies of the particular social, political, or cultural context within which certain ideas took root. Students react by understanding this introduction to the discipline as a 'necessary preliminary' to the study of 'real' contemporary archaeological theory and practice rather than something fully integral to an archaeological education. Ultimately, a knowledge of the history of their chosen discipline may be something they perceive as useful only for formal examination rather than something to carry with them into professional life. The overall effect is to limit students' grasp of the significance of the past of the field for its present and future.

One of the key ideas in European prehistoric archaeology is the so-called 'Three-Age System', devised originally for Denmark by Christian Jürgensen Thomsen in the early 19th century. This was an important element in the development of a 'scientific' archaeology based especially on developmental theories of evolution, and in the development of cultural-historical approaches to the deep past. Today, we are familiar with the sequence of cultural and technological development that places lithic technology prior to metallurgy, and, within the latter, copper and bronze technologies prior to that of iron. Later scholars developed the idea further: dividing the age of stone into a palaeolithic and a neolithic, and later still inserting a mesolithic to carry us over the transition between the two. Subsequently, the ages of copper, bronze, and iron all gained their regional subdivisions, too. Thomsen's story is well known and has been told many times (eg in Daniel 1975; Daniel and Renfrew 1988; Schnapp 1996; and especially Trigger 1989: 75–86).

In 1816 Thomsen was appointed to catalog the collection made by the Danish Royal Commission for the Preservation and Collection of Antiquities. He did so by starting with what he called 'closed finds' – deposits of objects that could reasonably be inferred had been made at the same time. By identifying which objects repeatedly appeared with which in such sealed contexts, he was able to infer which objects were in use (or at least available to be buried) together. The further study of changes in the style and form of objects in relation to their context of discovery allowed him to devise a chronological scheme for all of Danish prehistory. In all there were five stages rather than three: an early stone age, a later stone age, a bronze age, and an earlier and later iron age (the last of which continued into known historical times). First published as a guidebook to Scandinavian antiquity and translated almost immediately into German and then into English in 1848 (Ellesmere 1848), Thomsen's work was spread by his compatriot Jens Worsaae who influenced, among others, Daniel Wilson in Scotland (the inventor of the term 'prehistory') and Swiss investigators of the so-called 'Lake Dwellings' in that country. It went on to influence the rise of prehistoric archaeology in England and elsewhere. The scheme and its methodology fitted neatly into ideas about human social evolution and led the way to the construction of culture histories, an approach that would dominate much European and Anglophone archaeology until well into the 20th century.

The long-term and ongoing significance of Thomsen's scheme is that for the first time there was a methodology for the construction of a relative chronology on the basis of material remains alone. Previous schema had relied upon biblical or classical references for their linkages, but his was one that had no need of external reference. Instead, it relied upon making connections between assemblages on the basis of their co-appearance in the same context. The study of stylistic change – from relatively simple to more complex designs and their variations – provided a 'fine tuner' to allow the idea of gradual change over a flow of time rather than sudden alterations in cultural form. In other words, it was an entirely 'material culture' approach to a material culture issue: none such had existed previously. In many ways it represents the first example of 'archaeology as archaeology' (as advocated, for example, by Clarke 1968; Hodder 1986) rather than as an offshoot of historical, classical, biblical, art-historical, or folklore studies.

The exercise presented here – called the Game of Context for reasons that will become apparent – is intended to overcome some of the problems of the traditional approach to the teaching of the history of archaeology. It is intended to supplement the formal lecture with an activity that involves and engages the students, and to replicate in a small manner the conditions of uncertainty under which the early practitioners of archaeology labored. It also connects with the practical and theoretical concerns students will encounter elsewhere on their course of study.

THE EXERCISE IN CONTEXT AND PRACTICE

The Game of Context is constructed to be part of an ongoing course in the historical development of archaeology as a discipline and, especially, that part relating to developments in the 19th century in Europe. Accordingly, this exercise does not stand alone but has been used as part of a series of introductory lectures to undergraduates specializing in archaeology and also with adult continuing education (evening class) students studying the development of archaeological theory. In particular, it has been used as a means of making the 19th-century history of archaeology 'come alive' by turning the narrative of a known past event into a puzzle with no predetermined outcome. After an initial lecture covering the antiquarian tradition and its biblical connections, the Three-Age System is introduced to students in a second lecture as part of other key developments in 19th-century study. In particular these include the discovery of 'deep time' in the form of establishing the antiquity of the earth and, out of that, the antiquity of humanity as a species; and the consequent search for an explanatory mechanism for cultural change, resulting in the eventual take-up of Darwinian evolutionary theory. The role of Thomsen's typological scheme is here seen as a way of 'filling up' the great void of time evident in the prehistoric human past. The idea that it also represents the first truly and exclusively archaeological dating system is also introduced, but not dwelt upon.

In the introductory lecture, the Three-Age System is covered in outline rather than being explicated in depth. The point is to locate it in its historical context and indicate its significance but not to explain it fully: in this way the exercise – which aims to replicate the processes of thought involved – comes to students without providing them in advance with the means to complete it. It places them, so far as possible, in something like the same position as Thomsen when he began his work. That there is to be a practical exercise relating to Thomsen's work is announced at the same time as it is first mentioned, and the idea that it is meant to be an enjoyable and hopefully challenging alternative to a formal lecture style (rather than a test of ability) is also emphasized. At the end of the formal presentation of developments in 19th-century archaeology – the borrowing of ideas about stratigraphy from geology, the establishment of the age of the earth and of the human species, the focus upon field-work as an appropriate methodology – students are presented with a sheet containing appropriate advice and information (see Figure 7.1).

As indicated, students are expected to construct a relative chronology for the sequence of funerary practices and the objects provided. Only one clear stratigraphic relationship is included (of Find 4 to Find 1), and this provides the directionality of the sequence: it transpires from work with students that the relationships can all be inferred accurately from other information given, but without at least one indicator of stratigraphic sequence there is no information as to which Find is prior to which. In all tests of the exercise, both undergraduate and continuing education students were able to infer the sequence, and all arrived at the same conclusions by the same processes of thought and inference. In other words, the exercise works!

So far, the exercise has always been carried out as a 'whole group' activity taking up only part of a session: half of an hour-long lecture session with undergraduates or the latter segment of a two-hour session with continuing education students (in reality after coffee, running about 45 minutes). There is no reason why it cannot be offered as an exercise to be carried out in groups, with each group given a certain amount of time to offer a solution and report back, or some other arrangement. There is no reason why it could not also be developed into an exercise to take up an entire teaching session if thought appropriate, depending upon the students concerned and the structure of the course in which it has its place. A vital point is, however, that finding the solution is in itself not the aim, but rather to identify the processes of thought involved, the inferences it is possible to draw from the information given, and the manner in which such inferences may be reliably drawn. Throughout, therefore, whenever a solution or partial solution is offered or an inference drawn, it is essential to enquire how the solution was reached or on what basis the inference is made. Accordingly, the crucial element in the recognition that Find 4 must post-date Find 1 (the only piece of relative dating evidence provided) is how that inference is drawn. It is insufficient to simply 'know' it; instead, the student should be able to enunciate the stratigraphic relationship represented and how they infer the chronological relationship from it.

The specific content of the exercise does not relate to any known archaeological sequence. If by chance it should replicate a sequence from a local chronology, suitable changes should be made. It is important, however, that it should not replicate a known sequence, and also that this should be made clear to students carrying out the exercise, so that they will understand that successful completion of the task is not contingent upon previous archaeological knowledge (which might privilege certain students). Also, it is clear that this is an exercise in verbal reasoning. There are two reasons for this. The first is that as an exercise, solutions and contributions toward solutions will be offered verbally: the exercise is then set in the same terms as its resolution. The second is that use of images of real objects will privilege those who can identify them, but – more importantly from the point of view of encouraging (and indeed requiring) enunciation of the stratigraphic relationship represented – may also 'give the game away' too easily. An alternative to letters of the alphabet for objects is to use abstract symbols – circles, rectangles, triangles, etc.

OUTCOMES

The solution (Figure 7.2) depends upon making logical (or at least reasonable) inferences from the information available. The key term in the opening rubric is 'typical', meaning that where two or more objects are co-present, it is usual for them to appear together in that context. Therefore it can be assumed that where one appears but not the other, then the latter has either not yet come into, or has passed out of, use. The

Figure 7.1. The exercise.

OBJECTS IN CONTEXTS:

A PUZZLE OF ARCHAEOLOGICAL INFERENCE RECREATING THE THINKING BEHIND THE CREATION OF THE 'THREE AGE SYSTEM' AND THE INVENTION OF RELATIVE DATING IN AR-CHAEOLOGY

The following typical finds have been recorded. Your task – using the following information, which is all that has been provided, and such logical inferences as you are able to draw – is to determine (a) the likely sequence of the four different burial rites represented, and (b) some idea of which objects were in use at the same time.

Find 1

A central burial under a mound. Objects deposited: A, B, C

Find 2

A cremation in a flat grave. Objects deposited: D, E, F

Find 3

A deposit at the bottom of a posthole. In a pot of type G, objects A, H

Find 4

A cremation in a pot of type G in the upper part of a Find 1-type burial mound. Objects H, I

Find 5

A burial in a flat grave. Objects F, J, K

Find 6

Objects buried in a pot of type G: E, I, L

HINTS: What characteristic do all these Finds have in common?
Certain objects can stay in use for long periods of time.
Burial rituals change over time.

hints offered point to three significant aspects. The first emphasizes the 'closed' nature of the finds: as sealed deposits it can be safely inferred that the objects in any particular Find were buried together at the same time. The second hint points to the potential longevity of certain objects, so that one particular object may have different 'partners' at different stages of its life. The third hint emphasizes that we are looking for chronological relationships, and especially and centrally that a change in burial rite is a clear indication that time has moved on.

We know from the stratigraphic relationship of Find 4 to Find 1 that the latter predates the former. We also know which objects co-appear and it is evident that the relationships between objects change with the kind of deposit. We can see that objects in Finds 1 and 4 – which, as indicated, have a clear stratigraphic relationship – are different: we can infer that those in Find 4 (G, H, and I) post-date the objects in Find 1 (A, B, and C). Since A persists into the time of G and H, we can infer that Find 3 (where these are found together) is contemporary either to Find 1 or to Find 4 or occupies the length of time between them. We can see also that the objects in Find 6 (E, I, and L) are also contemporary with the currency of pot G, although none also appears with A, B, or C (in fact, B and C only appear with A). We can infer provisionally that E, I, and L may appear after A goes out of use and therefore after Find 3. E also appears with D and F, suggesting that Find 2 post-dates Finds 1, 3, and 4. Since F does not appear with G, we may provisionally infer that Finds 2 and 5 both post-date Finds 1, 3, and 6. The presence of G and E in Find 6 but not A, however, places Object A later in the period of G's currency. We know that E is present at the time of G and also possibly the later phases of A, but E is not present in Find 5. Therefore, we can infer that Find 5 post-dates Find 2.

The full solution is set out in Figure 7.2. In sequence, it is Finds 1, 3, 4, 6, 2, and 5. It can be seen that objects A, E, F, and G all have overlapping life spans. Object A is available for deposit in the burial under a mound and for deposit in a posthole but may still be present at the time of the secondary cremation burial in the mound. Object G is available for the posthole deposit, the secondary cremation burial, and to be used for the hoard. Object E is present from the time of the secondary cremation burial to that of the flat cremation burial. Object F is present from the time of the flat cremation burial into that of the flat interment, which ends the sequence.

Learning outcomes go beyond the solution and include more than merely gaining an idea of how to construct a relative chronology out of relationships and inferences drawn from them, although this is not in itself a meager result. The principles applied are essentially those from which any stratigraphic or typological scheme is developed: they are the fundamental building blocks of archaeological inference and interpretation. Students also, however, gain a sense of the realm of uncertainty within which the founders of the discipline worked and of the lack of a pre-existing framework within which to place the material they had encountered. By constructing a fictional sequence, we provide no extraneous material on which students can draw or rely for advice as to how to proceed. Instead, they are thrown onto their own (and their fellows') intellectual resources. It requires them to make connections where none previously exist, and to take small risks by trying out ideas to see if they fit any kind of viable scheme. It requires them to work as a team (or, if broken down into smaller groups, as teams) and thus builds a sense of community among the class. Requiring them to enunciate each stage of their thinking process in making connections and building toward a solution, helps to develop some of the skills they may need later as researchers.

The experience of conducting this exercise is one that confirms student enjoyment and engagement. Throughout, there is inevitably a lot of noise, with students calling out ideas to the lecturer or each other, or passing comments upon the suggestions made. There is a significant amount of laughter – not in my experience directed against individuals by others but more often as the significance of an idea becomes evident. Initial confusion (accompanied sometimes by frowns of concentration) is replaced by clarity as suggestions and solutions begin to fit together. Keeping a close eye on interactions allows the identification of any student not participating: they can be drawn in with a directed question or comment. Overall, it is clear that students do understand the aims of the exercise and appreciate the particular skills involved in its completion. It does make the history of the discipline – or at least a part of it – come alive for them.

There are two further serious aspects. By breaking the narrative sequence of spoken lectures and by concentrating on an exercise about types of remains, the activity relocates material culture at the center of students' attention. This is, after all, what archaeology is about, and what archaeologists concern themselves with, rather than the relation of a purely historical sequence of events. This exercise also presents students with a particular idea of time as commonly represented in archaeology, deriving from the Western tradition. This is time as an arrow moving in one direction, an idea that has had particular implications for the nature and, from the perspective of its past, the future of the discipline.

Figure 7.2. The solution.

BURIAL RITE	INTERMEDIATE DEPOSIT	OBJECTS IN USE (AND MAYBE STILL IN USE)
Under mound (1)		ABC
	Posthole deposit (3)	
	(GAH)	
Cremation in mound (4)	GHI (AEL)	
	Hoard in pot (6)	
	(objects GEIL)	
Flat cremation (2)		DEF
Flat burial (5)		FJK

BEYOND IMMEDIATE OUTCOMES: LOOKING FORWARD TO THEORY

The experience of the exercise is that it has educational value, and students have indicated that they find it quite fun to do. It does also seem to teach them what is intended: that the historical development of archaeology as a field of enquiry is not the inevitable working-out of fate but a product of particular modes of thought in a particular historical context; and that our predecessors were at least as clever as we are and probably more so. It also helps to build a spirit of cooperation among lecture groups. What it does not do is tell them anything specifically about archaeology – especially European prehistory – or the details of the discipline's history. These, however, it is not specifically intended to do; but an understanding of these things can be achieved on the basis of the principles taught through the exercise. The educational value could perhaps also be enhanced by taking some aspects further: by making use of 'counterfactual' scenarios; in the consideration of archaeological approaches to material change; and in considering concepts of time as applied in the field, such as the distinction between absolute dates and relative chronologies or the implications of working with long-term histories.

The presentation of history as a series of 'facts' also offers the possibility of a 'counterfactual' approach. The experience of the exercise and the knowledge of previous developments derived from accompanying lectures can be used to consider the future shape of the emerging discipline. In particular, it should be possible to predict the kinds of key interests and approaches to be developed in the next phases of the discipline's history (whether students know the correct terminology or otherwise), such as evolutionary schemes (eg Evans 1875; Lane-Fox 1875) and culture histories (eg Childe 1929). Where students do not predict these particular forms, their alternative ideas can be used as a basis to approach the actual line of development of the field and how and why that came about, rather than any alternatives they may have proposed (for ideas, see the accounts in Daniel 1975; Daniel and Renfrew 1988; Schnapp 1996; and for an alternative account see Carman 1993; 1997).

The methodologies of archaeology revolve around issues of relative dating and rely especially upon change as measured – or at least identified – over time. Indeed, for an archaeologist, change is often synonymous with time, and this is in part a legacy of the framework of thought within which Thomsen's work resides. Stylistic change – one of the aspects studied by Thomsen – was to emerge as a key focus of theoretical discussion in the 1970s and 1980s, first among processualists and subsequently as part of the processualist/postprocessualist split (Conkey and Hastorf 1990). The specific function of style was taken to be that of a means of communication (Weissner 1983; Wobst 1977). In general, its nature was agreed to be a residue left after functional aspects had been accounted for (Sackett 1990) or simply something added (Shanks and Tilley 1987: 173). Nevertheless, the value of style as an indicator is recognized by Hodder (1990) and by others. Ferguson's (1991) studies of 18th-century pottery among African American slaves allows him to use stylistic difference as an indicator of slave resistance to white hegemony, contributing to 'the building of [a distinct] African American culture' (Ferguson 1991: 37). Similarly, Yentsch (1991) uses differences in pottery styles among white Southern Americans in the 18th century to identify gender and class differences, while Beaudry *et al's* (1991) study of tobacco-related artifacts and household ceramics allowed them to identify the different social discourses of the emergent American working class at home and outside it. All of these applications of the idea of 'style' to understanding social and ideological factors take us beyond Thomsen's contribution, but ultimately derive from the framework of thought he represents.

Although central to archaeology as a discipline, time as a concept has come in for relatively little consideration by archaeologists (although for examples of more thoughtful approaches, see Bailey 1983; Fabian 1983; Murray 1999). Thomsen's relative chronology for northern Europe offered no measurement of the passage of time during prehistory, and much effort was spent subsequently in establishing absolute dates for archaeological events. The emergence of radiocarbon dating, especially as supported by dendrochronology, was a significant breakthrough and provided specific timetables into which particular kinds of objects and deposits could be placed. The place of Thomsen's scheme is crucial here, and goes beyond his achievement in developing a methodology for relative chronology. From the outset his work aimed to construct a conceptual framework for the display of ancient remains: Thomsen adopted a chronological one, and by doing so closed other possible avenues. His success – and the general applicability of his scheme across Europe and indeed elsewhere – committed archaeology to a concern (one way or another) with chronologies and the developments that arise from them. By recreating the conditions of Thomsen's work, these aspects re-emerge for scrutiny and deeper consideration by our students and ourselves.

CONCLUSIONS

The Game of Context offers a convenient practical alternative to the conventional lecture in presenting the events of the early development of archaeology as a discipline. It also opens an opportunity to consider the form the discipline has taken in the light of these early developments, by allowing concentration on the ideas that lie at the core of relative dating techniques. These include such notions as 'change', especially stylistic change, and ideas about time as represented in archaeological discourse. These are issues that arise in discussing the theory of archaeology, providing a good reason for students (and indeed lecturers) to bother with the early history of the discipline.

ACKNOWLEDGMENTS

Thanks are due to Heather Burke and Claire Smith (editors of the volume) for accepting this contribution and kindly criticism. I must also thank students of Cambridge University, UK, for acting as 'guinea pigs' and responding so well to the challenge of the Game of Context. Finally, but not least, I am grateful to Patricia Carman for all her advice on classroom and lecture-hall techniques over many years and for reading this chapter. Any errors – of logic, fact, style, or grammar – are exclusively those of the author and to be laid at the door of no one else.

REFERENCES

Bailey, GN (1983) 'Concepts of time in Quaternary prehistory', *Annual Review of Anthropology* 12, 165–192

Beaudry, MC, Cook, LJ and Mrozowski, SA (1991) 'Artifacts and active voices: Material culture as social discourse', in McGuire, RH and Paynter, R (eds), *The Archaeology of Inequality*, Oxford: Blackwell

Carman, J (1993) 'The *p* is silent – as in archaeology', *Archaeological Review from Cambridge* 12, 29–38

Carman, J (1997) 'Archaeology, politics and legislation: The British experience', in Mora, G and Diaz-Andreu, M (eds), *La Cristalizacion del Pasado: Genesis y Desarollo del Marco Institicional de la Arquelogia en España*, Malaga: Universidad de Malaga

Childe, VG (1929) *The Danube in Prehistory*, Oxford: Oxford University Press

Clarke, DL (1968) *Analytical Archaeology*, London: Methuen

Conkey, MW and Hastorf, CA (eds) (1990) *The Uses of Style in Archaeology*, Cambridge: Cambridge University Press

Daniel, GE (1975) *A Hundred and Fifty Years of Archaeology*, London: Duckworth

Daniel, G and Renfrew, C (1988) *The Idea of Prehistory*, Edinburgh: Edinburgh University Press

Ellesmere, Earl of (1848) *Guide to Northern Archaeology*, London: Bain

Evans, J (1875) 'The coinage of the Ancient Britons and Natural Selection', *Proceedings of the Royal Institution of Great Britain* 47, 76–87

Fabian, J (1983) *Time and the Other: How Anthropology Makes Its Object*, New York: Columbia University Press

Ferguson, L (1991) 'Struggling with pots in Colonial South Carolina', in McGuire, R and Paynter, R (eds), *The Archaeology of Inequality*, Oxford: Blackwell

Hodder, I (1986) *Reading the Past: Current Approaches to Interpretation in Archaeology*, Cambridge: Cambridge University Press

Hodder, I (1990) 'Style as historical quality', in Conkey, MW and Hastorf, CA (eds), *The Uses of Style in Archaeology*, Cambridge: Cambridge University Press

Johnson, M (1999) *Archaeological Theory: An Introduction*, Oxford: Blackwell

Lane-Fox, A (1875) 'The evolution of culture', *Proceedings of the Royal Institute of Great Britain* 7, 496–520

Murray, T (ed) (1999) *Time and Archaeology*, London: Routledge

Sackett, JR (1990) 'Style and ethnicity in archaeology: The case for isochrestism', in Conkey, MW and Hastorf, CA (eds), *The Uses of Style in Archaeology,* Cambridge: Cambridge University Press

Schnapp, A (1996) *The Discovery of the Past*, London: British Museum Press

Shanks, M and Tilley, C (1987) *Reconstructing Archaeology: Theory and Practice*, Cambridge: Cambridge University Press

Trigger, B (1989) *A History of Archaeological Thought*, Cambridge: Cambridge University Press

Weissner, P (1983) 'Style and social information in Kalahari San projectile points', *American Antiquity* 49(2), 253–276

Wobst, HM (1977) 'Stylistic behaviour and information exchange', in Cleland, CE (ed), *For the Director: Research Essays in Honor of James B Griffin*, pp 317–342. Museum of Anthropology Anthropological Paper 61, Ann Arbor: Museum of Anthropology, University of Michigan

Yentsch, A (1991) 'The symbolic divisions of pottery: sex-related attributes of English and Anglo-American household pots', in McGuire, RH and Paynter, R (eds), *The Archaeology of Inequality*, Oxford: Blackwell

8

The Simulated Excavation: An Alternative to Archaeological Site Destruction

Bradley F. Bowman and Glenna Dean

INTRODUCTION

One of the most popular educational concepts ever designed to teach archaeology, the simulated excavation, or 'mock dig', is suitable for students of all levels and can be conducted in the classroom or in the outdoors. This simulated archaeological experience, in which excavators use one or more data-recovery techniques to find planted artifacts, has been popular for years in the United States because it is relatively easy to produce and is an exciting, enjoyable experience for all who participate. Cobblestone Press (2004) maintains a list of many of the better programs presented in the United States. The methodical exposure of 'clues to the past', supervised by a trained archaeologist, is meant to inculcate a preservation ethic ('archaeology is more than artifacts and if you move too quickly, you will lose important information'). The careful scraping with trowels, screening, measurements, and drawings is meant to demonstrate science in action.

But by focusing on artifact recovery and rewarding the 'thrill of discovery' (necessary to ensure participant satisfaction), the mock dig sends the participants several wrong messages. One is that archaeology is excavation (and excavation is automatically archaeology). Another is that the purpose of archaeological excavation is to recover artifacts. Yet another is that laboratory analysis of artifacts is too difficult to teach but that anyone can perform scientific archaeological excavation. Lastly, that archaeological excavation in and of itself contributes to our understanding of the past and is a form of preservation without artifact analysis. In essence, the most destructive part of archaeology is promoted to students and the public as the single aspect of archaeology that they can learn to do 'just like real guys' in a short time (and without the tedium of college courses).

Since the inception of mock digs, the shape of holes dug by looters in search of artifacts has changed from being haphazard to something that resembles the scientist's square unit (Figure 8.1).

This suggests that the mock dig can be counterproductive without deliberate planning by dig sponsors and directed discussions with participants. Poorly designed mock digs, promoted by schools and avocational archaeological groups as a way to attract students or engage the public, foster a superficial understanding of the science of archaeological excavation. At best, the diverse discipline of archaeology is reduced to mere excavation. At worst, individuals with good intent end up training looters in 'scientific techniques'. The fun, excitement, and in many cases passionate energy generated by the mock dig can have devastating effects on archaeological sites if the experience is not directly linked to an understanding of ethics, historic preservation, and the concept of the value of an artifact beyond what someone will pay to buy it. This is especially true in the United States where archaeological sites on private land are considered the property of the landowner and are not protected by state or national laws (King 1991). The thrill of discovery, followed quickly by a desire to own a piece of the past, can become a personal quest, perverting the search for knowledge and distorting the real purposes of the discipline of archaeology.

Figure 8.1. Pothunter's excavation, Cibola County, New Mexico (photograph by Bradley Bowman).

The simulated excavation presented at the Museum of Archaeology and Material Culture (Museum) and summarized here has been refined over more than eight years of teaching individuals ranging in age from kindergarten to adult. This program, conducted in a museum setting, specifically addresses the problems outlined above by assigning the same values and research goals to the mock dig that professional archaeologists develop in a research design (why must we dig and why are we digging this particular site?), excavation strategy (how are we going to dig this site to learn the most with our research dollars?), accumulation of data to address the research questions through laboratory analysis (how will analyses be tailored to best provide the desired data?), tribal consultation for archaeological sites of American Indian affiliation, and curation of artifacts and records for future researchers. The simulated excavation, if presented in the context of professional and ethical standards, can instill some of the values necessary for student comprehension of the value of our past, our shared archaeological heritage, and the discipline of archaeology.

THE PROGRAM

Realizing a program that is positive for both the participant and the science of archaeology requires that the institution and program promoters disseminate the values upon which our science is built. The simulated excavation should not be conducted without a professional knowledge of the discipline, and of the many negative consequences that can occur when a student is allowed to believe that digging for artifacts and conducting archaeology are analogous.

Ethics

The Society for American Archaeology (SAA) adopted eight ethical principles (Kintigh 1996), which should be incorporated into all aspects of the program from the point of inception throughout the exercise, reinforcing professional ethical standards at every opportunity. These principles are:

1. Stewardship: Promote at every opportunity the importance of protecting archaeological materials, sites, records, and reports. Foster an understanding and support for long-term preservation.

2. Accountability: As archaeologists we are responsible to the public and should consult actively with groups affected by our activities.

3. Commercialization: We cannot support the commercial sale of archaeological materials, as this activity is directly responsible for the destruction of archaeological sites and the information they contain.

4. Support public education and outreach: Encourage the participants of the program to share their experiences with others.

5. Intellectual property: The result of our research and materials recovered should be made available to others and is not personal property.

6. Public reporting and publication: The results of our activities must be made available to the public in a way that will not place archaeological resources in danger.

7. Records and preservation: We need to work toward the long-term preservation of archaeological materials and promote preservation of collections, records, and reports.

8. Training and resources: Given the destructive nature of many archaeological activities, we must insure adequate training and experience with facilities and support necessary to conduct any program of research in a manner consistent with the other seven principles.

The simulated-dig program, from its pre-excavation discussions through excavation, analysis, and the final interpretations, must be thoroughly thought out and presented as if interlocking parts of a single puzzle. College-level application of this exercise should be presented with the complexities encountered by professional researchers, with emphasis focused on mapping, site layout, analysis, and interpretation. Recovering cultural materials through excavation of a mock site should be taken with the same degree of seriousness as if it were an authentic cultural deposit. Students who intend to become professional educators may wish to produce a version of this program during their teaching careers. These individuals will be faced with the task of presenting the major concepts of the program in a way that is appropriate for participants of varied ages and intellectual development. It is important to discourage individuals who wish to soften the focus on preservation and ethical standards.

The program as offered at the Museum has been attuned successfully to groups of varying ages by reducing intricacy and the use of jargon. The basic premise of the program, which presents archaeological excavation within a holistic context from research design to interpretation, is not compromised under any circumstances and if the students are not intellectually capable of understanding, we do not present the program.

PREREQUISITE INSTRUCTION

Students will require an understanding of the temporal affiliation of the recovered cultural materials and a comprehension of the cultures to be explored. Time is an abstraction that is difficult for many of us to grasp, and often is dealt with by simply memorizing dates. The program defines time as linear. An imaginary line is presented to the participants stretching from a mark on the floor to the horizon. A centimeter represents one year on our line. For example, an eight-year-old has been alive for eight cm on the line, which can be measured off in the presence of the students; the educator may be 50 years of age, and so 50 cm are measured off. Dinosaurs are thought to have been extinct at the end of the Cretaceous, or 65 million years ago; 65 million cm equals 65 km, or the distance from one landmark familiar to the students to another, and so on. Analogous references between linear distance (reference points within sight of the excavation) and time are brought up frequently during the exercise. A visualization of time in this manner helps define the abstract, elicits conversation, which can eliminate chronological misconceptions, and presents a visual image useful when discussing the age of the archaeological deposits.

Prior to excavation, participants are introduced to the human histories that are represented in the deposits and to examples of representative material culture. The Museum's program utilizes an exhibit for this purpose, a 12,000-year Native American Indian timeline. Students are escorted through the timeline discussing chronological changes in Native American Indian subsistence strategies, associated toolkits, and resulting social and demographic changes. During this phase of the program, opportunities arise to address current issues concerning social development, ethnic diversity, and related topics. Often students reveal their deepest concerns, and your, the educator's, response may open many intellectual doors. Discussion emphasizes portions of the timeline associated with the planted archaeological materials, thus beginning a conscious base for the analytical phase of the program. Time markers are introduced at this point. In the southwestern United States, the introduction of maize, the bow and arrow, and the production and general use of ceramic vessels correspond with dramatic shifts in Pre-Columbian lifeways. Throughout this phase of the program, students are repeatedly asked questions, which require answers that incorporate these corresponding dates. The redundancy of the questions and the focus on time markers consciously initiates the building of a cultural-temporal framework from which the student will develop an ability to associate cultural entities to recovered excavated materials. Material objects that are not included in the excavation may be included in the discussions related to the projected goals, but we never include artifacts in the excavation that are not discussed during this phase of the exercise. Student knowledge of the dates of artifact classes and the ability to recognize specific artifacts initiates the analytical process at this early stage of the exercise, shifting the focus of the excavation process from collection to interpretation.

Museum exhibits will probably not be available to most educators, and it will require effort to replicate the necessary information in a format suitable for the classroom. Cultural materials can often be borrowed from a local resource, augmented by photographs of artifacts and culturally related biological material taken from publications and institutional collections.

It is important from the inception of contact with any archaeological materials to stress value only in terms of what the artifact represents. The use of reproductions, or broken or average artifacts, in the exercise is preferred over using beautiful or outstanding authentic examples of an artifact type, as the former mute the desire to collect. Questions about the 'current market value' of an object are counterproductive to this exercise, stimulate a treasure-hunter mentality, and are downplayed or not addressed. Discuss artifacts in these terms: 'We are detectives – what would this artifact in association with this fragment of mammal bone tell us?'; 'What would this artifact reveal if it were associated with this hearth, or this structure?'; 'What is the true value of this information?' This line of inquiry often will elicit the question, 'What importance does the past hold for us today, as modern people running through our day-to-day lives?' This is an issue that educators must honestly address, and that may require some soul searching. We respond by saying that 'Cultures develop through time in direct response to their collective pasts. Our language is based on past events, as are our beliefs, prejudices, and perception of the world around us. A different past would alter our thought processes, creating a far different reality than the one we presently perceive'. The study of the past can reveal insight not only into other cultures, but into ourselves.

FIELDWORK INTRODUCTION

Upon completion of the initial prerequisite instruction, the students should be in possession of a rudimentary understanding of their responsibilities, time periods in history or prehistory, a specific native or historic group, and they should be able to understand and identify a cultural activity from physical objects located *in situ* in archaeological deposits. It is of utmost importance that the students understand legal and ethical issues surrounding site excavation. The disturbance of any archaeological deposit reduces its ability to provide information. Digging to collect artifacts, even from your own land, is stealing; valuable deposits are destroyed and ultimately everyone is robbed of the priceless knowledge of our past. At this point we also divulge the legal ramifications of collecting antiquities and penalties as prescribed by law, and reiterate the ethical standards as they apply.

The definition of an archaeological site is taught to the students, and a discussion as to *why* we are going to excavate the site is presented. Real-life examples are given: 'There is a road that will be built and it will destroy the site. It will be our job today to gather as much information as possible before the road graders arrive and destroy the site forever. We are not treasure hunters; we are scientists collecting information about the people who occupied the site and we will document on paper all that we find for future researchers to review. Before we are through, you (the students) will be able to describe who was here, when, and what activities are evidenced at the site'. By challenging the students' intellect in this way, and stressing the importance of their work, they should begin to forget that the project is make-believe, and begin to function as a conscientious field crew.

THE EXCAVATION

The simulated excavation is presented in a real format. There is no limit to the complexity that can be introduced into the exercise. The advantages of a simulated experience over real excavations are many. Archaeological resources are not destroyed for the purpose of college credit. The instructor has control over the outcome of the exercise as the number of possible conclusions is known before the exercise begins. A pre-existing knowledge of the deposits allows the instructor the option of quantifying a student's performance as in a written test. In contrast, authentic archaeological deposits contain an unknown quantity and quality of cultural material, from which the field worker may overlook an unknown amount of archaeological data. These uncontrolled variables can only allow for a speculative evaluation of a student's performance.

    Simulated excavations can be conducted in the classroom in meter-square sand boxes or outdoors in soils with designated units, as in a scientific excavation. We recommend the second method to provide an authentic experience. The facility at the Museum has a permanent, replicated ruin (Figure 8.2).

    Advanced students begin by mapping the site with a transit or compass and tape, laying out a grid, and establishing a datum with an arbitrary elevation of 0.00 m. Horizontal controls are established by assigning each unit a designation number. In our program, we use standard field designations, which contain both direction and distance in meters from a distant point beyond the site boundary. For example, Unit 1000N / 1000E indicates a unit 1,000 m north and 1,000 m east of some arbitrary point. The adjoining unit north of unit 1000N / 1000E would be designated as 1001N / 1000E. The adjacent unit east of unit 1001N / 1000E would be designated 1001N / 1001E, and so on. We employ the large number 1000 over the number one to avoid negative unit designations, a common source of confusion and mistakes. The datum provides reference for vertical control. This can be accomplished by placing a string and a line level on each unit's northeast corner stake. The strings should be placed at a known distance below datum, which is recorded in the site records.

Figure 8.2. Replicated ruin associated with the Museum (photograph by Bradley Bowman).

Figure 8.3. Strings and a line level in use for vertical and horizontal control (photograph by Bradley Bowman).

Vertical controls are recorded for each unit by measuring from the extended level string, as dictated by the line level (Figure 8.3) to any identified element of a feature, anomaly, or artifact. This information is recorded on graph paper (Figure 8.4). An accurate record of feature and artifact location is of primary importance in the analytical phase of the program. The graph paper (Figure 8.4) represents a square-meter unit subdivided into a 10 cm grid, which assists in the accurate plotting of recovered materials.

Excavated soils are screened through metal mesh or hardware cloth. Artifacts collected in this manner are placed in labeled paper bags and any observations are cross-referenced and recorded in the field notes. If time does not allow for formal mapping and unit layout as described, units can be numerically predetermined. Vertical recording with the string and line level, combined with spatial recording of any recovered materials on graph paper, are mandatory for this exercise. The educator determines what cultural group or groups are to be represented in the excavation and lays out artifacts, or reproductions of artifacts, identical to those presented in the Prerequisite Instruction portion of this exercise. The artifacts are then buried, bearing in mind their associations with other artifacts and features in the unit. Examples of temporal cultural change as reflected in the archaeological record might be:

1. Aspects of artifact types change due to changing cultural values – eg, ceramic designs in the southwestern United States correspond to the introduction of the Kachina Cult introduced from Central America (LeBlanc 1999: 285).

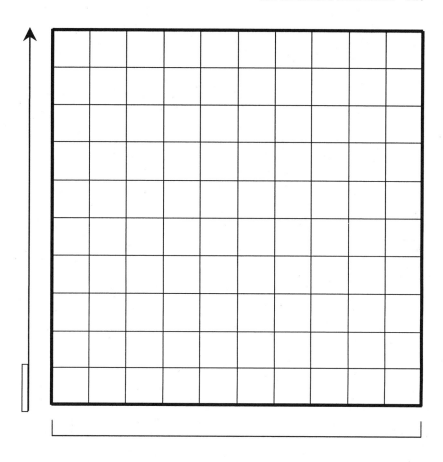

N   **1 m**

Unit Designation

Elevation

Figure 8.4. Graph paper for recording recovered materials.

2. Diagnostic projectile point typologies exhibit technological changes associated with the replacement of the atlatl and dart with the bow and arrow (Turner and Hester 1993; Whitaker 1993).

3. Changes in subsistence strategies are observed when there is a temporal change in the frequency of recovered wild animal remains associated with quantities of stone projectile points (expected with hunter-gatherer groups) to remains of domesticated species or evidence of a change to agriculture associated with ceramics indicative of more recent groups (Cordell 1984: 160–169).

As excavations progress, students are questioned about what they have discovered and the previously memorized time markers are brought into use. Students begin to formulate an evaluation of the deposits during excavations using information retained from the initial instruction. For example, ceramics found next to a hearth in close association with charcoal and maize suggest that food preparation was conducted at the site by an agricultural society after the introduction of maize and during the time diagnostic ceramic types in the area were produced. Observation is a learned skill and participants are quizzed in a way that forces them to open their eyes. For example, upon close examination animal bones recovered from the excavation are seen to bear cut marks.

'Stratigraphy provides the relative temporal and spatial framework on which to organise all archaeological data by separating temporally distinct assemblages of artefacts, ecofacts, and features that record the human history at a site' (Waters 1992: 60). Stratigraphy as applied to our exercise is based on the simple concept that artifacts deeper in cultural deposits were deposited at an earlier time than those above them. This can be replicated in two ways:

1. Soils are positioned in the units with earlier materials placed deeper in the deposits than those representing later occupations.

2. Stratigraphy constructed as above can have an 'erosional gully' placed through it in the form of terraces, exposing the layer-cake stratigraphy on the slopes (Figure 8.5). This method of constructing a multi-component site gives the illusion of stratigraphic superposition, but is far easier to produce than filling in deep pits with a chronology of archaeological materials. This option is used in our programs, and the different elevations are easily recognized when the students map the site and establish their vertical controls.

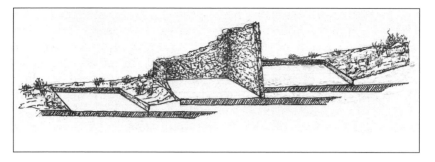

Figure 8.5. Using terraced units to provide an illusion of stratified cultural deposits.

ANALYSIS

The analytical portion of the exercise is conducted by comparing provenienced artifacts, animal bone, or other material recovered from the excavation to the photographs or collections used in the prerequisite phase of the project. The introduction and recovery of unidentifiable material from the excavation can frustrate and confuse the student and, without a specific purpose, should be discouraged. The Museum's program approaches analysis from a 'hands on' perspective. We use our exhibits and artifacts held in open storage, augmented by selected photographs and publications, for this purpose – for example, the basal portion of a projectile point of a specific type known to occur during a particular period of time was found in close association with an artiodactyl femur. The student looks through a chronology of projectile points until the artifact is identified, supplying an approximate date for the deposit. The artiodactyl's femur is then compared to photographs of a number of femora belonging to a variety of species, resulting in its identification as being deer. B. Miles Gilbert produced a publication, *Mammalian Osteology*, which includes multispecies illustrations of major skeletal elements suitable for this exercise (Gilbert 1980). A close examination of the deer femur reveals cut or butchery marks. The analyst can easily deduce from this information that a deer was butchered during a particular temporal period and its remains introduced into the site's deposits. Deer are known to inhabit certain environments within close proximity of the site, suggesting human exploitation of that environmental zone. The substitution of the deer remains for faunal material presently absent from your immediate area might provide evidence that a dramatic climatic shift occurred after the abandonment of the site (Klein and Cruz-Uribe 1984: 77).

This phase of the exercise may be broadened, limited only by time and the educator's desire and resources. Analytical classroom activities can include a variety of standard laboratory techniques – eg charcoal and other biological materials recovered by means of water flotation from excavated soil samples can be identified with the aid of a low-power binocular microscope. The microscope can also aid in the identification of ceramic tempers (Shepard 1995: 160), or the detection of use-polish on surfaces of lithic artifacts from the recovered assemblage (Hayden 1979).

INTERPRETATION

At the completion of the analytical phase of the project, all participants share with the class their collected materials and documentation as recorded in their field notes and graph paper. This can be done individually or in assigned groups. Each student is given the opportunity to describe his or her interpretations, with time allotted for the entire class to discuss the validity of those interpretations. The instructor leads the discussion by asking questions and evaluating the thoroughness of each student's performance. Did each student recover all of the information available? Was science conducted on a professional level, collecting a quantity of data suitable for documentation and replication of the site on paper? Will the quality of this documentation be of value to future researchers? Encourage the participants to reflect on the primary issues of the project, ethics, preservation, and the implications of inevitable site destruction. Students often remark on the significance of what they previously perceived as unimportant. A fragment of bison bone in association with a hearth and a diagnostic projectile point can become an interpretable moment of the past. They deduce, 'If any single element of this story were collected and removed from the site prior to excavation, a correct interpretation of the remaining evidence would be impossible'. The level of intellectual stimulation maintained by the students during the excavation and analytical portions of the exercise can become intense. In an attempt to understand the evidence, students often initiate heated discussions among themselves, unknowingly presenting a scenario (hypothesis) and using their discoveries (scientific data) to support their arguments. The intellectual environment created by the exercise initiates a natural progression resulting in the application of the scientific process.

DISCUSSION

This program has been presented to thousands of students of all ages and is designed specifically for individual stages of intellectual development and molded to suit the educator's desired goals. The exercise imparts a practical understanding of primary archaeological concepts and ethics, and provides a foundation from which competent field skills can be built. We feel our success rate far exceeds that of many similar programs, as archaeology is presented as a vehicle to communicate an awareness of social issues, specifically cultural understanding, ethics, and preservation of archaeological resources. The format, as presented here, allows the educator the flexibility to include related issues that might be required by imposed curricula, and is limited only by one's creative abilities.

One issue that recurs repeatedly during these exercises is the monetary value of artifacts. In many cases, students come from families that have long histories of artifact collecting as a recreational pastime and feel this is part of their heritage. The educator must provide convincing arguments to set seeds that can and will begin to change this pattern. Prosecution has not been successful in the elimination of illegal artifact collecting (King 1991). Only through education and an understanding that everyone has 'an obligation to weigh the consequences and impact of their actions on the irreplaceable evidences of past cultures' (SAA 1995) can we expect a change in public sentiment concerning our archaeological resources.

The mental exercises and excitement generated by an educational experience of this type have demonstrated benefits of positive change. Former program participants frequently bring otherwise uninterested friends and relatives to tour our facility, reciting to their guests important issues learned during the course of the program. Participating students' thought processes are elevated to an academic level of awareness focused on the intellectual value of archaeological materials. The act of data recovery and the associated analytical process stimulate this change in perspective. The exercise creates an understanding of the importance of our archaeological heritage, and provides its participants a glimpse into the diverse world of scientific disciplines brought to bear on the interpretation of the past.

REFERENCES

Cordell, LS (1984) *Prehistory of the Southwest*, San Diego: Academic Press
Cobblestone Publishing Company (2004) *Dig's State-by-State Guide to Archaeology and Paleontology Events for Kids,* Peterborough, NH, Available on-line at: www.digsite.com/guide/

Gilbert, MB (1980) *Mammalian Osteology*, 709 Kearny, Laramie, WY: B Miles Gilbert

Hayden, B (ed) (1979) *Lithic Use-Wear Analysis*, New York: Academic Press

King, TF (1991) 'Some dimensions of the pothunting problem', in Smith, GS and Ehrenhard, GS (eds), *Protecting the Past*, Available on-line at: www.cr.nps.gov/seac/protecting/html/3b-king.htm

Kintigh, KW (1996) 'SAA principles of archaeological ethics', 14(3) *Society for American Archaeology Bulletin*, Available on-line at: www.saa.org/publications/saabulletin/14-3/saa9.html, accessed 31 March 2005

Klein, RG and Cruz-Uribe, K (1984) *The Analysis of Animal Bones from Archaeological Sites*, Chicago: University of Chicago Press

LeBlanc, SA (1999) *Prehistoric Warfare in the American Southwest*, Salt Lake City: University of Utah Press

Shepard, AO (1995) *Ceramics for the Archaeologist*, Pub 609, Washington, DC: Carnegie Inst of Washington

SAA (Society for American Archaeology) (1995) *Guidelines for the Evaluation of Archaeological Education Materials*, Washington, DC: SAA

Turner, SE and Hester, TR (1993) *A Field Guide to Stone Artifacts of Texas Indians*, Second edition, Houston: Gulf Publishing Company

Waters, MR (1992) *Principles of Geoarchaeology, a North American Perspective*, Tucson: University of Arizona Press

Whittaker, JC (1993) *Flintknapping: Making and Understanding Stone Tools*, Austin: University of Texas Press

Digging Your Own Grave: Generic Skills from an Archaeological Simulation

Clive Orton

INTRODUCTION

The relationship between archaeology and statistics has been a long, but at times uncomfortable, one (Orton 1999). It can be traced back at least to the 1950s, but was formalized (the metaphor of an engagement party comes to mind) by the conference *Mathematics in the Archaeological and Historical Sciences*, held in Mamaia, Romania, in 1970 (Hodson *et al* 1971). The 1970s were a decade of optimism and experimentation, but in the 1980s the post-processual backlash against the 'New Archaeology' of the 1960s and 1970s led to 'the result that methodologically useful babies were unfairly thrown out with the theoretical bathwater' (Baxter 1994: 7). Opinion in the 1990s and since has been divided, perhaps just reflecting the fragmentation within archaeology itself that characterizes this period.

Nevertheless, I remain convinced that statistics has a key role within archaeology. Archaeology is a data-based discipline, and where you have archaeological data you also have uncertainty. To make sense of data in a climate of uncertainty, you need statistical techniques and insights. 'Eye-balling' data is simply not good enough; the human eye is all too good at seeing some patterns, even when they are not actually there, while easily missing others. Further, statistics is not just about data analysis, it is also about model-building, research design, and data collection, concerning itself with questions such as the quantity of data needed to answer a particular question. Nothing annoys statisticians more than to be asked how to analyze a pile of badly collected, possibly biased, inadequate or irrelevant data, and nothing annoys archaeologists more than to be told that it can't be done. Clearly, dialogue is needed at a much earlier stage than is often the case. Finally, statistics has something to say about how the outcomes of analyses are presented to various audiences, knowing from experience that nothing closes minds faster than an incomprehensible table or graphic.

In teaching archaeology, one has to acknowledge that many of the students will not go on to work in archaeology or related disciplines. Employers expect graduates to bring a set of transferable skills that they have acquired in the course of their degree studies, whatever their particular subject may have been. Such skills include the ability to analyze and assess the reliability of data, to work together in teams, and to present their conclusions cogently, both orally and in writing. Further, these are valuable general 'life skills', which help the individual to find their way in an increasingly complex world. These needs should not be overlooked in the teaching of archaeology students, especially as they are also part of what goes to make up a good archaeologist.

It is from this position that I have been teaching statistics to archaeologists, formally since 1985, but informally for much longer. The task is two-fold: to convince archaeologists that they need a dialogue throughout their research with what they may well feel to be an alien discipline, and to provide them with some useful analytical tools, and the knowledge of when and where to look for help. The formal part of the teaching has been mainly through two optional courses, one for third-year undergraduates and one for MA/MSc students; the informal part has been through innumerable consultations with students at all levels, as well as staff. Recent changes in the syllabus have allowed me to expand this teaching.

CONTEXT

This chapter is about a second-year 'core' (ie compulsory) course for the BA and BSc in Archaeology at University College London Institute of Archaeology, called 'Research and Presentation Skills in Archaeology'. Together with a parallel course, 'Interpreting Archaeological Data', it seeks to impart skills that students will need for their third-year dissertation, for further study, and for a career in archaeology. 'Research and Presentation Skills in Archaeology' also seeks to provide some transferable skills that will be valuable in any career, as outlined above.

The 'Research and Presentation Skills in Archaeology' course centers on the stages of the 'Research Cycle': model-building, research design, data collection, data analysis, interpretation, and presentation (Orton 2000: 10). It is assessed by means of a portfolio, comprising data collection (sampling), data analysis (statistics), critiques of research designs, of tabular and graphical presentations, and of an oral presentation (five topics in all). Since these are very general concepts, which are taught in many disciplines, it could be argued that they could be taught in a cross-disciplinary context. However, experience (particularly of using text books that do not have archaeological case studies) suggests that these skills need to be taught to archaeologists in an archaeological context. So what was the context to be – field survey, excavation, post-excavation? real or simulated data? Despite the attractions of using real data, I decided on a simulated excavation, so that all the topics I wanted to teach under the headings of 'data collection' and 'analysis' could reasonably be tackled from the same dataset, thus ensuring a strong 'story line' to the course. The alternative was to choose particular datasets to illustrate particular points, which would have given the course a fragmented feel (one of the criticisms of *Principles of Analysis in Archaeology*). Thus was born the cemetery of *Allemenschen*, very loosely based on the Iron Age cemetery of Hallstatt (Hodson 1990) but with similarities to some Saxon cemeteries in England (Brenan 1985). The name was taken from Beethoven's *Choral Symphony*, itself taking the words of Schiller's *Ode to Joy*.

Allemenschen is presented as an Excel (.xls) file, and statistical analyses use the 'Analysis Toolpak' Add-in. Students should be familiar with Excel, having been taught its basic use in the first-year core course 'Introduction to Field Methods and Techniques', in the context of a costing exercise. The use of more advanced packages, such as SPSS and Minitab, is reserved for the third-year option, 'Statistics for Archaeologists'. The data file consists of 500 rows (one for each grave in the cemetery, although this number could easily be varied) and 14 columns representing the following variables:

- ID no. (a unique identifying number running from 1 to 500)
- Easting (the location of the center of each grave, as meters east of an arbitrary datum)
- Northing (the location of the center of each grave, as meters north of an arbitrary datum)
- Orientation (the orientation of each grave in degrees clockwise from north, eg 90 means due east)
- m/f (male or female burial)
- spear (there follows a small selection of artifact types, whose presence is indicated by a 'y' for 'yes'. This list could be extended indefinitely.)
- shield
- sword

- knife
- key
- bracelet
- brooch
- pendant
- phase (for this cemetery, there are five phases, A to E; since the phasing is based on the artifacts, not on stratigraphy, any graves with no 'diagnostic' artifact types – ie with no artifacts, or with just a knife, which is not considered diagnostic of phase).

The variables listed above, which go to make up the description of the cemetery, each have both a deterministic and a stochastic (random) element. For example, the orientation of the graves decreases linearly from west to east across the cemetery (representing the intended alignment of each grave), but on this simple pattern is superimposed a random deviation (representing a failure to align the grave exactly on the intended alignment). This obscures the underlying pattern so that it is not easy to spot visually, but it can be detected statistically. Artifacts of different types are allocated to graves on a probabilistic basis, the probabilities depending on the osteological sex of the burial, as well as the presence of artifacts of 'lower' types (eg the probability of the presence of a sword depends on the presence of a spear, but not vice versa). This means that it is possible (but not likely) that a male burial could contain 'female' artifacts; various interpretations are possible (recording errors in excavation, incorrect osteological sex, or even cross-dressing, as suggested by one student). The relative importance of the deterministic and stochastic elements can be varied easily in Excel through varying the size of the parameters used in the random number generator to create the site, and the random element means that a 'new' cemetery can be generated every year if required.

In this course, the cemetery is specifically designed as a vehicle for teaching the following topics:

- sampling – simple random, stratified, systematic, and cluster sampling
- statistical approaches – exploratory and confirmatory (ie hypothesis testing)
- statistical techniques – *t*-test, binomial test, linear regression, contingency tables (chi-squared test)

These choices may appear arbitrary, but they are based on a career of statistical consultancy in archaeology, and cover a high proportion of archaeologists' needs. A wider range of topics is taught in the third-year option 'Statistics for Archaeologists'.

PREPARING THE EXERCISE

The material for this exercise consists of:

- The file *Allemenschen.xls*, which is made available on the Institute intranet (password-protected), and can be downloaded by students to their personal accounts. It comprises three sheets: sheet 1, on which students select a sample of graves from the cemetery according to their chosen strategy; sheet 2, on which they enter the identity number of their graves; and sheet 3 (which is hidden), which contains details of each grave (see below). When a grave's identity number is entered on sheet 2, the details are automatically copied from sheet 3 and 'appear' in the appropriate columns of sheet 2.

- A Portfolio Pack, which is distributed to students at the start of the course, and is also available on the intranet in case of loss. This contains all the instructions and information needed to complete the portfolio, including critiques of research designs and of tabular and graphical presentations, which are not based on *Allemenschen*.

APPROXIMATE LENGTH OF THE EXERCISE

For the purposes of this exercise (and other work contributing to the portfolio), the class is divided into small groups of about eight students, each led by a group facilitator (either the course tutor or a graduate teaching assistant). The groups meet five times, each for an hour.

At the first meeting, the groups discuss five possible questions that could be asked about the cemetery (see below), and which sampling strategies might be appropriate for trying to answer such questions. The story line is that, for reasons of time and resources, only 10% of the cemetery can be excavated. A strategy is then allocated to each student, the facilitator ensuring that each strategy is taken by at least one student in the group. Students then select their own samples in their own time.

At the second meeting, students discuss which exploratory (ie visualization, such as scatter plots) and which confirmatory techniques (ie hypothesis-testing, such as t-tests) would be appropriate for trying to answer each of the five questions, and assign questions and techniques so that each question is answered by at least one student in the group. The facilitator ensures that no one chooses an inappropriate technique. Students then carry out their own analyses on their own samples in their own time.

The third meeting is to critique published examples of tabular and graphical presentation, so does not concern us here. It is designed to reinforce the teaching of the basic principles of good/bad presentation of data.

At the fourth meeting, students share their results with the others, and plan a joint presentation of their collective results and conclusions. In their own time, they prepare the necessary materials (acetates for overhead projector, PowerPoint presentation, or whatever medium they choose), and may hold a further informal meeting (without the facilitator) to finalize details.

The fifth meeting is the presentation. Each group makes a 10-minute presentation to at least one other group (it was to two other groups in 2003/04 and to three other groups in 2004/05), with time for questions. The final part of the portfolio is to write a short critique of another group's presentation. The presentations themselves cannot form part of the assessed coursework because their assessment cannot be moderated by an External Examiner.

The total time allocated to the exercise is thus:

- Group meetings – four hours, ie 20% of the total of 20 contact hours of the entire course; this could be cut to two hours by omitting the presentations;
- Private work – 40 hours for *all* coursework, but this varies enormously according to the ability and inclination of the individual student.

THE EXERCISE

The following excerpt from the Portfolio Pack sets the scene:

The inhumation cemetery of *Allemenschen* has been discovered by aerial photography in advance of a motorway project. There appear to be about 500 graves affected by the motorway project, occupying an area of about 80 m east-west by 12 m north-south. Each grave has been given a unique ID number. The resources (time, money, and personnel) are available to excavate 10% of the cemetery.

In this course you will select a sample of the site for excavation, then 'excavate' your chosen sample using a spreadsheet, analyze certain aspects of the data, and present your findings to the other groups in your 'hour'. The details of each stage are given on separate sheets.

Sampling

The sampling exercise is introduced by the following excerpt from the Portfolio Pack:

How you design your sample depends on your research aims, so it is important to clarify them first. Possible aims for our example include:

- To discover the chronological sequence of the cemetery (in what order was it laid out?)
- To discover the topographical basis of the layout of the cemetery (is there a pattern to the orientation of the graves?)
- To ascertain the gender balance of the cemetery (more males? more females? separate areas?)
- To determine whether there is a hierarchical structure to the cemetery (are there 'classes' of differing 'richness' in terms of grave goods?)
- To discuss possible chronological changes in burial practice (eg do graves become 'richer' over time?)

Four sampling strategies are available to you: Simple random sampling, Stratified random sampling, Systematic sampling, Cluster sampling.

There follows instructions on how to use Excel to select a sample of 50 graves using each of these strategies. They are:

1. Simple random sample

    In this case, you need 50 random numbers between 1 and 500 (inclusive).

    Open the file Allemenschen.xls.

    Type 'ID number' in cell A1 of Sheet 1.

    Type '=RANDBETWEEN(1,500)' in cell A2.

Use *Autocomplete* to repeat this formula in cells A3 to A51.

Then copy column A of Sheet 1 to column A of Sheet 2, using *Paste Special.../Values* when you paste, not the usual *Paste* command.

2. Stratified random sample

   First, decide into how many strata you wish to divide the cemetery. I suggest a number between 5 and 10 (inclusive). The strata do not have to be all the same size (have the same number of graves), but it will make your life simpler if they are.

   Suppose you have 10 strata of 50 graves each. Stratum 1 will consist of graves 1–50, stratum 2 of graves 51–100, and so on. (Note that in this stratification, the strata run west to east; you could use a different criterion, eg north to south, but the numbering would be more difficult). You need a sample of five graves from each stratum (in real life you could vary the sampling fraction between strata, but we will not do so here).

   Open the file *Allemenschen.xls.*

   Type 'ID number' in cell A1 of Sheet 1.

   Type '=RANDBETWEEN(1,50)' in cell A2.

   Use *Autocomplete* to repeat this formula in cells A3 to A6.

   Type '=RANDBETWEEN(51,100)' in cell A7.

   Use *Autocomplete* to repeat this formula in cells A8 to A11, and so on until you have 50 random numbers in cells A2 to A51.

   Finally, copy column A of Sheet 1 to column A of Sheet 2, using *Paste Special.../Values* when you paste, not the usual *Paste* command.

   You may notice that the same ID number has been chosen more than once. This is what is called *sampling with replacement*. It is theoretically valid but a practical nuisance. What you need is *sampling without replacement*, in which no number can be chosen more than once. The simplest adjustment is to replace any duplicates by adding one (eg if ID 56 occurs twice, replace the second occurrence by 57). If that causes another duplicate, repeat the procedure until there are no duplicates.

3. Systematic sample

   In this case, you need for a starter one random number between 1 and 10 (inclusive).

Open the file *Allemenschen.xls*.

Type 'ID number' in cell A1 of Sheet 1.

Type '=RANDBETWEEN(1,10)' in cell A2.

Type '=A2+10' in cell A3.

Use *Autocomplete* to repeat this formula in cells A4 to A51.

Then copy column A of Sheet 1 to column A of Sheet 2, using *Paste Special.../Values* when you paste, not the usual *Paste* command.

4. Cluster sample

In this case, you have the choice of selecting ten clusters of five graves each, or five clusters of ten graves each (other cluster samples are of course possible, but they have not been written into the program).

Open the file *Allemenschen.xls*.

Type 'C5' in cell A1 of Sheet 1 if you want clusters of five graves each;

type 'C10' if you want clusters of ten graves each.

Type '=RANDBETWEEN(1,100)' in cell A2 if you want clusters of five graves each.

type '=RANDBETWEEN(1,50)' in cell A2 if you want clusters of ten graves each.

Use *Autocomplete* to repeat this formula in cells A3 to A11 if you want clusters of five graves each; or A3 to A6 if you want clusters of ten graves each.

This gives you the ID numbers of the clusters you have selected in cells A3 to A11 or A3 to A6, and the ID numbers of the graves you have selected in cells B2 to F11 (clusters of five graves each) or in cells B2 to K6 (clusters of ten graves each).

You may notice that the same cluster number has been chosen more than once. This is what is called *sampling with replacement*. It is theoretically valid but a practical nuisance. What you need is *sampling without replacement*, in which no number can be chosen more than once. The simplest adjustment is to replace any duplicates by adding one (eg if cluster 6 occurs twice, replace the second occurrence by 7). If that causes another duplicate, repeat the procedure until there are no more duplicates.

Finally, type into cells A2 to A51 of Sheet 2 the ID numbers of all the graves in the clusters that you have selected.

The pros and cons of different sampling strategies in relation to different research questions are discussed at the first meeting, and again (with the benefit of hindsight) by the students in their first submitted piece of coursework. For example, some students are disappointed by the spatial 'gaps' that often appear in simple random samples, and would in retrospect prefer the more even coverage produced by samples stratified by easting (since the excavated portion of the cemetery is an east-west swathe). Systematic sampling, which appears to offer a very even spread across the cemetery, may disappoint by leaving 'stripes' of unexcavated graves running east-west, or diagonally, across the site. Cluster samples may appeal to the practically-minded, since a 'block' of 10 contiguous graves should be easier to locate, excavate, and plan than 10 random graves across the cemetery, but again they may leave large areas unsampled. Does this matter? It's all up for discussion.

Analysis

The statistical analysis exercise is introduced in the Portfolio Pack by the following:

> Your dataset consists of the following information for each of the graves you have selected:
>
> - Column B: location of center of grave (meters east of an arbitrary datum)
> - Column C: location of center of grave (meters north of an arbitrary datum)
> - Column D: orientation of grave (in degrees clockwise from north, eg 90 is due east)
> - Column E: sex assigned to the skeleton by the osteologist (f = female, m = male)
> - Columns F to M: presence of various artifact types in the grave (y = yes, blank = no)
> - Column N: phase assigned to the grave by the finds specialist, based on the artifact types present. Note that knives are the same in all phases.

The artifact types listed in the dataset are very simple, simplistic even. There are three 'male' types: spear, shield, and sword, and three 'female' types: brooch, bracelet, and pendant, as well as two 'unisex' types: knife and key. Even with so few types, it is difficult to detect patterns in only 50 graves, and more types would make it almost impossible. Approaches to the five aims given above are set out as, for example:

> Topic 2: the topographical layout of the cemetery
>
> Data: the locations of the graves (eastings and northings), and orientations of the graves.
>
> Archaeological question: what is the relationship between location and orientation?
>
> Statistical questions: what are the types of data?
>
> Does the orientation of graves vary as easting varies? Or as northing varies?
>
> What exploratory techniques might shed light on this question?
>
> What confirmatory techniques might support a conclusion?
>
> Statistical conclusion: the relationships between orientation and easting and between orientation and northing can be described as ...
>
> Archaeological interpretation: what does the statistical conclusion tell you as an archaeologist? Can you spot a pattern in the way that the cemetery was laid out?

These detailed tasks are followed in the Pack by accounts of the analytical techniques provided, with instructions on how to carry them out in Excel, and linked to worked examples (of other datasets) which can be downloaded from the intranet.

REFLECTIONS ON THE EXERCISE

A disproportionate amount of time and effort, and considerable *angst*, went into the analysis aspect, from both students and staff. Although it was worth only 20% of the assessed marks of the course, I estimate that for some students this took up to half of the course's workload. Much of this can be put down to a fundamental error in my teaching strategy. Based on experience with the third-year course 'Statistics for Archaeologists' and a comparable Masters' course (both of which are options), I had come to believe that the answer to getting statistics across to nonspecialists was to use plenty of worked examples based in the parent discipline (in this case, archaeology). This approach was not, however, adequate for a compulsory course. For example, most students found it difficult to grasp that the statistical techniques demonstrated in some worked examples (which were deliberately *not* about *Allemenschen*) could be transferred to mathematically analogous problems in the analysis of *Allemenschen*. The problem seemed to be a lack of a sufficient level of abstract thinking, which prevented them from seeing the abstract similarities in physically very different situations. Whether this is something that can be taught, or something that people are born with (or not), I don't yet know. But it took me by surprise, and an extra class had to be put on at short notice to go through the questions and relate them to the detailed application of specific techniques.

What I *had* anticipated was the difficulty encountered in understanding the concept and operation of a hypothesis test. I hold no brief for them as a general approach, but they are so firmly embedded in the methodology of science, yet are so widely misunderstood, that I feel an understanding of them is an essential part of the education of anyone living in an 'evidence-based' society. Their logic is peculiarly convoluted, and does not always give the sorts of answers that students expect or want. One day, user-friendly software permitting, they may give way to a more intuitively appealing Bayesian approach (Buck *et al* 1996) but for the time being we have to help students to live with them.

Some changes have been made for 2004/05, both to the dataset and to the ancillary material. Some 'leveling' of the patterns was needed, making some more obvious to detect and others less so, to balance the workload between that various questions, and to make for a more interesting story. Some searching final questions, such as 'do you think that this question can be adequately answered from a sample?' would stretch the more able students. More detailed annotation of the worked examples was requested, including animation – this is likely to stretch *me*.

Mention should be made of the graduate teaching assistants in the course, who were not selected for their statistical expertise. They led their groups very well, fielding awkward questions and guiding gently rather than giving formal instruction. They were able to empathize with the students' problems and to communicate with them at an appropriate level. Without them the course would not have been nearly so successful, and they also got a lot from it, in terms of both knowledge and personal skills.

DISCUSSION

Simulated datasets, with embedded patterns overlaid by random variation, have a valuable role in teaching archaeologists how to look at and analyze data. The use of sampling means that each student's dataset will be different, and that they may even contradict one another (if 20 students answer the same question, on average one can be expected to reject a true null hypothesis – and they did). Having demonstrated the value of statistical techniques, it is useful also to demonstrate that they are not infallible. An interesting spin-off from the use of samples is that it reduces the risk of plagiarism, since everyone's results should be different, and there are no absolutely 'right' answers.

The *Allemenschen* dataset could of course be expanded. At present, it exists only as a fairly basic spreadsheet, and all sorts of enhancements would be possible. For example, a clickable site plan would enable students to select graves just by pointing at them (not by typing in numbers), and the artifacts could appear as images (rather than yes/no boxes). But would it be worth the effort? I'm a firm believer in the 80/20 principle (you get 80% of the functionality from the first 20% of the effort, and the remaining 80% of the effort gives you only 20% more functionality). So I think I shall concentrate on making the principles and practices as comprehensible as possible, and steer clear of the 'whizzy' effects. This should also help to make the dataset as platform-independent as possible, and help to prolong its shelf life.

REFERENCES

Baxter, MJ (1994) *Exploratory Multivariate Analysis in Archaeology*, Edinburgh: Edinburgh University Press

Brenan, J (1985) 'Assessing social status in the Anglo-Saxon cemetery at Sleaford', 21/22 *Bull Inst Archaeol* 125–31

Buck, CE, Cavanagh, WG and Litton, CD (1996) *Bayesian Approach to Interpreting Archaeological Data*, Chichester, England: Wiley

Hodson, FR (1990) *Hallstatt: the Ramsauer Graves: Quantification and Analysis*, Bonn: Habelt (Monographien/Römisch-Germanisches Zentralmuseum. Forschungsinstitut für Vor- und Frühgeschichte)

Hodson, FR, Kendall, DG and Taŭtu, P (eds) (1971) *Mathematics in the Archaeological and Historical Sciences*, Edinburgh: Edinburgh University Press

Orton, CR (1999) 'Plus ça change – perceptions of archaeological statistics', in Dingwall, L, Exon, S, Gaffney, V, Laflin, S and van Leusen, M (eds), *Archaeology in the Age of the Internet CAA97 Computer Applications and Quantitative Methods in Archaeology*, pp. 25–34. BAR Int Ser 750

Orton, CR (2000) *Sampling in Archaeology*, Cambridge: Cambridge University Press

Part IV

Hands-on Activities

10

Playing with Ochre:
Some Problems Associated
with the Analysis of Indigenous
Rock Markings

Michael Diplock and Abigail Stein

The history of the analysis of ancient rock markings[1] is replete with many examples of the subjective and erroneous interpretation of their meaning (eg Leroi-Gourhan 1968; Lewis-Williams *et al* 1986; Macintosh 1977; Sharpe 2004). This exercise is designed to show that, although the function of some rock markings can occasionally be discerned (particularly when relevant ethnographic data is available), the *original* intended meaning of the marks rarely survives their production (Grant *et al* 2002). Indeed, distortions to the rock marker's intended meaning occur immediately as they begin the process of marking the rock to depict an idea. This transformation of original meaning generally arises in the first place because of constraints imposed by the available media and intensifies as the production of the rock markings unfolds. This is due to other, more 'social' restrictions, which demand further compromises of the rock marker.

Original meaning is further altered when this two-dimensional visual representation of an idea is interpreted or given meaning by another person. Primarily, this is because the viewer of the marks will always see them through the filter of their own particular cultural and cognitive biases (culture is used here in the sense of the non-genetic transfer of practice). This distortion of intended meaning increases with the passage of time since the marking event, because not only does the viewer become increasingly unfamiliar with the marking conventions of the rock marker's society but also, inevitably, according to taphonomic logic,[2] a part of the motif, the motif itself, or the rock will degrade naturally until it ceases to exist.

Because of these problems, Bednarik (2001: 151) argues that the interpretation of ancient rock markings is a meaningless and subjective exercise and that '... [i]ts only scientific function [is] to study the perception, cognition and cultural conditioning of the interpreter'. Macintosh's (1977) experience at Beswick Creek Cave in Arnhem Land certainly lends weight to a view of the futility of iconographic interpretation. Prior to consultation with the artist, Macintosh attempted to identify motifs in terms of the faunal species they represented. Following consultation he found that he erred in nearly 90% of his interpretations.

The exercise described in this chapter highlights some of the innate complexities encountered in archaeological investigations. The original lecture from which this chapter evolved focused on both the production and analysis of rock markings. This exercise, however, can be used to teach a broad range of archaeological concepts and is particularly suitable for topics in the field of cognitive archaeology. In addition, the exercise is well suited to classrooms outside Australia. Indeed, because of its emphasis on the futility of interpretation (due to the interpreters' culturally specific 'baggage'), it lends itself to any cultural setting. The practical and collaborative nature of the exercise also generates an understanding of the social negotiations that the artifact producer (in this case the rock marker) engages in to produce the artifact and then to situate it in a socially meaningful context. Throughout the exercise, ideas of how this approach can be applied in other areas of archaeological investigation are presented in italics.

PREPARING THE EXERCISE

The materials required for this exercise (below), are based on a class size of 20 students.

- Several lumps of red, yellow, and white ochre. An alternative, if ochre is unavailable, is to use similarly colored chalks.
- 60 brown sheets of paper – two for practicing and one for the final design. If chalks are used rather than ochre, then a large river pebble for each group could be used for their final work, as this would add a tactile (and fun), dimension to the exercise to replace the activity of grinding and mixing ochre.
- 12 large, flat shells or other containers for grinding the ochre (or chalk).
- 12 smooth grinding stones (pestles).
- 20 paint brushes.
- Small water containers for washing brushes and mixing ochre. If chalk has been used, the ground chalk should be mixed with clear-

drying wood glue before use, to give a similar consistency to ochre and water.

- Secret printed instructions for each group (see below).

APPROXIMATE LENGTH OF EXERCISE

The length of this exercise is about one hour. This is broken down in the following manner:

- Introduction: 10 minutes
- Practical component: 20 minutes (five minutes for organizing groups with instructions; five minutes to demonstrate ochre preparation; 10 minutes to help each group produce their motifs)
- Discussion: 20 minutes (five minutes for each group)
- Summation: 10 minutes.

Where there is a need to accommodate a larger number of students or to analyze the issues in greater depth, the time allotted to each of the above components can be extended. However, where it is necessary to conclude the exercise in one hour, the lecturer should adhere rigidly to the suggested times.

THE EXERCISE

After the introduction, the class is initially formed into small groups of three to five students. Each group is then allocated a group identity and purpose (based on the demographics of a traditional Indigenous community), both of which are kept secret from the other groups. Each group is expected to produce at least one 'rock art' motif in accordance with their secret instructions. Following this, each group's 'rock art' motif(s) are analyzed by the other groups, in terms of their possible meaning and/or function. A discussion of the salient issues arising from this analysis will conclude the exercise.

PLAYING WITH OCHRE

Introduction

A 15-minute introduction focusing on the ability of archaeologists to sometimes manage to decipher the function but rarely the meaning of ancient rock markings, using whatever examples are appropriate to the region or course.

(Introduction to any archaeological issue the teacher wishes to pursue).

Practical Component

Each student is then allocated to one of the following groups:

> **Group 1:** Exclusively female
> **Group 2:** Community A
> **Group 3:** Community B
> **Group 4:** Exclusively male

Note. To promote more effective 'in-group/out-group' dynamics, groups 1 and 4 should be composed exclusively of female students and male students, respectively.

(Groups could adopt different theoretical perspectives on a range of archaeological issues or perhaps divide according to kinship/sex/age or other groupings relevant to the aspect of archaeology being explored).

When the grouping of students is accomplished, the lecturer demonstrates the grinding and preparation of the ochre before distributing (in an envelope), the secret nature and identity of each group and the task expected from them. During this, one representative of each group collects the required materials and returns with them to their respective group.

After a reminder from the lecturer that the students are to imagine they are members of an ancient Indigenous population that has no system of writing, each group is instructed to open their envelope and begin work. The contents of each envelope are as follows:

> **Group 1.** You are all involved in a women's secret totemic ritual. Design and produce a rock art motif(s) that reflects this by encoding information that is ritual in nature and only known to the members of your group.
>
> **Group 2.** Design and produce a motif(s) for use as a boundary marker between your community and that of your friendly neighbors.

Group 3. Design and produce a motif(s) for use as a boundary marker between your community and that of your extremely hostile neighbors.

Group 4. You are relaxing around the fire, idling away the evening together after a successful day of hunting. One of you scrawls a meaningless doodle on a rock as he listens to his mates bragging about their tracking ability. Design and produce such a motif(s).

As the students begin discussing among themselves what motif(s) they will produce, I like to offer the following suggestions and hints:

- A selection of symbols used in the Western Desert region of Australia (Bardon 1989: 104), are displayed on an overhead projector. I suggest to the students that they can use one or more of these symbols, or they can reject them all as unsuitable and create their own.
- I also mention at this point that Howard Morphy (1998: 95), working in northern Arnhem Land, has found that ritual or sacred markings usually take the form of geometric symbols and can often represent and maintain ancestral connections.

(Any other hints relevant to the specific archaeological topic under discussion can be given here).

Discussion

At the conclusion to the practical component, the four groups' motifs are displayed in front of the entire class. At this point they can dispense with imagining that they are Indigenous people from another time, marking the multidimensional landscape within which they live their lives. Now, they must become contemporary 'rock art' researchers, imbued with a spirit of scientific enquiry based on rigorous, epistemologically informed analysis of the evidence. In turn, each of the four paintings is analyzed in terms of their possible meaning and/or function by the class. During this analytical process, the group who produced the motif(s) under discussion remain silent.

(Each group could bring a different theoretical approach to a current archaeological debate – for example, one group could pursue a processual approach in their analysis of the other groups' motif(s), while the other groups employ either a postprocessual or poststructural perspective).

The discussion is kept focused by asking the same four questions about each of the four paintings:

1. What do you think is the message intended by the person (or people), who produced this motif?
2. Why?
3. What do you think is the social function of the motif?
4. Why?

Summation

The lecture is wound up with a 10-minute summation, in which the students are invited to revisit the questions: 'Is the meaning of a prehistoric artifact ever truly understood?' and, 'If we can get an idea of function, does meaning matter?' When Diplock has taught this exercise, the class discussion usually agrees that:

- Invariably, the search for the original, absolute meaning of rock markings becomes, in and of itself, a meaningless exercise.
- Largely due to the patterning that underlies the residues of past human activity, we can sometimes discern the function of such markings, or rather what their position was within the overall social fabric. In this way, 'meaning' can be understood within the context of the creation of a cultural landscape and the social interaction that accompanies this.

REFLECTIONS ON THE EXERCISE

In terms of its basic aims of fun and active learning, the exercise was a success. Judging from the dirty hands and intensity of collaboration within each group, the exercise was also successful in generating a high level of student participation and enthusiasm. The structure of the exercise facilitated detailed teacher/student discussion as well as stimulating student-to-student dialogue. In turn, this constant discourse ensured that all members of all groups were (fairly) equally informed about the relevant issues before they participated in the concluding inter-group discussion. As well, the students' engagement in the process of producing rock markings provided a large measure of understanding of the complex cultural, artistic, and practical hurdles to be negotiated or resolved by the rock marker in order just to get their message 'out there', let alone to accurately communicate it to others.

The practical activity was also successful in terms of the goals it achieved. These were to center the learning experience in a lighthearted and fun environment, both to maintain the interest of the students and the teacher, as well as to increase the students' level of attention to, and retention of, the information presented.

The results of the exercise indicated that original meaning is not retrievable, and that even when rock markings are tied to some contemporary ethnographic data, such data is no guarantee of correct interpretation (Corbey *et al* 2004). In fact, the students learned that to render the marks as meaningful requires of the viewer the same translation process (idea ➤ design) that the marker brought to the production process, only in reverse, and with the added burden of using a mind which is governed by a different heuristic or set of cultural beliefs.

On the other hand, however, the students had gleaned some idea of the function of several of the motifs, for example, as a means of allowing differential access to information or resources by members of a community, or as a boundary marker on the landscape. They also learned that a prerequisite to this process of ascribing function is the need (on the part of the researcher), to develop an understanding of the multilayered nature of a humanized landscape.

DISCUSSION

In short, this exercise demonstrates the futility of trying to interpret the original meaning of rock markings of unknown origin. This is achieved by role-play, which fosters a perspective that emphasizes a scientifically rigorous approach to the analysis of such markings. During the initial part of the exercise, when the student is an ancient rock marker, she is encouraged to appreciate the difficulties inherent in communicating symbolically with her fellows. Simultaneously, she also comes to appreciate that her behavior and framework of reality are largely culturally determined. Later, when she becomes a contemporary scientific researcher, she understands more clearly both the culturally insular nature of the rock markers and their marks, as well as her own culturally determined biases and assumptions. In short, this exercise teaches the student (in a fun and nonthreatening way) more about themselves by allowing them to become someone else.

The structure of the exercise also allows it to be employed for the teaching of other archaeological topics, as is shown by the suggestions in italics throughout the text. One way this could be done is for each group to bring a different theoretical stance to their analysis of the other groups' motifs. If this was attempted, however, the students would need time beforehand to research their particular school of thought. Alternatively, each group could emphasize different avenues of investigation in their analysis of the other groups' motifs. For example, one group could attempt to delineate various styles, another group could examine the techniques and materials used, while another could focus on hypothetical dating opportunities.

Although the exercise is designed to run for one hour, it could easily be extended. Ideally, the exercise could be run in the field for a whole day. The students would mine, prepare, and trade their ochre between groups, before applying it as motifs in places of their own choosing: an act which would imbue those places, and consequently the larger landscape as well, with meaning. This broadens the scope of the exercise to include discussions on other related issues, such as precolonial trade and Indigenous use and perceptions of landscape, in addition to allowing a deeper understanding of questions of meaning and function.

In terms of cognitive archaeology, the exercise can be used to convey some of the theoretical perspectives relating to theories regarding the timing of human language acquisition. In particular, it could be used to examine whether syntactic, complex language is a prerequisite to the development of multicomponent tools (Davidson and Noble 1992a; Lieberman *et al* 1992; Marshack 1989). If this idea is followed, the exercise needs to be adapted in the following manner: The students are allocated to only two groups. Both groups are given the same task, which is to design, construct, and then successfully use a multicomponent artifact. One group is instructed not to use any form of complex syntactic language for the duration of the task, while the other group would have no such restriction.

Most importantly, the structure of this exercise establishes a learning environment that is student centered and that promotes a relaxed and open forum for discussion. By using role-play, the exercise becomes a learning tool which allows the students to appreciate the extent of cultural conditioning that informs their framework of reality. It is hoped that this awareness will engender greater scientific rigor in their future archaeological investigations.

NOTES

1. *Rock markings* is used throughout this exercise in preference to *rock art* as *art* embodies Eurocentric connotations. Indeed, *art* generates a subtext relating to culturally specific marking techniques such as perspective or the use of the 'golden ratio' (the ratio 1:1.6). *Markings*, however, recognizes and emphasizes the true status of humanly marked rocks as artifacts whose function includes that of symbolic communication.

2. *Taphonomic logic* is a form of logic viewing rock art as the surviving remnant of a cumulative population that has been subjected to continuous degradation that selects in favor of specific properties facilitating longevity (Bednarik 2001).

REFERENCES AND FURTHER READING

Bednarik, RG (2001) *Rock Art Science: The Scientific Study of Palaeoart*, Turnhout, Belgium: Brepols Publishers n.v

Bardon, G (1989) *Mythscapes: Aboriginal Art of the Desert*, Melbourne: National Gallery of Victoria

Corbey, R, Layton, R and Tanner, J (2004) 'Archaeology and art', in Bintliff, J (ed), *A Companion to Archaeology*, Oxford: Blackwell Publishing

Davidson, I and Noble, W (1992) 'Why the first colonisation of the Australian region is the earliest evidence of modern human behaviour', *Archaeology in Oceania* 27(3), 135–142

Grant, J, Gorin, S and Fleming, N (2002) *The Archaeology Coursebook: An Introduction to Study Skills, Topics and Methods*, London: Routledge

Leiberman, P, Laitman, JT, Reidenberg, JS and Gannon, PJ (1992) 'The anatomy, physiology, acoustics and perception of speech: essential elements in analysis of the evolution of human speech', *Journal of Human Evolution* 23, 447–467

Leroi-Gourhan, A (1976) [1968] 'The evolution of Paleolithic art', in Fagan, B (ed), *Avenues to Antiquity, Readings from Scientific American*, San Francisco: WH Freeman and Co

Lewis-Williams, JD and Loubser, JHN (1986) 'Deceptive appearances: a critique of Southern African rock art studies', in Wendorf, F and Close, A (eds), *Advances in World Archaeology*, volume 5, New York: Academic Press

Macintosh, NWG (1977) 'Beswick Creek cave two decades later: a reappraisal', in Ucko, PJ (ed), *Form in Indigenous Art*, Canberra: Australian Institute of Aboriginal Studies

Marshack, A (1989) 'Evolution of the human capacity: the symbolic evidence', *Yearbook of Physical Anthropology* 32, 1–34

Morphy, H (1998) *Aboriginal Art*, London: Phaidon Press

Sharpe, K (2004) 'Line markings: human or animal origin?' *Australian Rock Art Research* 21(1), 57–70

Perspectives from a Pot: Introducing Archaeological Theory Through Visual Interpretation

Melinda Leach

Several years ago, a university colleague from another discipline asked me how I approached the problem of theoretical ideas in my introductory archaeology courses. Surely, he proposed, ideas in my discipline weren't that important to freshmen – what students needed most was a comfortable grounding in the facts of prehistory and the dirt methods of archaeology, not exposure to the confusing controversies, debates, and downright brutal arguments of the leading theoreticians in my field. He was skeptical when I told him that not only did I believe 'difficult theory' had a place in an introductory course, but that it could be introduced relatively painlessly. Moreover, after some background lecturing and small group discussion, my students usually were able to successfully apply their working knowledge of the rudiments of the major debates in my field within a class session or two. Further, I argued, this was an important component of my class because I wanted students to realize how *perspective* shapes *interpretation*, an awareness of which I thought was essential to critical thinking in archaeology or any other field.

What follows is a brief description of a small group activity that I use in 'Introduction to Archaeology', a university 'general education requirements' course taken by undergraduate students of all ranks and majors, including Anthropology majors. This small group activity requires students to take on the persona of an archaeologist who espouses the perspective of one of several major theoretical schools that have shaped archaeology as a discipline. Through that persona students are asked to interpret (faithfully within the boundaries of their theoretical school) a particular artifact – in this case, a prehistoric southwestern American Mimbres pot (see Brody 1977; Cordell 1997; Fewkes 1989) with a somewhat ambiguous design motif. My purpose is to help students think about how working within a theoretical school (with its own critical questions, biases, assumptions, perspectives, and methodologies) shapes one's questions, data collection methods, and interpretation of evidence. I am also hoping that students will come to understand, if only in quite simplified terms, several of the key theoretical frameworks that are operating today in the discipline of archaeology.

Traditionally, I have used this exercise in the early weeks of the semester after some discussion of the goals of, and ethical issues in, archaeology and several lectures on the roles of models, hypothesis-testing, and theory in archaeological explanation. After this exercise and throughout the remainder of the semester, I will frequently refer back to how taking a theoretical perspective alters the interpretation of a particular problem or data set in light of larger questions about culture and culture change.

PREPARING FOR THE EXERCISE: PROVIDING SOME BACKGROUND

Prior to the class exercise, some groundwork must be laid by the instructor and by the students. From their textbook (I use Ashmore and Sharer's *Discovering Our Past: A Brief Introduction*) and my introductory lectures, students are provided with a basic overview of key theoretical perspectives and the paradigmatic shifts that have moved the discipline through the last century. Several lectures introduce 'What is Theory?' and provide an overview of three central schools of theoretical thought that have shaped American archaeology – culture history, processualism, and postprocessualism (including contextualism, cognitive, gender, and interpretive archaeologies, among others). These lectures are followed by a take-home worksheet and/or a quiz and some further class discussion about the uses/goals/purposes of theory and explanation in archaeology. Students then have some basic recall grounding in theory.

What students need next is some experience in the application of theoretical perspectives; this is where the following small group activity comes into play. Through this activity, students build their knowledge and grasp of theory cumulatively, reaching a more complex understanding of how theory works. Because this is an introductory general education class, with relatively few Anthropology majors, I deliberately oversimplify the core ideas, attempting to show the starkest contrast between theoretical schools. In reality, the three approaches should be seen as complementary and interdependent, even though their debaters sometimes get into heated arguments about the rightness of their own approach. Each subsequent school has relied on the achievements and insights of the earlier approach, and our discipline grows as they continue to interact and interweave in the pursuit of common problems (Ashmore and Sharer 2000; Preucel 1991; Thomas 1998).

Each of the three approaches asks questions in different ways and appeals to different kinds of explanations for cultural phenomena. A culture historian, for example, is concerned about outlining the details of the past: the what, when, and where of culture development (Ashmore and Sharer 2000; Renfrew and Bahn 2000; Thomas 1998; Willey and Sabloff 1980: 101). Often working from specific observations (inductive reasoning) to derive general arguments about historical trends, the building of cultural chronologies and the definition of complex regional styles and geographical relationships dominate culture historical studies (see, for example, Hawley 1934; Irwin-Williams 1967; Kidder 2000[1924]). The painstaking description of ancient lifeways examines technology and organization via normative and idealized models of culture. Styles of pottery, for example, reflect cultural rules passed between generations and identify cultures and variations in time and space. Culture change is usually ascribed to migration and/or diffusion of ideas from surrounding regions, or to environmental change. Traditional cultural historical studies are highly descriptive; attributes of artifacts are meticulously recorded and compared in detail to determine stylistic change through time. The spatial and temporal distribution of stone tool or pottery styles is worked out region by region to show relationships (eg trade and contact) between cultures.

A processualist, in contrast, seeks to go beyond mere historical description to provide complex, systemic (perhaps even universal) explanations of how cultures work and why they change over time (Ashmore and Sharer 2000; Renfrew and Bahn 2000). Concepts of adaptation and materialist models emphasize the interrelatedness between components (eg social, economic, or political) of culture and external phenomena like environmental change. Deductive, rather than inductive, reasoning is employed. Multiple hypotheses are advanced and tested with the scientific method, and specific data are identified that will support or refute each hypothesis (see, for example, Binford 1962, 1967, 1972; Flannery 1976).

Postprocessual archaeologies also attempt to account for why cultures change, but many of them reject the procedures of the scientific method to do so and, instead, seek to validate multiple interpretations and perspectives (Hodder 1985; Johnson 2000). These diverse approaches emphasize culture as a construct of individuals who should be viewed as active decision makers and agents of culture change (Hodder 1995; Preucel 1991; Whitley 1998). The perspective of the ancient peoples themselves is important, as their views are layered with culturally specific meaning and significance. This cognitive model of culture requires archaeologists to examine cultures as sets of meanings that people put together for making sense of their lives. Symbols and the use of space become powerful 'windows' into these meanings. If symbolic world views guide people's lives and behaviors, then changes in material expression (pottery styles, burial practices, house form, etc) reflect particular cultural values, attitudes, and beliefs (Hodder 1985; Leone 1982). Age, class, and gendered relationships become significant shapers of the patterned material record. The individual, the family, and the ethnic group are the units of examination, rather than whole societies, as in culture historical and processual analyses (Hodder 1986).

THE EXERCISE

I set up the exercise by describing three personalities who espouse the central ideas of the key theoretical schools. For example, because of my interests in the American Southwest and my desire to include one female theoretician, I have chosen Florence Hawley Ellis, an early culture historian who helped work out time-space relationships for that region. Lewis Binford is an obvious choice as the ardent vocalist of the New Archaeology, or processualism, as is Ian Hodder, the British archaeologist who became disenchanted with the goals and claims of the New Archaeology and who has articulated many themes for the diverse approaches encompassed by postprocessualism. I find that students are particularly interested in biographical details, and relish hearing about hard-hitting debates, controversies in the field, and heated arguments that have arisen between famous archaeologists (Binford and Hodder, for example).

The exercise takes between one and two hours, depending upon how much discussion is encouraged. A two-hour activity allows plenty of time for group set-up, final presentations, and follow-up discussion for a class of about 50. Students are clustered in groups of four or five, are assigned a persona, and elect a spokesperson. They are asked to use notes, the text, and their creative minds to collaboratively reconstruct the significance of the artifact, from an assigned theoretical perspective. I provide a worksheet (Figure 11.1) and a photographic image (on an overhead transparency) of the artifact to be interpreted (Figure 11.2).

I deliberately select an ambiguous archaeological image. I enjoy using the image of a particular Mimbres pot, shown in Figure 11.2, because the design motif presents so many elements to which the students might potentially respond: technology, style, function, economy, ideology, contextual interpretation, gender roles, subsistence, etc. Many interpretations are possible and the students are encouraged to be creative in their

Figure 11.1. The activity worksheet.

Introduction to Archaeology

Your Name _____

University of North Dakota

Dr. Melinda Leach

INTERPRETING A MIMBRES POT THROUGH THE LENS OF THEORY

My purpose with this exercise is to help you think about how working within a theoretical school (with its own 'critical' questions, biases, assumptions, perspectives, and methodologies) shapes one's data-collection methods and interpretation of archaeological evidence. I am also hoping that you will come to understand the key theoretical frameworks that are operating today in the discipline of archaeology.

In class, we have discussed (and you have read about) the three key theoretical 'schools' that have shaped this century's archaeology – culture history, processualism, and postprocessualism. And you have viewed each of these through the eyes of their chief proponents (Drs. Florence Hawley Ellis, Lewis Binford, and Ian Hodder, respectively).

Group Activity:

First, gather into groups of four or five. Note the archaeological 'persona' assigned to you and identify yourself (Dr. Ellis, Binford, or Hodder) and your theoretical 'school':_____.

Now, consider that you are one of these world-renowned archaeologists who is presenting your latest interpretation of a puzzling artifact at the Society for American Archaeology meetings in New York. You pride yourself in being a particularly outspoken representative of your theoretical school (culture history, processualism, postprocessualism).

Now, consider this ceramic pot (shown on overhead transparency) made by a member of the Mimbres Culture of southwestern New Mexico. Its maker may have lived sometime between A.D. 1000 and A.D. 1150. Given your particular theoretical training, how would you interpret the significance of this pot? Discuss with your group members for approximately

20 minutes. Remember, stay faithful to the questions and research orientation of your theoretical school. Try to identify, in detail:

    a. What questions would you ask about the pot? What ideas/terms would you use in discussing it?

    b. What archaeological field or lab methods might you employ to study it, given your specific research questions?

    c. What context would you posit for this artifact – where do you think it was found? How might it have been used?

    d. What could you posit about the organization, economy, world view, or other details about the culture and lifeway of the Mimbres people?

    e. What is the pot's ultimate significance to archaeology, in your theoretical view?

Now, select a spokesperson from your group and present your conclusions to the professional meeting (the class) at large.

Activity Assessment Response:

What did you learn from this activity? Do you think it was useful in helping you distinguish the major schools of thought that have shaped the discipline of archaeology? Why or why not? What might be more useful in future exercises like this one? (Continue on the back if desired.)

Figure 11.2. Mimbres polychrome bowl. Woman carrying antelope in burden basket. H: 3 1/4" D: 11 1/4". Source of image: Plate 16 in Brody 1977; Photograph by Fred Stimson; from the collection of the Historical Museum and Institute of Western Colorado, Grand Junction, CO.; Redrawn by Douglas Hunter, University of North Dakota, 2004.

cultural reconstructions, keeping in mind that they should remain as faithful to their assigned theoretical orientation as possible. I tell the students virtually nothing about the Mimbres culture, the context of the pot, or the significance of the hole in its interior (ie the pot's ritual 'killing' before it was placed over the head or face of an individual at burial [Fewkes 1989]). The challenge is for them to create context and significance for this artifact. Whether or not their reconstruction is 'true' is immaterial; it should merely be authentic and theoretically justified.

During the small group work and discussion, the students discover and define the boundaries of their particular theoretical approach, devising some key questions and positing an interpretation of the pot. I wander from group to group and guide them back on track when I hear them veering from their assigned approach. If, for example, I hear a culture historian group reflecting on the meaning, symbolism, ideology, and gender roles revealed in the motif, I remind them that these are not questions that typically guide culture historians.

It is vital to give the students adequate time to work through some difficult concepts and to come to consensus in their group. After 20–30 minutes we reconvene and each group's spokesperson makes a formal presentation as Dr. Ellis, Binford, or Hodder. Because multiple groups will have been assigned the same persona, I usually ask all the Dr. Binfords, and so forth, to stand at once and make a joint presentation, involving some debate and discussion among the spokespersons. Thus, the rest of the class readily observes the variability of interpretations and ideas advanced by a single theoretical approach. I might offer a few guiding questions and a summary, before moving onto the next group.

REFLECTIONS ON THE EXERCISE

I am frequently amazed by the ideas that beginning students generate and share during this activity. In the third week of their first archaeology course, many students are able to make subtle cultural observations and posit big questions that get at the heart of the theoretical debates. They observe that they are 'thinking like an archaeologist'. While the spokespersons might sometimes waver and wander over into another theoretical orientation, their group members usually rein them in, thereby clarifying some of the key differences between the approaches, questions, methods, and interpretations.

Even misguided claims by spokespersons can lead to some interesting discussion, revealing assumptions and biases held by students. For example, some students readily propose that the human figure (see Figure 11.2) is a male hunter bringing home his quarry. They fail to notice the obvious breasts or the pregnant stomach, so distracted are they by their first observation that this is a hunter (and therefore, of course, a male). During the discussion we confront our common assumptions about gender roles in the past and our difficulty in seeing how these roles might differ from those in our own society. Invariably, a good discussion ensues about how our own cultural lenses can blind us to other possibilities in the past. And, of course, this point often opens up discussion about the androcentric bias recognized in archaeological research and the profession at large (see Conkey and Spector 1984; Wylie 1992).

In their final activity assessments, students reflect on the learning value of the hands-on experience of applying theory to a real case. They report that they are able more readily to distinguish between theoretical approaches, and the application of basic knowledge to a concrete problem helps considerably their understanding of difficult theory:

> I feel that this exercise brought me from just listening to lectures and reading the book, to a more active learning. I think it was helpful in the attempt to distinguish the different schools of thought, because we were forced to pick out one and compare it to the others.

It gave me a better understanding of the theoretical perspectives as opposed to just memorizing a definition. I learned that there are different ways an archaeologist studies an ... object and uses various methods to obtain their information. This provides a different perspective on how they see the past.

The activity was fun and engaging. It's really awesome to get a teacher who does more than lecture. It was useful for me in that I was engaged in what I was learning. I had to reason ... based on criteria set out by the cultural historians and that really stimulated a lot of critical thinking skills and also attached the information to previous associations in my memory.

In addition, students recognize and are sometimes surprised by how much complex cultural detail can be reconstructed from the analysis of a single artifact:

From this exercise I learned how to look at a piece of archaeological evidence with the intention of answering questions ... such as what was the structure of the society, when and where did it come from, was there trade involved, etc.

... If you put all these [approaches] together, an interesting story might be able to be put together about the culture you may be looking at or studying. ... you might be able to really understand the whole society and put together a full view of what life might have been like for the Mimbres.

It is vital to give the students adequate time to work through some difficult concepts and to come to consensus in their group. The small groups provide valuable opportunities for peer teaching and collaboration (see Brookfield and Preskill 1999): '... [t]hese group activities are excellent in fostering a better understanding; we each contribute our own ideas and learn from the others. Other people's creativity can make you think in other ways'.

Too, students recognize the potential richness of ideas and perspectives in archaeology, and the ultimate value of looking holistically at a problem from many viewpoints. Ultimately, students realize that each of the theoretical approaches offers something vitally important to the discipline. Indeed, the sense of being restricted to only one approach seems limiting and ultimately sterile. Students invariably argue that the use of multiple perspectives enriches interpretation:

By doing this activity I learned that studying artifacts solely from a single school of thought is extremely difficult. I found that I kept asking questions that would apply to other schools of thought other than the one I was looking and studying the pot from. It also made me realize that the best way to study the artifact is by using all three schools of thought. In a way it did help me to distinguish between the three schools of thought by realizing that for each school of thought I need to ask different questions.

I learned that when you are working within a single theoretical school your questions, study methods and views are narrowed because of the framework of the particular school. By putting yourself into one of these schools, one can really see how you must think a little differently when answering questions and studying cultures.

I learned that analyzing and interpreting artifacts is more difficult than it looks, but you can actually learn a lot about a culture by just looking at a bowl. I thought it was quite useful because not only did we get to discuss our school of thought within our group, we got to hear about all of the viewpoints from the other groups.

CONCLUSIONS

Broaching archaeological theory with students in an introductory course can be fraught with difficulty; students at best are often novice critical thinkers, ill-prepared, and predisposed to panic when the notion of 'theory' is mentioned. But I have found that approaching theory as a process of discovery, built upon cumulative understanding, critical discussion, and concrete application can be quite successful. Moving from simple information recall and comprehension to role-playing with application and collaborative analysis helps solidify and enrich first-year students' understanding of theory, explanation, and interpretation in archaeology.

My observation of the deeper and more critical thinking that results from this 'active learning' exercise has convinced me of the value of giving up lecture time and transforming my classroom into a more student-centered arena. This particular exercise combines elements of several strategies that have been well reviewed in the growing literature on active learning, including problem-solving discussion, team work, role-playing, collaborative learning groups, case-based learning, and the like (see for example, Bonwell and Eison 1991; Brookfield and Preskill 1999; Center for the Advancement of Teaching 2004; Felder and Brent 1996; McKinney 2004; Meyers and Jones 1993; Stein and Hurd 2000). With this exercise, students (regardless of their major course of study) are given the opportunity to practice analytical and interpretive skills that are relevant far beyond this introductory course in archaeology.

REFERENCES AND FURTHER READING

Ashmore, W and Sharer, RJ (2000) *Discovering Our Past: A Brief Introduction to Archaeology*, Third edition, Mountain View, CA: Mayfield Publishing Company

Binford, LR (1962) 'Archaeology as anthropology', *American Antiquity* 28, 217–225

Binford, LR (1967) 'Smudge pits and hide smoking: the use of analogy in archaeological reasoning', *American Antiquity* 32, 1–12

Binford, LR (1972) *An Archaeological Perspective*, New York: Seminar Press

Bonwell, CC and Eison, JA (1991) *Active Learning: Creating Excitement in the Classroom. ASHE-ERIC Higher Learning Report No. 1*, Washington, DC: George Washington University

Brody, JJ (1977) *Mimbres Painted Pottery*, Albuquerque: University of New Mexico Press

Brookfield, SD and Preskill, S (1999) *Discussion as a Way of Teaching: Tools and Techniques for Democratic Classrooms*, San Francisco: Jossey-Bass Publishers

Center for the Advancement of Teaching (2004) 'Teaching tips: Active learning. Illinois State University', Available on-line at: www.cat.ilstu.edu/teaching_tips/, accessed 12 November 2004

Conkey, MW and Spector, JD (1984) 'Archaeology and the study of gender', in Schiffer, M (ed), *Advances in Archaeological Method and Theory*, volume 7, New York: Academic Press

Cordell, LS (1997) *Archaeology of the Southwest*, Second edition, San Diego: Academic Press

Felder, RM and Brent, R (1996) 'Navigating the bumpy road to student-centered instruction', *College Teaching* 44(2), 43–47

Fewkes, JW (1989 [1914–1924]) *The Mimbres: Art and Archaeology*, Albuquerque: Avanyu Publishing

Flannery, KV (1976) *The Early Mesoamerican Village*, New York: Academic Press

Hawley, F (1934) *The Significance of the Dated Prehistory of Chetro Ketl, Chaco Canyon, New Mexico*, University of New Mexico Bulletin, Monograph Series No 1, Part I, Albuquerque: University of New Mexico Press

Hodder, I (1985) 'Postprocessual archaeology', in Schiffer, M (ed), *Advances in Archaeological Method and Theory*, volume 8, New York: Academic Press

Hodder, I (1986) *Reading the Past: Current Approaches to Interpretation in Archaeology*, Cambridge: Cambridge University Press

Hodder, I (1995) *Theory and Practice in Archaeology*, London: Routledge

Irwin-Williams, C (1967) 'Picosa: The elementary southwestern culture', *American Antiquity* 32(4), 441–457

Johnson, M (2000) *Archaeological Theory: An Introduction*, Oxford: Blackwell Publishers

Kidder, AV (2000 [1924]) *An Introduction to the Study of Southwestern Archaeology*, New Haven: Yale University Press

Leone, MP (1982) 'Some opinions about recovering mind', *American Antiquity* 47, 742–760

McKinney, K (2004) 'Active learning', Center for the Advancement of Teaching, Illinois State University, Available on-line at: www.cat.ilstu.edu/teaching_tips/handouts/newactive.shtml, accessed November 12, 2004

Meyers, C and Jones, TB (1993) *Promoting Active Learning: Strategies for the College Classroom,* San Francisco: Jossey-Bass

Preucel, RW (1991) *Processual and Postprocessual Archaeologies*, Center for Archaeological Investigations, Southern Illinois University at Carbondale, Occasional Paper No. 10

Renfrew, C and Bahn, P (2000) *Archaeology: Theories, Methods and Practice*, Third edition, London: Thames and Hudson

Stein, RF and Hurd, S (2000) *Using Student Teams in the Classroom: A Faculty Guide*, Bolton, MA: Anker Publishing

Thomas, DH (1998) *Archaeology*, Third edition, Fort Worth: Harcourt Brace College Publishers

Whitley, DS (1998) *Reader in Archaeological Theory: Post-processual and Cognitive Approaches*, London: Routledge

Willey, GR and Sabloff, JA (1980) *A History of American Archaeology*, Second edition, San Francisco: WH Freeman and Company

Wylie, Alison (1992) 'The interplay of evidential constraints and political interests: Recent archaeological research on gender', *American Antiquity* 57, 15–35

Culture of Litterbugs

M. Jay Stottman, Sarah E. Miller,
and A. Gwynn Henderson

Anthropology and archaeology are dynamic sciences whose practitioners generate field data through observation and construct narrative descriptions and interpretations of that data for both professional and public audiences. This lesson was born out of the belief that, in addition to traditional classroom instruction, undergraduate anthropology courses must involve students directly in the process of data collection and interpretation. By turning students into participant-observers of their own anthropological education, out-of-classroom exercises serve as productive links between students' lives and abstract anthropological and archaeological concepts.

The objectives of this lesson are:

1. to provide students with an out-of-classroom hands-on activity linked to in-class learning;
2. to connect archaeology students with the broader discipline of anthropology;
3. to demonstrate how anthropology and archaeology can effect social change; and
4. to relate the content of an introductory course directly to students' lives.

This lesson explicitly covers four of the seven principles outlined by the Society for American Archaeology that should be addressed when teaching today's students: social relevance; written and oral communication; fundamental archaeological skills; and real-world problem solving (Bender 2000).

Studying contemporary litter as part of an introductory archaeology course is a little quirky, but it plays to college students' sense of their world. Instructors should not underestimate litter's educational value:

it is a tangible, and legitimate, source of data that students can easily and often obviously link to human behavior that they see themselves. From an analytical standpoint, litter also rates highly: it is easily identifiable, and students do not require special knowledge of material culture to successfully study it.

Contemporary material culture studies are not new to archaeologists. In the 1970s, champions of the 'New Archaeology' found the study of contemporary material culture an excellent way to test their theories of cultural process (Rathje and McCarthy 1977). Noted 'garbologist' William L. Rathje continues to use archaeological practice and process to study contemporary culture through garbage (Rathje 2002; Rathje and Murphy 1992).

This lesson builds on these ideas, providing students with an opportunity to participate in a real-life, hands-on application of archaeological research. The findings from their research can potentially benefit the public at large by solving real problems and promoting change in the culture they study (Derry and Malloy 2003; Little 2002). This lesson goes far beyond the passive, standard 'term paper': students develop a personal connection to research that gives them a sense of having accomplished something meaningful. This provides a critical theoretical framework for the lesson and allows for self-reflection (Potter 1994).

This lesson is perhaps most conducive to use in introductory courses and those focused on artifacts or material culture. It is best used throughout the course as an on-going class project that reinforces every step of the archaeological process taught in the classroom. However, its strength is its flexibility, adaptability, and applicability for any archaeology course: the lesson can be adapted easily for specific class periods that focus on particular aspects of archaeology. Because the lesson also includes the collection and evaluation of ethnographic data, it also has clear connections to other courses and fields within and outside the discipline of anthropology (ie cultural anthropology, applied anthropology, ethnography, sociology, and environmental studies).

PREPARING FOR THE EXERCISE

The instructor will need trash bags and gloves for each student and the following forms:

- Data Collection Sign-up Sheet (Handout 1)
- Artifact Code Key (Handout 2)
- Artifact Catalog Sheet (Handout 3)
- Project Report Specifications (Handout 4).

Before beginning the course, the instructor should consult with school officials about any administrative concerns they may have regarding student participation in litter collection and identify the location of litter collection location site(s) (ie on or off campus). If the ethnographic data collection component of the lesson will be included, the instructor also should consult with school officials about the institution's guidelines or policies regarding human subjects (see Dunn and Chadwick 2002) and its policies regarding student-conducted interviews.

Before introducing the lesson to students, the instructor should make some basic decisions about:

1. whether students will work alone or in groups;
2. the length of the exercise; and
3. how the exercise will be integrated into classroom lectures, if at all.

APPROXIMATE LENGTH OF THE EXERCISE

This lesson is best conducted for the full duration of the course and takes place largely outside of regularly scheduled class instruction. The instructor should reference lesson activities during classroom instruction to illustrate relevant concepts. It is recommended that time be allotted during scheduled class meetings throughout the course to provide guidance to students and to check on their progress.

Instructors can, however, adapt this lesson for use during shorter periods of time with good results. Some steps can be abbreviated, while others can be omitted to reduce the time required to complete the exercise. Alternatively, specific steps or sections of steps can be used independently to illustrate particular aspects of the archaeological process. For example, to demonstrate data analysis, the instructor can ask students to catalog a sample of litter from the classroom's trash receptacle during a single class period. Other steps have similar potential as single class period activities.

THE EXERCISE

In this exercise, students experience, first-hand, the process of archaeological research by studying a contemporary community's littering behavior. Students devise a research design, select a study area, collect archaeological and ethnographic data, analyze the data, make interpretations, and present their findings in a final report. The lesson's seven main components mirror a typical archaeological research project. They consist of the following:

1. Problem formulation
2. Study area selection
3. Data recovery
4. Data analysis
5. Data interpretation
6. Reporting results
7. Curation

Begin the lesson with a presentation about archaeological research, research design, and the research reporting process. This helps introduce the exercise to the students and outlines what will be required of them as they pursue their study over the duration of the course. Be sure the students understand that the exercise is intended to complement what they are learning in the classroom by demonstrating archaeological concepts. Remind them that they will be conducting real research during this exercise, that the information they collect will lead to a better understanding of littering behavior in the study area, and that their research will provide potential solutions to address real community concerns.

Problem Formulation

The first step in conducting any kind of scientific inquiry is to develop a research question or problem. Therefore, near the beginning of the course, the instructor should devote at least one class period to working with the students to develop a problem focus for the exercise. Working within parameters set by the instructor, lead a discussion that facilitates the development of the kinds of questions the study of littering behavior might address. Ask students to formulate research questions, such as: 'Where does the litter come from?'; 'Who is littering?'; 'When are they littering?'; 'Why are they littering?'; 'What kinds of activities are associated with littering?'; 'What factors contribute to litter problems?'; 'How can the results of this kind of research affect public policy regarding litter?'; and so forth to facilitate the development of the research questions. Through classroom discussion, identify the major research questions that will be addressed.

Once the class has decided on the research questions, turn to a discussion of how these questions can be answered. Ask students to consider issues related to where they should collect their data; what kinds of data they should collect; and how they should collect it. This discussion should challenge students to think about how they will use archaeology to address their research questions, about research logistics, and about the planning that goes into conducting research.

Study Area Selection

Selection of an appropriate study area is crucial to the success of this exercise. Although, theoretically, any place that has a litter problem could be the study area, litter alone is not enough. Many factors need to be considered when identifying a study area, including logistics of the class (such as availability of transportation, class schedules, and number of students) and study area features (such as access, safety, and litter controls already in place). Any area considered for study should target a particular location on campus or a particular area in a neighborhood that has a chronic litter problem. The study area also must have clear boundaries, so that all students collect their data from the same area and don't introduce data from other areas. Planning and successful execution of the exercise can be enhanced if the instructor is personally familiar with locations of high research potential. Study area selection can be approached in two ways: each student or group of students can study an area of their choice; or the class as a whole or the instructor can select a single study area where everyone will work. There are advantages and disadvantages to each approach.

Allowing students to choose their own study area provides them with a great deal of flexibility. It eliminates problems with transportation and data collection scheduling, thereby permitting students to use the location that is best for them. However, it is difficult for the instructor to monitor multiple study areas and, more importantly, using multiple study areas greatly reduces the potential for the exercise to produce data that can be used to address research goals targeting public benefits.

The selection of one study area that the whole class uses is the preferred approach: it allows for the collection of extensive data from one location, and therefore has a higher potential for the successful development of viable solutions that can benefit the public. However, this approach is logistically more complicated for the instructor. He/she must ensure that data are collected evenly over the time permitted and without overlap. The instructor also has to ensure that the study area is accessible to all students.

Data Recovery

Students collect two different types of data during this exercise: the physical litter (artifacts) and ethnographic data about the human behavior that generated it. Prior to data collection, the instructor should lead a class discussion focused on the kinds of information that should be collected/recorded. This provides a good opportunity for students to consider the relationship between research questions and research logistics, and between artifacts and human behavior. Ask students if they think different littering behaviors might occur in different sections of the study area: for instance, in a residential section compared to a commercial section. Are there specific times and days that one might expect to find more (or less) litter?

As a class, decide when data collection should take place and establish time limits. If class size is large (ie over 40 students), the length of time devoted to data collection should be adjusted to ensure that everyone gets a chance to collect data (alternatively, students may work in groups).

Archaeological Data

Before students begin collecting the litter, discuss the research questions to be answered with these data (ie 'Who is littering?'; 'When are they littering?'; 'What kinds of activities are associated with littering?', 'What factors contribute to litter problems?') and what kind of data to collect and not collect. This discussion will introduce students to how data collection relates to research questions and to issues of sampling (sampling is particularly useful when dealing with thousands of cigarette butts and chewing gum wads!). Also discuss a standardized way of labeling bags, paying particular attention to provenience (spatial designations). Schedule student data collection sessions so that enough litter can accumulate between sessions. It is recommended that a sign-up sheet be used to manage data collection in a single study area (Handout 1). Students should use the trash bags and gloves provided when they collect the litter.

Ethnographic Data

Before students begin collecting information on littering behavior, lead an in-class discussion about the research questions to be answered with these data (ie What are people's attitudes toward litter and littering? What are the processes involved in the creation of litter? What are the positive effects of individuals who pick up litter?) and the kind of information the students will need to collect to answer them. Also, thoroughly discuss with students the various ethnographic methods and techniques for recording the information and, as a class, select one method: interview, survey, or observation. Take time to discuss with students how they might deal with situations when curious subjects approach them. Collecting ethnographic data provides an excellent opportunity for the instructor to discuss site formation processes and the connection between archaeological research and other disciplines within anthropology.

If interviews or surveys are the techniques selected, develop questionnaires that will elicit the information needed to answer the research questions. These instruments can be developed through in-class discussion or by each student or group of students. A single questionnaire that every student uses is preferred, however, as it will provide more consistent and reliable data. If observation is the technique selected, discuss as a class what basic observations should be made (they may include recording the proximity and condition of trash receptacles, weather conditions, littering behavior, cleaning-up behavior, and behavior associated with the proper disposal of litter) and create a checklist.

As mentioned previously, before students begin to collect ethnographic data, the instructor should ensure that the class complies with the institution's guidelines concerning interviews or surveys conducted by students. Each institution may have a different policy regarding this issue.

Data Analysis

During this part of the exercise, students sort and organize both sets of data to identify patterns and trends that can help answer the research questions.

Archaeological Data

These data provide an opportunity for in-class discussion on a variety of topics: material culture, artifact analysis using contemporary material culture; how archaeologists organize their data into computer databases; and how to use databases to search for patterns that relate to the research questions. In particular, this is the time to discuss issues in artifact classification and typology development, since depending on the research questions posed, data can be sorted into any number and type of categories (ie by material type, functional categories, size, form, and so forth).

For this exercise, each student can devise their own typology or, as a class, a single typology can be developed that all students use. Each approach has its advantages and disadvantages. Allowing students to devise their own artifact typologies provides an opportunity for them to be creative and for the class to see the diversity of classification schemes. However, the individually developed typologies will be different from each other, which will make it more difficult to combine the data into a single database for the entire class to use. Developing a single typology through class discussion ensures consistency. This approach is preferred, as the data easily can be combined into a single database, even though this approach may restrict individual student creativity. Based on the typology devised, develop an artifact coding system. Require all students to use this system when they code their data for entry into their databases (Handouts 2 and 3).

Ethnographic Data

Method of data collection will determine how the students analyze their ethnographic data. Much like the archaeological data, data collected through interviews or surveys can be easily quantified to view patterns and trends, by creating a response typology related to the research questions. Ask students to devise a response typology for the ethnographic data, either individually or as a class.

Observational data is more difficult to quantify, but broad typologies can be created for information collected using this method. These may include categories such as 'actions in the study area', with options such as 'littering', 'properly disposing of litter', and 'instances of picking up litter'. Qualitative ethnographic data (perhaps best generated through observation, although also accessible through interviews and surveys) is also an important source of information, because it provides students with an opportunity to understand the dynamics of littering and how litter accumulates. The combined use of qualitative and quantitative ethnographic data limits observer bias and provides different kinds of data that can be compared and contrasted for interpretive use.

Data Interpretation

Based on the results of their data analysis, students interpret the patterns and trends they identified in the archaeological and ethnographic data, answer the research questions, and draw conclusions about the litter problem in the study area. This part of the exercise also asks them to apply the knowledge they gained from their research to develop solutions to the litter problem in the study area. This aspect of the exercise connects the students' research to the community: they will have not only studied about, but also experienced, how archaeological research can have real and tangible public benefits. Set aside time for students to discuss their interpretations and solutions in class.

Reporting Results

The culmination of the exercise is each student's report of the results of the study. Distribute a Research Report Specification Sheet (Handout 4), which outlines the report's format and content. Review the handout in class within the context of a discussion about archaeological reporting standards and issues in contract archaeology. Be sure they realize that their report format mirrors that of regional professional archaeological reports prepared to comply with national and/or state cultural resource management regulations (cf Sanders 2001). Consider using a role-playing activity that asks students to pose as archaeologists submitting a report for approval. Give students the option of presenting the results of their research in public: at a neighborhood meeting or to school officials. This becomes not only a way for students to further connect with the community, but illustrates that there are many ways to disseminate the results of research.

Curation

Keeping true to the archaeological research process, the final activity in the lesson addresses curation. Ask students to consider, now that their research is completed, what they should do with their archaeological data (bags of litter) and ethnographic data (filled-out observation forms), as well as all supporting documentation and materials they generated as a result of their research. While it is not likely that they will curate these materials, as is typical for materials generated by professional archaeological projects, use this question to generate a discussion about the curation process and current issues regarding curation/ownership of artifacts.

Encourage students to use the knowledge they have gained from the exercise: dispose of the litter properly (at a ceremonial "disposal" event attended by the whole class). Alternatively, ask students to think about recycling the litter and how such behavior affects the formation of archaeological sites. Finally, as a class, ask students to select particularly significant artifacts found during the course of their research and prepare sets of artifacts that could be used in the future to illustrate important archaeological concepts.

Assessment

The report is the instructor's major tool for assessing student performance. Develop a rubric for grading that mirrors the archaeological report review process for professionally prepared cultural resource management reports (cf Sanders 2001). Base student grades on completing all sections of their report to specifications (eg the presence and quality of required content, format, and interpretations). Divide the report into sections for grading (Required Content, Organization, and Results) and assign a point value to each section.

Epilogue

At the end of the exercise, the instructor should prepare a final report that combines the data and interpretations from the student reports. Submit this report to the appropriate university officials (ie campus grounds office), city agency (ie the health department), or neighborhood organization.

AN EXAMPLE

Although the lesson has been explained in detail above, this example is provided to demonstrate its application.

Stottman developed the lesson as a hands-on demonstration of material culture analysis for an undergraduate Anthropology class on material culture he taught at the University of Louisville (Kentucky) during the spring of 2003. The class met twice a week for one hour and 15 minutes. Thirty-five students with a range of experience in archaeology (from none to very experienced) registered for the class. He chose a locale near his neighborhood as the study area because he was familiar with that neighborhood's chronic litter problem. The study area consisted of a Commercial Section (which included bars, restaurants, a coffee shop, post office, and bank) and a Residential Section (a middle-class urban neighborhood of late 19th- to early 20th-century houses).

The litter situation in the study area had been the focus of community concern for some time. Residents did not understand the nature of the litter problem and had few solutions to combat it. Their general approach was to find the cause of the litter and to place blame. Thus the lesson was designed not only to provide students with hands-on experience in analyzing material culture, but also to provide a service to the community. Collecting litter would make the neighborhood cleaner; providing information would help residents understand the causes of litter; and suggesting solutions could help combat the litter problem.

Stottman introduced the lesson to his students during a portion of a class session specifically designed for this purpose. After discussing the purpose and goals of the lesson, he showed the students a PowerPoint presentation that described the study area, its two different sections, and its boundaries. He also discussed the chronic litter problem in the study area and the residents' frustration with it. He emphasized that this project was not merely a class assignment: through this exercise, the students would help this neighborhood handle its litter problem and contribute to the community in a positive way.

During that class session, students formulated research questions and devised methods and strategies for collecting data. The research focus was on learning more about how and why the study area had a litter problem: What kinds of behavior were associated with littering? Where did the litter come from? Who was littering? How can the litter problem be solved? The students decided that they would study the spatial distribution of litter by collecting artifacts from both the Commercial Section and Residential Section. Since they considered that timing might be an important issue for identifying who was doing the littering and where it came from, they decided to conduct their research (ie collect the litter) at different times of the day and on different days of the week. They concluded that this strategy would provide a better understanding of the dynamics of littering in the two distinct sections of the study area.

Stottman decided that ethnographic data could also provide additional insights into the litter problem. After consulting with the department chair, he determined that this information was best collected through observation, since university regulations and guidelines required no special forms or permission for observing behavior. A list of factors that could affect littering was generated through in-class discussion: day of week, time of day, duration of littering activity, the weather conditions, and the condition and location of litter receptacles (Figure 12.1). Students decided that during their collection of ethnographic data, they would record occurrences of littering, instances of litter pick-up, instances of proper litter disposal, and general attitudes concerning litter. Students also decided that these observations would be conducted in one-hour increments using the same strategy of varying days and times as they would use for artifact collection.

Upon completion of this discussion of research design and data collection strategies, a sign-up sheet was prepared to ensure that litter was collected and that observations were made for all days and times (Handout 1). Students signed up for data collection days and times (at least one day/time per student) and were responsible for collecting their litter data and observational data at the scheduled day and time. The sheet also allowed the instructor to monitor the progress of the exercise, and he made periodic checks of the study area to make sure that students collected litter at their scheduled times (Figure 12.2). During the data

Figure 12.1. View of trash receptacle.

collection phase of their research, class time was set aside to discuss questions and problems as they arose.

Throughout the remainder of the course, Stottman referenced the exercise in class when it was relevant to the topic under discussion, such as research question development, data categorization, recording provenience, or artifact pattern identification. For example, during a discussion about how artifact categories are used in material culture studies, the class considered how to best organize the data they were collecting to answer their research questions. Suggestions for ways to organize the data were presented, such as functional and material type categories,

Figure 12.2. View of student collecting litter.

Figure 12.3. View of commercial litter.

but students were encouraged to devise their own typologies (Figure 12.3).

Toward the end of the semester, Stottman distributed the Research Report Specifications Handout (Handout 4). These reporting specifications were discussed in class with reference to regional professional archaeological reporting standards, and students were informed that the structure of, and information contained in, their reports would mirror professional reports. He used the report specifications to develop a rubric for grading student performance. After the course ended, Stottman compiled the information produced by the students into a single database using the coding system the class had developed (Handouts 2 and 3). He also produced a final report that was presented to city officials and neighborhood leaders.

As a result of having completed this exercise, students discovered that windy weather and overflowing litter receptacles were responsible for much of the litter. Smoking paraphernalia and fast food packaging constituted the largest litter categories. They found that people littered unintentionally and that many people picked up litter or went out of their way to dispose of litter properly. The prevalence of alcoholic beverage container litter increased on Fridays, Saturdays, and Sundays, but constituted only a moderate proportion of the total litter collected. Based on their research, the students suggested that installing more litter receptacles and emptying existing litter receptacles more often would help combat the litter problem in the study area. They also proposed placing cigarette disposal containers in various locations in the study area, particularly near the doors of some businesses.

REFLECTIONS ON THE EXERCISE

This exercise works well in an introductory archaeology class. It illustrates the entire archaeological process and complements in-class discussion, providing opportunities to demonstrate concepts taught in the classroom. It also works well in a special topics in archaeology course. As described in this example, referencing particular activities in the exercise when the complementary topic, such as data analysis, was being covered in class, stimulated classroom discussion. By conducting the analysis within the context of a wider research project, students learned how all the separate activities fit into the archaeological process as a whole.

An unanticipated product of this lesson was the variability in research design, methodologies, and study contexts utilized by the students. Different combinations of these components yielded different results and ultimately interpretations depending on what components were selected. Such is the case in professional archaeological research where different researchers arrive at different interpretations depending on how they use their data.

If time constraints or course structure do not permit devoting an entire semester to the lesson, it can be condensed into fewer class sessions by having students work in groups and by selecting a smaller study area with less litter. Parts of the lesson also can be condensed into stand-alone exercises focused on particular topics (ie sampling, research design, classification, and so forth). However, we recommend involving students in the long version of the exercise to maximize its benefits.

Perhaps the most important aspect of this lesson is its goal of using archaeological research to connect students to real-world problems. Although operationalizing the lesson and its various steps can be intricate and time consuming, it has the potential to make an ordinary class into a very enriching educational experience that leaves students with a new perspective on the role of archaeology and the study of material culture in today's world.

DISCUSSION

Most students enjoyed the lesson and its applications to archaeology and anthropology. It gave them an opportunity to get out of the classroom and actually get their hands into real research. They found that it helped them better understand archaeological and anthropological concepts and the relevancy of these "classroom" concepts to real world situations. Others were inspired by the sense of community benefits. College students tend to have a "save the world" kind of attitude: this lesson gives them a chance to put their studies into action.

Understandably, not all students responded favorably to the exercise. These individuals tended to be those who had little to no prior archaeology or anthropology coursework, who frequently questioned the value of these disciplines, or who did not understand them. Others had an aversion to collecting litter or handling litter (for some students, the litter was just plain gross!). While these students were perhaps not as enthusiastic about the exercise as their classmates, nevertheless they did feel that it left an impression on them, and they consequently gained a greater respect for how research is conducted by having taken part in the lesson.

As most instructors know, it is difficult to teach archaeology successfully using only books and lectures: it only really can be learned by doing. Within the context of a regular university course, this lesson provides students with an opportunity to experience, first-hand, how archaeologists study culture. It is what teaching archaeology in the 21st century is all about.

REFERENCES AND FURTHER READING

Bender, SJ (2000) 'A proposal to guide curricular reform for the 21st century', in Bender, SJ and Smith, GS (eds), *Teaching Archaeology in the 21st Century*, Washington, DC: Society for American Archaeology

Derry, L and Malloy, M (eds) (2003) *Archaeologists and Local Communities: Partners in Exploring the Past*, Washington, DC: Society of American Archaeology

Dunn, CM and Chadwick, GL (2002) *Protecting Study Volunteers in Research: A Manual for Investigative Sites*, Second edition, Boston: CenterWatch

Little, BJ (ed) (2002) *The Public Benefits of Archaeology*, Gainesville: University Press of Florida Press

Potter, PB Jr (1994) *Public Archaeology in Annapolis*, Washington, D.C.: Smithsonian Institution Press

Rathje, WL (2002) 'Garbology: The archaeology of fresh garbage', in Little, BJ (ed), *The Public Benefits of Archaeology*, Gainesville: University Press of Florida

Rathje, WL and McCarthy, M (1977) 'Regularity and variability in contemporary garbage', in South, S (ed), *Research Strategies in Historical Archaeology*, San Diego: Academic Press

Rathje, WL and Murphy, C (1992) *Rubbish: The Archaeology of Garbage*, New York: Harper Collins

Sanders, TN (ed) (2001) Specifications for Conducting Fieldwork and Preparing Cultural Resource Assessment Reports, Frankfort: Kentucky Heritage Council. www.state.ky.us/agencies/khc/specs_reports.htm

HANDOUT 1

LITTER PROJECT
DATA COLLECTION SIGN-UP SHEET

Date/Day	Time	Name
Sept. 14 or 15 Sunday or Monday	Anytime	
Sept. 16 or 17 Tuesday or Wed.	Afternoon	
Sept. 18 Thursday	Afternoon/Evening	
Sept. 19 Friday	Afternoon	
Sept. 20 Saturday	Afternoon	
Sept. 21 or 22 Sunday or Monday	Anytime	
Sept. 23 or 24 Tuesday or Wed.	Afternoon	
Sept. 25 Thursday	Afternoon/Evening	
Sept. 26 Friday	Afternoon	
Sept. 27 Saturday	Afternoon	
Sept. 28 or 29 Sunday or Monday	Anytime	
Sept. 30 or Oct. 1 Tuesday or Wed.	Anytime	
Oct. 2 Thursday	Afternoon/Evening	
Oct. 3 Friday	Afternoon	
Oct. 4 Saturday	Afternoon	
Oct. 5 or 6 Sunday or Monday	Anytime	
Oct. 7 or 8 Tuesday or Wed.	Anytime	
Oct. 9 Thursday	Afternoon/Evening	
Oct. 10 Friday	Afternoon	
Oct. 11 Saturday	Afternoon	

HANDOUT 2

LITTER PROJECT
ARTIFACT CODE KEY

A. Materials

1. Paper
2. Plastic
3. Metal-Other
4. Other Synthetic
5. Plastic and Metal

6. Fabric
7. Styrofoam
8. Glass
9. Wood
10. Rubber

11. Latex
12. Aluminium
13. Iron
14. Cardboard
15. Leather

16.
17.
18.
19.
20.

B. Form

1. French fry box
2. Placemat menu
3. Condiment packets
4. Napkins
5. Misc. food wrappers
6. Straws
7. Straw wrappers
8. Cups
9. Cup lids
10. Fork
11. Knife
12. Spoon
13. Spork
14. Container lid
15. Food bag
16. Stirrer
17. Take-out container

18. Coffee sleeve
19. Soft drink can
20. Water bottle
21. Pizza box
22. Cigarette butt
23. Cigarette butt-filter
24. Cigar butt
25. Matches
26. Cigarette pack/box
27. Cigarette pack wrapper
28. Lighter
29. Chewing tobacco contr.
30. Rolling paper
31. Cigarette carton
32. Cigar filter
33. Cigar wrapper
34. Pill pack

35. Pill wrapper
36. Lozenge wrapper
37. Medicine bottle
38. Toothbrush wrapper/box
39. Prescription label
40. Eye drop package
41. Wet wipe package
42. Condom
43. Face cleaning p
44. Bandage
45. Medical tape
46. Surgical mask
47. Cotton swab
48. Tissue
49. Diaper
50. Bottle label
51. Bottle cap

52. Milk chug
53. Gallon jug
54. Soft drink bottle
55. Juice bag
56. 12-pack box
57. Stay tab
58. 6-pack holder
59. Newspaper
60. Newspaper bag
61. Magazine
62. Newsletter
63. Misc. Publication
64. Parking pass
65. Bus pass/transfer
66. Bank receipt
67. Receipt
68. Check stub

HANDOUT 2 (continued)

LITTER PROJECT
ARTIFACT CODE KEY

B. Forms (continued)
69. Misc. stubs
70. Air freshener
71. Motor oil bottle
72. Tire
73. Car Seat part
74. Oil change sticker
75. Misc.
76. Candy/snack wrapper/box
77. Lollipop sticks
78. Beer can
79. Beer bottle

80. Advertisement
81. Price tag
82. Time card
83. Name tag
84. Miscellaneous cards
85. Menus
86. Coupons
87. Handbills
88. Ink pen
89. Envelope
90. Tape
91. Bubble wrap/peanuts

92. Post it notes
93. Paper clips
94. Pencil
95. Rubber band
96. Flat glass
97. Curved glass
98. Pet tag
99. Foil
100. Coins
101. Pie pan
102. Wash cloth
103. Towel

104. Nails
105. Washers
106. Hanger
107. Weed whip string
108. Fire works
109. Toys
110. CD
111.
112.
113.
114.

C. Category
1. Fast Food/Take-out
2. Smoking
3. Candy/Snacks
4. Alcoholic Beverages
5. Non-Alcoholic Beverages
6. Advertising/Promotion
7. Publication
8. Automotive
9. Receipts
10. Office Materials
11. Medicinal
12. Entertainment
13. Household
14. Miscellaneous

D. Location
1. Residential
2. Commercial

E. Markings?
1. Yes
2. No

HANDOUT 3

LITTER PROJECT
ARTIFACT CATALOG SHEET

Initials_____   Page_____

#	Date	Day	Time	Dur.	Coll.	N=	A	B	C	D	E	Prod./ Brand	Comments

HANDOUT 4

RESEARCH REPORT SPECIFICATIONS

The final product of the research project is a report of your findings. This report will essentially be a paper that is 5–10 single-spaced pages long including figures and tables. The organization of this paper is outlined below.

INTRODUCTION

Your paper will begin with an introduction that states the purpose of the project and presents the research questions. Describe the study area (where is it, what are the two parts, give a description of businesses, the location of litter cans, parking lots, alley, etc). Provide the date, time, and duration of data collection (for both litter and observations of littering behavior).

H2 Methods
In this section, you will describe the methods you used during your research. What methods did you use for data collection (litter and observations of littering behavior)? What methods did you use during the analysis (classification system used, how artifacts were identified, counted, etc)? What did you do with the litter after the analysis? Where did you conduct your observations of littering behavior? What kinds of behavior were you looking for?

ANALYSIS

Present the tabulated data you collected in this section. Litter should be listed in a table with text that characterizes the assemblage. Compare and contrast your data categories (you can use percentages). For example: 'Fifty percent of the total litter collected consisted of fast food packaging, with 25% of that category consisting of packaging from one particular restaurant.' You also could do other analyses, such as measuring the relative distance of litter from a specific place. For example: 'Most of the fast food packaging originated from restaurants located within a half kilometer of the project area.' Also mention any anomalies you see in the data, such as litter that was obviously transported over a long distance. Compare and contrast litter categories in the two areas.

Observations on littering behavior also should be categorized and tabulated in either text or table form or both. As you did with the litter data, compare and contrast the observational data. For example: 'There were five instances of littering observed during the observation period, while there were ten instances of proper litter disposal observed.'

CONCLUSIONS AND RECOMMENDATIONS

This is where you will synthesize the data (litter and observations of littering behavior) and make interpretations that will address the research questions. Characterize the litter problem, if there is one, and the people who visited the study area during your observations. Make some interpretations about litter behavior, good and bad. Make interpretations about the source of litter, the effects of weather on littering behavior, and identify particular problem locations. Explain why you think these patterns exist. For example: 'Based on the location of fast food packaging along street curbs and in the parking lot, and since most fast food restaurants are located more a half kilometer away from the study area, the litter was probably deposited by someone in a car.'

Finally, make some recommendations about how to solve the litter problem. For example: 'The addition of more litter cans of a different design could improve the litter problem in the residential area.'

Please feel free to use photos of the study area and the litter, or maps and other illustrations, but don't overdo it. I don't want 10 pages of photos.

If you have any questions, feel free to see me during office hours or e-mail me.

Toilets as Tools of Teaching

H. Martin Wobst

This chapter presents some examples of how to integrate toilets creatively into the classroom teaching of archaeology. In particular, I report on how to use toilet paper as an inexpensive tool to simulate the passing of geological or human history, and how to use public toilets to understand material culture as a force in constituting individuals and social groups. The teaching goals of these two examples are obviously quite distinct. They are not intended to exhaust the kinds of creative uses to which toilets, as basic and accessible parts of our material world, can be put in innovative teaching at the university level.

Toilets work well in teaching, because everybody is familiar with them, and they are a part of everyday life. Toilets are particularly useful because, while they are designed to zone bodily functions, they also intensively engage the mind in Anglo-American culture. The very mention of the work 'toilet' evokes reactions of prurient interest, mirth, and/ or aversion. In the minds of listeners, toilets set in motion chains of association and disassociation with purity, dirt, cleansing, cleanliness, taboo, public, and privacy. The very word must rank close to the top, if English words were rank-ordered by the number of their synonyms, suggesting that it is highly context-sensitive, and that it is used to constitute social contexts among speakers. In short, where the word is heard, the listeners' minds are engaged.

Compared to the richness of the cultural engagement with toilets in everyday talk and life, Anglo-American archaeologists have paid relatively little attention to toilets in their research and teaching. Some recent professional publications deal with toilets in classical antiquity (see, for example, Koloski-Ostrow 2001 or Shanks 2002); or with privies encountered in historical archaeology (see, for example, Neudecker 1994 or Wainwright 2003); historic privies are the focal points of intense avocational interest (for example, Scott's Privy Page [2003] and privydiggers.com [2003] have elicited several hundred thousand hits); and the literature on the social history of toilets is expanding (see, for example, Colman 1994; Hart-Davis 1997; Horan 1996; Reyburn 1974; Wright 1960). But, in the polite halls of Anglo-American archaeology, toilets remain off-color, *sub rosa*, illicit, a topic so smelly that it is avoided altogether. This chapter is a modest attempt to increase professional interest in toilets via experiential learning.

EXERCISE I: THE TOILET PAPER EXERCISE

The first example illustrated here employs toilet paper. It is earmarked for introductory archaeology courses in which students are exposed for the first time to concepts of time and its measurement. The exercise helps students to internalize, for their own experience, the inordinate amounts of time that archaeologists deal with, compared to the fleeting moments that their own experience and memory keeps accessible. I have used it to advantage in our entry-level introductory undergraduate course, 'Introduction to Archaeology and Prehistory', at the University of Massachusetts. The course introduces archaeological theory and methods and human cultural evolution for beginning undergraduates. Although the course has discussion/lab sections, I have always used this exercise in a lecture (for about 150 students).

Preparing the exercise

The materials for this class are:

- The requisite number of rolls of standard commercial toilet paper so that the total number of sheets is 4,500. While other combinations are possible, the numbers are easiest to follow if there are nine rolls of 500 sheets each. I have always placed the rolls before the exercise secretly behind the lectern, for better effect.
- An overhead or a slide (see Figure 13.1) that is also passed out to the students in a hand-out, summarizing the information presented below.

Approximate Length of Exercise

The exercise should not take up more than about twenty minutes of a one-hour lecture class, but it could be spun out for dramatic effect.

Figure 13.1. Earth history on toilet paper.

Each roll has five hundred sheets
Each sheet is the record for 1 m.yrs of history

DATE	EVENT	TOILET PAPER ROLL # AND SHEET #
12.5 b.y.	Origin of universe	—
4.6 b.y.	Origin of earth	1
3.6 b.y.	First bacteria	2, sheet 400
3 b.y.	First oxygen	3, sheet 400
2.4 b.y.	1st O dependent bacteria	5, sheet 100
1.3 b.y.	1st sexual reproduction	7, sheet 200
700 m.y.	1st marine critters	8, sheet 300
500 m.y.	1st fish	9, sheet 1
400 m.y.	1st amphibians	9, sheet 100
350 m.y.	1st reptiles and trees	9, sheet 150
225 m.y.	1st dinosaurs	9, sheet 275
180 m.y.	1st mammals and birds	9, sheet 320
70 m.y.	Last dinos, 1st primates	9, sheet 430
50 m.y.	Mammals 'explode'	9, sheet 450
5 m.y.	1st human-like primates	9, sheet 495
1.6 m.y.	Genus Homo	9, sheet 498.4
40-150k	Homo sapiens	9, sheet 499.85-96
10 k.y.	Agricultural origins	9, sheet 499.99
5 k.y.	Cities, written history	9, sheet 499.995
200 yrs.	Industrial revolution	9, sheet 499.9998
21 yrs.	1984, no big problems	
20 yrs.	The students were born	
15 yrs.	Gorbachev deposed	
6 yrs.	Millennium	
3 yrs.	Iraq invaded	
? yrs future	Iran invaded?	

The Exercise

Students are told that the kind of time that geologists and archaeologists talk about, thousands to millions if not billions of years, is something that most people have a very difficult time internalizing. Nothing in their experience remotely relates to more than four billion years of earth history, or even to the few centuries that already separate us from the industrial revolution. They will hear that 'such and such took place 1.5 million years ago', but that number will enter one ear and leave the other, without having interacted with anything significant in between. In their lives and from their own experience, there is nothing to help them to really imagine, and intelligently interact with, durations of such magnitude.

I suggest that we need something that everybody is familiar with from their own experience, to help us imagine time intervals of varying lengths, including geological ones, to bring out their relationships and contrasts and, thus, to truly understand and internalize the kind of time we will be talking about in class. 'Thus', I continue my lecture, 'instead of presenting you with a simple boring list of what happened when in the earth's history, let us now imagine that the earth's history were written down on something quite prosaic, in everyday use, easy to grasp, ... like toilet paper'. At that point, an assistant or I myself suddenly reveals nine rolls of toilet paper. 'Let us imagine that each sheet of toilet paper describes events within 1 million years. On standard institutional issue tissue, we would thus need about nine rolls at five hundred sheets each. Let us now read earth's history, from its very beginning, to the gory end which is us, the present, sheet after juicy sheet!'

I either make a pyramid of the toilet paper rolls right in front of me, and remove the rolls as their information is pretend-read (as on a scroll) or, for greater drama, have two assistants unroll (and actually read) the earth's history as it unfolds: 'There is nothing much to read on the first or second roll', or so I go, 'just lots of hot rock; not even oxygen yet. Lots of unrolling needs to take place – you have to unroll all sheets of roll 1, and then the first 400 sheets of roll 2, so, before the first bacteria are described', etc, etc.

It takes an excruciatingly long time to get through the entire history of the world. Moreover, the historic end of history that the students actually know from personal experience will be found only on infinitesimally small pieces of toilet paper. These pieces are so small as to be utterly useless for their originally intended function. In short, the immense lengths of time of earth and human history become graspable in the student's mind, and humans, recent humans, and even industrial humans become imaginable as extremely short-term phenomena.

Reflections on the Exercise

Years after I teach about time, students always remember this toilet paper lecture, even if they don't remember anything else about the course. Students connect with it, discuss it afterward, and walk away with a sense of wonder and engagement about a topic that otherwise is often criticized as being painfully plain and boring. If one had materialized time most other ways (including the traditional clock image), every trace of that lecture would have left their memory.

The actual unrolling takes considerably more time than just pointing to the rolls, and reading off where on the roll something would have been written down. But that also more effectively embodies the vastness of time. It is quite doable for a large class, with a pair of assistants. If it were done in a very small class, and one were not averse to unrolling and thus wasting lots of toilet paper, it should work quite well to actually have nine rolls for every pair of students, and have them each individually experience the passing of *lots* of time by unrolling their rolls.

Discussion

Teachers of archaeology often think that something they have an easy time grasping, others will have an easy time grasping, too. Teaching introductory courses has taught me that this usually is not so. At a given time, each category of material, set of methods, and bundle of theory has its optimal heuristic for presentation. That toilet paper works well for explaining geological and archaeological concepts of time does not mean that it will work well for anything else in introductory archaeology teaching. Only self-critique, experiment, and research will establish what works well for other topics.

EXERCISE II: THE PUBLIC TOILET FIELD TRIP

I have used toilets constructively in my teaching in a completely different way, in a field work course called 'The Archaeology of Us'. The course is directed toward third-year undergraduate students (not necessarily archaeology, or even anthropology, majors). The class has a size limit of 30 students. It is designed to have students experience how material culture interferes in one's life and helps to constitute us as individuals and members of social groups (in contrast to the standard representation of artifacts as passively 'reflecting' human behavior). The course starts from the inside out, from university publications (what kinds of students they are designed for and help to construct), to classrooms (how they classify producers and consumers of knowledge differently), and to campus architecture and landscaping, and then moves out into the local communities, their front yard sculptures, playgrounds, children and pets (interpreted as social artifacts), etc., and the 'wilderness' that surrounds it all (and how that artifact constructs New Englanders socially). Our first field trip always looks at university toilets, because toilets make the class topic more easily accessible.

Preparing the exercise

Before looking at actual toilets, students do some standard readings on artifacts as social tools and begin to critique the notion that artifacts are dead-end products of a construction process. Specifically, the standard interpretation is applied to toilets, as repositories for artifacts and other materials, as automatic results of design, and as terminal points of causal chains. Thus, the students approach the exercise with the understanding that standard artifact analysis (specifically toilet analysis) feeds an image in which artifacts and humans are neatly segregated, the one as mind, the other as matter; the one as input, the other as output; the one as subject, the other as object. In a society that is probably the most materialistic society ever, standard toilet analysis, they learn, alienates the *'us'* from *'artifacts'*. It actively deflects from understanding how we are shaped by artifacts, and what our artifacts tell us to think, say, do, or not do.

As teacher, I have to explore a range of toilets within walking distance from class beforehand, and get a sense of their usage pattern, so that this particular class size will fit into the available toilet space, and to learn how not to disturb the normal users of the facilities by invading their space with a bunch of undergraduates. It is ideal to have a range of toilets for inspection, differing in date of construction/last renovation, gender, and class. Students are handed a study guide with questions that are designed to sensitize them to the problems encountered. When we enter a gendered toilet, we make sure that there is nobody in it, and then, while we are discussing that toilet's materialities, we divert potential users. If the class is large, students are taken into the toilet in groups appropriate to its size.

Approximate Length of Exercise

I usually have this field trip take up the major part of a one-hour-long class. With a class of 20 to 30 students, five to seven toilets can be visited and discussed in detail in that length of time. The exercise could not be done during times of heavy toilet usage, such as during the times when classes begin and end, or during lunch hour.

The Exercise

When we look at the actual toilets of Machmer Hall (at the University of Massachusetts, Amherst) where the course meets, we can begin to grasp to what degree our image of person, status, power, gender, and privacy, among many other components of our ego, is shaped by and insepa-rable from material inputs to our lives. Toilets massively contribute to these dimensions in our daily lives, and much of that contribution is implicit, subconscious, unanalyzed by us. The field trip, with its guided discussions, exposes this.

We note for example that there used to be public toilets for faculty, and separate toilets for everybody else. This binary constructs and con-veys power to those who have or want it, and it privileges them with control over space and right to privacy. In contrast, lack of access to privileged space, and homogenized space for the many, are the marks and makers of underprivilege.

The toilets of Machmer Hall make gender 'real', that is, they turn it into a thing and, thus, make it imaginable as an essential, rather than a cultural, attribute. The simple differentiation 'Men' vs 'Women' on toilet doors does not *reflect* male and female difference as much as it helps to imagine it and provide a script for enacting it. Upon entering, the two stereotypic genders can validate for themselves that toilets materially define gender roles. For example, our female toilets exclusively contain baby-associated materiality (females should be child raisers?), all of the non-toilet sit-down places (females are the weaker sex?), and all of the bidets (females are cleaner than males?). Only male toilets separate spa-tially the elimination in front from the elimination in back (males are under greater time pressure?).

Our discussions at the site of elimination bring out that Machmer Hall toilets help to constitute the personal spatial halos that people con-sider inviolable, in the toilet space for either sex, or in the peeing spaces for males. Where does a person's privacy end, and the public's right to see begin? Toilets for both sexes permit, if not require, feet to be seen, most likely as surveillance to prevent sexual activities there. Heads, on the other hand, are usually made invisible in public toilets. When uri-nating, males can watch each other's behinds without objection. In most material constructions of the urinating wall, they even have visual ac-cess to the stream of urine generated, often including its source. This provides another significant material input to personhood and adds to a male's growing pains.

Toilets are places constructed to make look clean and wholesome that which the vernacular knows to be dirty and objectionable. Thus, toilets play a significant part in reifying the whole concept of cleanliness. They turn it into a thing, so that we can grasp it and imagine it. Both the cleanliness and the dirtiness, of course, are culturally constructed. Toilets function as the devices that 'hard-wire' those arbitrary categories into our brain as if they were natural ones.

The Machmer Hall public toilets are designed to keep people on the move, to make it as hard as possible to linger, or to enjoy what they have to do. They talk to us about productivity and efficiency, and to please-not-grow-roots. For the taxpayer, they help to make state-funded education look frugal (as opposed to the toilets in expensive private colleges). Although different ends of the alimentary tract are involved, in the public university setting they are thus very similar to the classrooms that carry similar messages to the taxpayer. As we return to one of those classrooms after the field trip, we recognize that, as vehicles in state-funded education, they are set up to facilitate the speedy consumption of academic input, the listening, the note-taking, and the cheat-free regurgitation. Public toilets are organized to facilitate the speedy elimination of what the body was fed. In that way, we discover that the artifacts of classroom and public toilet are icons of our age. They are artifacts and instruments of our alienation from our social context and history. They help us to think about our own strangeness and estrangement, about being continually bombarded with instruments that want to turn us from being three-dimensionally linked, multifaceted, creative, and thoughtful social beings, into unidirectional input or output devices. They make us and our society easier to think and to control.

Reflections on the exercise

Mechanically, it is not easy to give 20 to 30 adults visual access to the space provided by the usual public toilet, so care needs to be taken that a few people don't hog the space for the rest of them, and that class members circulate past what is to be observed.

The field trip is rich for an hour; students discover important angles of social process and their place in it. There needs to be time for digesting and internalizing that information. A useful follow-up would be an at-home exercise in which students individually are asked to analyze their own toilet, or toilets at one of the local private institutions of higher learning, to provide more context for the exercise, and more room to internalize potential conclusions.

DISCUSSION

There is no need for this exercise to be restricted to the class for which it was designed. It would serve well as an initial 'archaeological fieldwork' exercise, for discussion sections of introductory archaeology classes, exposing the social articulations of artifacts that are relatively long-lasting. By focusing on a variable that is usually outside polite discourse and learning from the exercise that this variable contains important keys for understanding society, the exercise is also useful for reifying and understanding the theoretical concept of hegemony, and for turning beginning students into self-propelled critical thinkers. The exercise is not designed to exhaust what one can learn by treating toilets as inputs into social life. A number of other material dimensions of toilets offer themselves for fieldwork. What these exercises do bring home is that toilets are useful learning devices, and interesting dimensions for archaeological research. They add fun in learning and catalyze student involvement in teaching and research. Even though they are designed to facilitate speedy elimination, they can be retooled to improve student retention. And, even though they are thought of as hidden and marginal, they are central instruments in constructing modern Anglo-Americans.

ACKNOWLEDGMENTS

This chapter is dedicated to my first TAs in Anthropology 102 ('Introduction to Archaeology and Prehistory') in the Fall Semester of 1971, at the University of Massachusetts in Amherst, Jerome C Rose and Stephen M Perlman. The toilet paper exercise had its origins in Jerry Rose, who knew about it before teaching with me at the University of Massachusetts and was happy when I took it to my intro students. I must have been an awful teacher then. Thanks for helping me. I also owe considerably to all of the other teaching assistants in 102 since then. Without you, I would not have been able to make it. Thanks also to the editors of this volume whose sense of humor is infectious, and who should be encouraged to add volumes on Research to delight and instruct and Service to delight and instruct. Those topics are in even greater need of levity!

REFERENCES

Colman, P (1994) *Toilets, Bathtubs, Sinks and Sewers: A History of the Bathroom*, New York: Simon and Schuster's Children's Books

Hart-Davis, A (1997) *Thunder, Flush, and Thomas Crapper: An Encycloopedia* [*sic*], London: Micheal O'Mara Books

Horan, J (1996) *The Porcelain God: A Social History of the Toilet*, Secaucus, NJ: Carol Pub. Group

Koloski-Ostrow, AO (2001) 'Talking heads': Interpreting the paintings in the Terme Dei Sette Sapienti at Ostia', *American Journal of Archaeology* 105(2), 261

Lupton, E and Miller, JA (1992) *The Bathroom, the Kitchen and the Aesthetics of Waste: A Process of Elimination*, New York: MIT List Visual Arts Center

Neudecker, R (1994) *Die Pracht der Latrine: Zum Wandel öffentlicher Bedürfnisanstalten in der kaiserzeitlichen Stadt*, Munich: Dr. Friedrich Pfeil Verlag

Ogle, M (2000) *All the Modern Conveniences: American Household Plumbing, 1840–1890*, Baltimore: Johns Hopkins University Press

Reyburn, Q (1974) *Flushed with Pride: The Story of Thomas Crapper*, London: MacDonald & Co

Scott's Privy Page (2003) Available on-line at: www.privymaster.org, accessed 6 June 2003

Shanks, H (2002) 'The puzzling channels in ancient latrines', *Biblical Archaeology Review* 25(5), 49–52

Wainwright, M (2003) 'Privy lifts lid on loo heritage', *The Guardian Home Pages*, 17 April 2003, Available on-line at: www.guardian.co.uk/arts/news/story/0.11711.938360.00.html

Wright, L (1960) *Clean and Decent: The Fascinating History of the Bathroom and the Water Closet, and of Sundry Habits, Fashions and Accessories of the Toilet, Principally in Great Britain, France, and America*, London: Routledge & Paul

14

Simple Ideas to Teach Big Concepts: 'Excavating' and Analyzing the Professor's Desk Drawer and Wastebasket

Larry J. Zimmerman

For archaeologists, many of the methods, techniques, and theoretical constructs we use seem so fundamental and straightforward that we believe they ought to be simple for everyone to understand. In actuality, some are based on 'big' concepts that can seem very complicated to novices. Many archaeological methods or techniques can be mastered by rote memorization or constant practice, but others require understanding at an epistemological – how we know what we know – level. That's more difficult.

For my 'Introduction to Prehistory' class, I 'resurrected' two hands-on activities to help students learn the epistemology behind the big concepts of stratigraphy, especially in regard to concepts of relative time, and archaeological classification. What more basic concepts are there in archaeology? Over three decades of teaching the class, I've discovered that both concepts pose problems for students because they often conflict with a student's 'received wisdom', that is, ideas about classification and time that they bring with them from everyday experience or learning from other sources. These problems likely originate from what seems to be an intuitive understanding of the basics of classification where the apparent need to classify objects in the world around us arguably can be called a human universal. Similarly with stratigraphy and its connection to relative time, the temporal primacy of a layer on the bottom of a pile of layers seems nearly common-sensical. To understand the concepts archaeologically, they have to 'unlearn' some things, and they have to cut through archaeological jargon to do so.

What do I mean when I write that I 'resurrected' the activities? I cannot claim these hands-on activities as new or original. They've been used and written about several times, but always in the context of elementary education as a way of teaching archaeological principles to children (see Browne nd for an example). For younger students they provide a fun way to engage students in thinking about the past, and I've discovered that the approach still works for university students. They enjoy the exercises, and as adults, you can make the exercises more germane to precise, actual examples from archaeological sites.

THE SIMPLE MAY NOT BE

The concepts of stratigraphy and classification might seem outrageously simple to most of us, even the students, but just how simple are they? With stratigraphy, we define the term for students as the layering of natural and cultural deposits in a site, and using the law of superposition, we can provide a relative age based on the stratigraphic position of one layer and the materials or artifacts it contains in relation to another. That's obvious, right? But we all know the reality of strata. Only rarely is it easily interpretable. Usually cultural- and bio-turbation have occurred, and sometimes, with the right geological or cultural processes, superposition can be turned upside down. Archaeological classification is a matter of grouping objects on the basis of their shared attributes; but what, exactly, is a shared attribute? Does it count if two attributes are 'sort of' alike? How or where do you draw the line? What kind of attributes should you use? Should you emphasize only material types such as stone and ceramic, or are other morphological traits such as size also important? Can we easily apply functional attributes? What do our groupings mean? Following the Ford and Spaulding debates of the 1950s in Americanist archaeology, do they represent the 'mental templates' used by the people who made and used the objects, waiting to be discovered by the archaeologist, or are they simply constructs of the archaeologist doing the classification? (See Willey and Sabloff 1993: 164–169 for an excellent summary of the debate.) None of these questions have easy answers.

Excavation of the Professor's Wastebasket and Analysis of the Professor's Desk Drawer bring some of these complexities forward without confusing or 'terrifying' students. The exercises come relatively early in the term, and on the syllabus they are usually called 'laboratories'. Part of the reason I do them early is also to promote a sense of camaraderie and teamwork among the students. They will need to work together on other activities later in the term. I call the activities 'labs' to promote the idea that method is important and that what we do is science. I personalize the exercise to myself as the Professor so they can get some insights into who I am. Looking into my trash makes them feel they know me better as a person and may show them that I have a sense of humor.

EXERCISE I: EXCAVATING THE WASTEBASKET

The key objectives of this exercise are to help students to understand the nature and complexity of stratigraphy, the law of superposition, and what strata can tell us about relative time. The exercise can be adjusted easily to add additional concepts such as minimum date, 'index' or type artifacts, and a variety of interpretive approaches based on disturbance of the strata by natural or cultural activities. A key to the exercise is a small take-home project in which students analyze the contents of a wastebasket in their residence.

Preparing the Exercise

The preparations for this exercise are very simple. I use my office wastebasket (dustbin, trashcan, rubbish bin, 'circular file') to collect a wide range of objects. I do not use the actual accumulation of material in my wastebasket; that is too difficult to control. A few days before the exercise, I begin to fill my wastebasket with items that normally get thrown away, but also with items that I 'plant' ('salt' is another term, but the idea is to carefully place particular objects and even arrange them in certain ways). I throw in a few food wrappers or relatively fresh items such as orange or banana peels, half-eaten sandwiches, or whatever happens to be at hand. All this gives it a semblance of authenticity.

I make certain that there are some fairly definite layers and in them some items with a calendrical date, such as papers with a date on them, a dated receipt, and the like. Coins with small monetary value are also useful. These allow me to discuss minimum dates. I have also used old computer diskettes, with an old 8' disk on the bottom, a 5.25' floppy, a 3.5', and a CD-ROM at the top (I've done this for several years; the technology has changed nicely so that I can keep things current). I use these to discuss stylistic change through time, a key concept in seriation. I do make certain to remove any item that contains confidential information, such as letters of reference for students or colleagues.

Very important is telling the custodians not to empty the wastebasket for a few days. Put a sign on it to remind them (more than once I have forgotten to do this, losing my work and some items I didn't want to get rid of!). I've even taken to hiding it in my laboratory. Sometimes I also let advanced students who have had the class before take care of the preparation of the wastebasket. They seem to enjoy trying to embarrass me or confuse the students. If you intend to raise additional concepts you can plan the basket accordingly, with objects that crosscut several strata, emulate folding, and the like. Trying to do too much, however, may detract from the simplicity of the exercise.

Approximate Length of Exercise

This exercise can be done in approximately 20–45 minutes. Much depends on the detail of concepts you try to work into the exercise and how much the students are willing to talk.

The Exercise

I make certain that students understand that archaeology is methodical and that knowing the vertical and horizontal context of artifacts is important. I ask for volunteers to excavate the wastebasket's contents and a note taker to record the position and nature of material removed. I ask them to describe each object and to hold it up for other students to see. Each object is removed and noted. As notes are taken, I ask the students to speculate about what happened that could account for items in the wastebasket, that is, what processes had to occur for the item to appear where it did. They also consider what had to happen before the next object could be placed on top of it, which hints at the concept of superposition. They go through the entire wastebasket this way. Having a sense of humor during this process helps to keep it from becoming tedious (let them learn that in their fieldwork!). I usually plant items that seem personal and revealing about me so the students can have a laugh at what they think is my expense.

I send the students away with an activity that calls for them to excavate a wastebasket in their own residence, do an inventory of contents, a 'profile' drawing of the strata they observe, and a short analysis of what they think the contents might say about the occupants of the residence. The objective of the activity is to reinforce the notions of stratigraphic analysis they've learned, but more importantly, to move toward analysis of material remains as a way of interpreting lifeways.

Reflections

The key ideas that you should make the students think about as you discuss the exercise are:

- the concept of uniformitarianism (that is, the processes that are going on now are the same as those that went on in the past)
- the law of superposition (that is, materials are probably older as you near the bottom)
- what relative time is
- how strata reflect relative time (that is, you know by position in the ground that something is older or younger than something else, but not by how much)
- exceptions are possible in superposition (that is, atypical events can disrupt the stratigraphic evidence and thus, interpretations of relative time).

There is almost no way for this exercise to fail if you pay attention to what students are saying and respond to or expand on their comments. The most difficult part is when you try to move them toward finer points of interpreting relative time from strata. For example, if an item cross-cuts several strata, they sometimes have difficulty distinguishing whether the strata might have built up around the item or whether the item was inserted at a later time. The notion of a minimum date can also be confusing, so you need to use caution when planting objects with calendrical dates.

The take-home activity is also potentially difficult. Students tend not to be as careful in their methodology as you'd like them to be, so you need to reinforce that you want them to take careful notes about the context of items they find, especially in vertical space. The problem with wastebaskets is that debris tends to accumulate rather quickly, so determining much about relative time can be difficult. Mostly, however, the take-home activity is meant to move them to the next step of interpreting lifeways from material objects and contexts. Students seem to have fun speculating about what an archaeologist might say about their habitation based on trash, and can quickly make the jump from the exercise to the realities of archaeological research, especially its limitations.

I try to debrief the students immediately after the in-class exercise to be certain the simple points have been understood, but also to set up the take-home activity. I also debrief after I return the take-home work, asking especially what they learned about the limitations of interpreting lifeways from material culture.

EXERCISE II: ANALYZING THE DESK DRAWER

The main objective of the desk drawer exercise is to help students to understand that classification of materials from archaeological sites follows classification strategies like those of other science disciplines, is systematic, and is a key to interpretations of the lives of people from the past. Ancillary objectives target the kinds of classification schemes archaeologists use, the reasons they are selected, and the limitations of each.

Preparing the Exercise

Ahead of the exercise, you need a desk drawer. I usually use the central drawer of my desk because it tends to accumulate the most 'junk,' even after a relatively short occupation of an office. Nothing about this is complicated. Some of it happens in the course of a university professor's daily work life. If you are like me, you can literally pull the drawer out and take it to class. If you don't have a desk with a drawer, you can fill a box with a wide range of items. Though it's not as personal, the goals are largely the same.

What's in the drawer? Ever since I have been a child I've had a 'junk' drawer where all the miscellaneous bits and pieces of daily life get thrown, just to get them out of the way. This changed little once I became a college professor, except perhaps that there were more things to put in the drawer, and their variety was substantially broader than when I was a child. The objects also became considerably stranger. You tend to keep the things you just can't throw away because you fantasize that they might be useful someday, they somehow might be valuable, they hold personal significance, or, as I discovered later, they might become useful to befuddle students. These are the badges from conferences, the plastic eating utensils or even metal ones liberated from the university cafeteria, a wide range of give-away pencils, pens, and 'do-dads' (defined as the odd items that businesses hand out at events to promote themselves), as well as the usual office supplies.

The location of these accumulated treasures is now the center drawer of my office desk. As colleagues learned about my use of the drawer in class, they would sometimes throw in the odd something-or-other to either embarrass me or to confuse the students. Sometimes I've also 'salted' the drawer with potentially difficult items such as a plastic 'spork' – that infamous Kentucky Fried Chicken combination spoon/fork eating utensil – or a laser pointer shaped like a pen.

Classification of Items 'Recovered' from Excavated Drawer		
Item #	Description of Item (eg size, color, weight, material, shape)	Possible Function of Item
1	medium, green/transparent, light, plastic	magnifying glass?
2	small/long with point, silver with black handle, metal	scissors?
3	small (square), black with silver 'slide', plastic/metal	computer diskette?
4	small with 'points', white, plastic	fork for eating

Possible Classification Clusters of Items Based on Attributes		
Cluster Name or Designation	Key Attribute(s)	Item # if grouped on this/these attributes
office tools	function	1, 2, 3
mostly plastic items	material	1, 3, 4
mostly metal items	material	2
small	size	2, 3, 4
with points	shape	2, 4

Figure 14.1. Sample forms for recording and clustering items in desk drawer classification (note: only the label segment of the form is reproduced here with sample entries).

That's really all there is to preparation. Just be sure that there is plenty of variety of both common and odd items. If you wish to make a particular point about classification, you can place items in the drawer to facilitate accomplishing that goal. I have also made up forms to help the students record their finds and their clusters, but mostly that's unnecessary.

Approximate Length of Exercise

This exercise can be done in approximately 45–60 minutes. The greater the number and variety of objects, the longer the exercise usually takes. If you have tried to work in complexities of classification, that can also add to time. Students usually talk more about the desk drawer than they do about the wastebasket.

The Exercise

As we begin a discussion of archaeological classification in my introductory archaeology class, I simply pull out the drawer and take it into class. At this point I have done no preparation with the class on classification terms or processes, so they come to the exercise 'cold'. This allows them to make connections between their intuitive or received knowledge about classification and more systematic archaeological approaches without my adding potentially confusing jargon or ideas until they are ready for them.

I announce where the drawer comes from and ask for a team of four to six 'excavators' whose job it is to take items out of the drawer and put them into categories, much as an archaeologist would at a site or in a lab. I give them absolutely no guidance as they do this. If the class is small, I invite other students to come closer to watch; if it's a large class in a large room, I encourage students to put their grouped objects on an 'elmo', that is, an opaque projector with the image enlarged and projected to be visible to the whole class. I ask one or two students to keep track of the groupings in a general way.

After the students have made their initial groupings, I begin to ask a series of questions, much like those an archaeologist might ask in classifying objects: Why does an object fit in a particular group? Does it share characteristics with objects in another group? Why did you put the object in this group rather than that group? Having a sense of humor about the questions and being willing to 'play' help, and you need to pay careful attention to the process the students use in their initial sorting so you can target specific questions. Eventually, the other students get the idea and start asking similar questions. They are often more pointed and critical than my own.

After several minutes of questions I ask them to try different groupings and we repeat the process. If others in the class wish to join in, all the better. When the class has done this at least twice, I then work through a debriefing where I ask them what they think they've learned from this and make key points about the problems or issues of the classification process.

Reflections

The key ideas that you should make the students think about as you discuss the exercise are:

- that classification is an important way for archaeologists to organize their observations;

- that classification follows rules;
- that the rules include specification of attributes used to cluster objects;
- that classification schemes can be numerous, depending on the archaeologist's research goals;
- that archaeologists try many different sets of rules before they arrive at conclusions;
- that making assumptions about function based on objects in the archaeologist's own culture can be erroneous;
- that categories created by archaeologists may or may not reflect the realities of the people who made and used the objects.

Students invariably group the objects according to categories that are familiar to them. For example, the eating utensils get grouped, writing instruments, and so forth, and the categories they choose are almost always functional groupings. If their categories are functional categories that American students might recognize, for example, I will rearrange the items into categories of material (ie plastic, metal, wood, etc) and ask if they can see the rationale for my arrangement. Often they can't easily see this because they are so locked into seeing the more familiar categories of function, or can't see how my classification might be useful. So, we put them back into their earlier functional groupings, but ask them to break these into smaller groupings. They might, for example, break the eating utensils into knives, forks, and spoons, but then they hit the 'spork' and puzzle over what to do with it. The laser pointer looks like a pen and in a way shares a similar function, but it is not a pen or a pencil. How should they deal with it? They try all sorts of arrangements with objects, led by my questions and those of fellow students.

They continually get asked why they are making the arrangement a particular way and often get suggestions about other ways to look at the objects. By the time they are done, they start to see the complexity of classification and how much more difficult it would be when we know little of the culture from the past that might have created and used a set of objects. They begin to understand the reasons that archaeologists almost always tend to fall back to categories of material first and move with great apprehension into function. I then raise questions about what these categories might mean or have meant to the people who made and used the objects. Students often have trouble doing this for items with which they are familiar, let alone for items that might be from another culture and time. When they finish the students usually recognize that categories are an invention of the analyst, not necessarily those of the creator or user of the objects. They recognize that there might be some overlap, but learn that one can't assume that analyst, creator, or user categories are congruent.

CONCLUSION

Hands-on activities more readily draw student attention and are often more memorable; they certainly are more fun for students than many other forms of learning. Frankly, they also are more fun for me than giving yet another dreary lecture (even one I can turn into a new PowerPoint or other presentation, which sometimes can be fun). Hands-on student learning is less passive, and manipulation of objects encourages them to develop meaning, that is, to restructure their epistemologies through direct interaction with phenomena, guided by discussion with classmates and exploration with the instructor (compare this with Haury and Rillero [1994] who provide an excellent discussion of hands-on learning from which I've drawn many of my general comments). Students tend to 'own' a concept better if they can connect it to contemporary life, to something with which they are very familiar and understand at perceptual and emotional levels. As a teacher, my task is to help students connect the perceptual and emotional to the intellectual.

By the time students get to college, however, the primary mode of teaching has become lecture and discussion. Hands-on activities are far less frequent. The reasons for this aren't entirely clear to me, but I suspect that much stems from the reactions of colleagues and peer pressure. Many have seen the wastebasket excavation before, which they remember as a way to teach elementary school students about archaeology. To me, some colleagues have been extremely harsh in their criticisms, telling me that I was 'dumbing down' the university curriculum. What they often don't see is that on my teaching evaluations students consistently have named these and similar hands-on activities as the most memorable parts of the class and those from which they felt they learned the most. More important, test results show that these concepts are among the best-learned and understood in the class. Some colleagues insist that university students should be more capable of learning complex ideas than elementary students, and I don't disagree. More complex ideas can be built into the hands-on exercises with relative ease and still do a better job of helping students learn than a lecture.

There is no high-powered conclusion to draw from my use of these simulated 'excavations' in classes. They do reinforce the idea that hands-on learning is more fun and memorable than most other forms of teaching. More important, hands-on learning promotes better understanding. As many of us may remember about our own training, our first field school – a fully hands-on experience with archaeology – was the most fun. The anticipation of discovery might have lured us into the discipline, but the hands-on experience of excavation or lab work is probably what kept us there. Elementary teachers know the power of hands-on learning, so as we teach archaeology to our university students we professors might do well to remember that simple, hands-on activities may be the most efficient and painless way to teach complex ideas.

REFERENCES

Browne, V (nd) *Lesson Plan 4: History Underfoot. The Story of Virginia*, Virginia Historical Society, Available on-line at: www.vahistorical.org/sva2003/lparch3.htm, accessed 19 March 2005

Haury, DL and Rillero, P (1994) *Perspectives of Hands-On Science Teaching*, Columbus OH: The ERIC Clearinghouse for Science, Mathematics, and Environmental Education, Available on-line at: www.ncrel.org/sdrs/areas/issues/content/cntareas/science/eric/eric-toc.htm, accessed 19 March 2004

Willey, G and Sabloff, J (1993) *A History of American Archaeology*, New York: WH Freeman

Part V

Creative Construction and Performance

The Draw-an-Archaeologist Test: Eliciting Student's Ideas About Archaeology

Susan Renoe

CONTEXT OF THE EXERCISE

All students enter the classroom with some sort of archaeological knowledge. Whether that knowledge is the result of family vacations to archaeological sites or from watching television, they all have some idea of what they think archaeology is and what archaeologists do. Dr. Jane Baxter states, '[I]t would be difficult to argue that there is a more popular image of an archaeologist than Indiana Jones. ... [He] has become the stereotypical image of an archaeologist. He is also very white and very male, and his character has become the racial and gendered stereotype of a "typical" archaeologist' (Baxter 2002: 16). Most people have no idea what archaeology is really like, and the truth often disillusions them. How do we get students to stop having Indy-vision and see with archaeological vision? In other words, how do we address the misconceptions that students bring into the classroom with them?

A student's previous understanding of archaeology has a profound effect on what that student will learn about archaeology in the future. Conceptual change theory (Strike 1983; Strike and Posner 1982, 1985, 1992) focuses on 'how ... learners make [the] transition from one conception ... to [another] conception' (Strike and Posner 1992: 148), and the 'interaction of the learner's conceptual ecology with ... new knowledge' (Kelly 1997: 358). In essence, new archaeological knowledge presented to students is filtered through their existing knowledge, which then guides them to make a judgment about whether to accept or reject that new knowledge. The best way to reinforce factual understandings about archaeology and to correct fallacious ones is to find out what students already know and address that directly.

Since students' existing conceptions weigh heavily in their decision whether to accept or reject new archaeological knowledge, it is important to know what those existing conceptions are. The Draw-an-Archaeologist Test (DART) is an easy and nonthreatening way to elicit students' conceptions of archaeology. This exercise is a great opening and/or concluding exercise for an introductory archaeology course. The DART (Dixon 2000, 2001a, 2001b; Judge 1988; Renoe 2003a, 2003b) is based on the Draw-a-Scientist Test (Chambers 1983), itself based on the Draw-a-Man Test created by Florence Goodenough (1926).

PREPARING THE EXERCISE

The materials needed for this activity are:

- Drawing paper
- Markers, crayons, paint, pencils, pens – whatever medium you or your students have available.

APPROXIMATE LENGTH OF EXERCISE

The time needed to conduct this exercise will vary from class to class. If the assignment is given as homework, then class time can be devoted to discussion. If the assignment is given in class, then time will need to be divided between the activity and the discussion. The activity can take anywhere from 5–15 minutes. Discussion can last from 10–60 minutes.

THE EXERCISE

The procedure for the DART is fairly straightforward: ask each student to draw what he or she thinks an archaeologist looks like, including any associated tools, artifacts, clothing, etc. When they finish their drawing, ask them to write a paragraph or short story about their archaeologist – either on the back of their drawing or on a separate sheet of paper. Ask them to describe what an archaeologist does and what is going on in their picture. Ask students to be explicit about their particular archaeologist (ethnicity, age, gender, etc).

When students are finished with their drawings and descriptions, ask them to present their archaeologists to the class. Do not be surprised by any drawings you receive. Most students will draw an archaeologist in the field, usually with a shovel or pickaxe. Some students may draw aliens, robots, and monsters instead of humans. These beings are perfectly acceptable; however you might point out that there are no *known* monster or alien archaeologists. Some students will draw archaeologists doing 'non-archaeological' things such as dancing or cooking dinner. This is a good time to remind them that archaeologists are people, too.

Make sure you take notes (mentally or physically) as they are talking so you can use the information to frame the introductory discussion. Be particularly mindful of the number of minority archaeologists and the ratio of men to women depicted in the drawings. This feedback will allow you to address issues of gender and ethnic equity and access in science. This is an important point that we will come back to further in our discussion. Another thing to note is the number of dinosaurs and Indiana Jones elements present in the drawings (whips, fedora hats, chalices, bones, etc). These drawings will allow you to address misconceptions students have about archaeologists and what they do. To clear up misconceptions, point out the following:

- Archaeologists do not study dinosaurs;
- Professional archaeologists do not usually keep the artifacts they find;
- Professional archaeologists are concerned with preserving the archaeological record, not making a profit from it.

Although the DART can be used any time during your discussion, it works best as the opening activity of an archaeology unit because it is a common place to start the discussion of what archaeology is and what archaeologists do. The DART can be used as an in-class assignment or given as homework. If the DART is given as homework, the methodology is the same except the drawing and writing are both done before class, and the responsibility for materials falls on the student, not the teacher. In this instance, the in-class time can range from 20–45 minutes, depending on the length of presentations and discussion.

I like to assign the DART shortly before the class in which I am going to talk about archaeology or gender and ethnicity in the archaeological record, because it gives me time to analyze the drawings and descriptions. This way I can use the results in my discussion. It also gives me a chance to seek permission from students to show their drawings to the class – especially if students are hesitant to display their drawings to the class themselves.

The DART can also be used as the concluding activity of an archaeology unit. It is a good way to compare change in student conceptions from the beginning of the unit to the end. If you intend to use the DART at both the beginning and the end of the unit, then you will need to double the materials for each student. Otherwise, the methodology is the same.

REFLECTIONS ON THE EXERCISE

I used the DART to elicit student conceptions in two settings over three courses. It was first implemented during the summer of 2000 in the Houston Museum of Natural Science (HMNS) summer course, *Archeology.com*. During that time, I was co-instructor of an introductory archaeology class for 10-, 11-, and 12-year-olds held at the museum. Classes were one week long and spanned the entire month of June. The main objective of the course was to introduce students to archaeology through a variety of activities including flint knapping, excavation, data analysis, research, and preservation. I administered the DART on the first day of each week as the introductory activity. Students were given blank pieces of paper and crayons or markers and asked to draw an archaeologist. Students were not given any other instructions. The archaeologists who taught the class, myself included, were not allowed to comment on or give advice about the drawings. After the students finished their drawings, I held up several of them and asked students to explain to the class what was going on in their picture. After the students explained their drawings, I led them in a discussion on the topic 'What is archaeology?'

The second time I administered the DART was to college-age students in my introductory archaeology discussion sections at the University of California-Santa Barbara (UCSB) during winter quarter 2001. The discussion sections were part of a larger course, 'Anthropology 3: Introductory Archaeology', at the university. Students were asked to draw an archaeologist and then write about his or her life. The following week, I asked them to stand in front of the class and describe their archaeologist.

There were several differences between the initial HMNS implementation of the DART and the implementation of the DART at UCSB. First, the methodology was different between the two sites. The college students were asked not only to draw an archaeologist but also to write a story about their archaeologist. Also at UCSB, the DART was assigned as an extra-credit homework assignment during week 8 of a 10-week quarter. Instead of using it as a way to introduce archaeology, I used the DART as a wrap-up activity to gauge students' conceptions of archaeology at the end of an introductory course.

I changed the methodology between the two sites to gain a better understanding of students' conceptions of archaeology. Having the students describe their archaeologists in written form allowed them a voice in my analysis. With the HMNS students, I had to extrapolate their conceptions from their drawings. With the UCSB students, I was able to use their own words to describe their conceptions.

The third time I used the DART was during the summer of 2001, again at HMNS, as part of *Vikings.com,* a course on Viking archaeology. The student population comprised 9-, 10-, 11-, and 12-year-olds from the Houston area. The classes were one week long and spanned five weeks across July and August. They were held in conjunction with the Smithsonian traveling Viking exhibit so students could view Viking artifacts as they participated in the course. The main objective of the course was to introduce students to Viking culture through archaeology. As the course was technically about Vikings, the DART was not an appropriate opening activity. However, on day two I brought archaeology to the forefront of the course by administering the DART. Students were asked to draw what they thought an archaeologist looked like and to write a short description of their archaeologist. I then asked them to describe what was going on in their pictures to the rest of the class. After the students finished talking, I used the DART to frame the introduction to archaeology.

I administered the DART differently in all three settings because each classroom situation was different. Time was a major factor in the museum courses. I had students only four hours a day for five days – only 20 hours a week. In the case of *Vikings.com*, I barely had time to administer the DART. In both museum courses, it would have been easier to assign the DART as a homework assignment, but that was not possible given that they were noncredit, summer 'fun' courses. The university setting was a little different because it was a 'traditional' classroom setting where grades were assessed and academic credit was given. One of the nice things about the DART is that it fosters discussion no matter when it is given. Although I have not done it yet, I would like to use the DART at both the beginning and the end of the term as an assessment tool.

DISCUSSION

Earlier, when discussing how to use the DART in the classroom, I mentioned the importance of making mental notes about students' drawings, especially concerning the number of female and minority archaeologists. When analyzing the DART from all three sessions, I was disturbed by the low number of female (34%) and minority (2%) archaeologists. I was especially disturbed because several minority students drew European-looking archaeologists, even though their teacher (myself) was a minority female archaeologist. I was concerned that minority students do not see archaeology as a viable profession for them. I discussed this with a colleague, and he suggested that maybe the low numbers actually reflected archaeology as a discipline, so I decided to test that hypothesis.

In 1994, the Society for American Archeology commissioned a census of its members to find out just who the 'American Archaeologist' was (Zeder 1997). Of the archaeologists who responded, Zeder (1997: 9) found that 64% were men and 36% were women. She also found that 98% of the respondents were classified as being of European ancestry (Zeder 1997: 13). Of the 1,644 archaeologists surveyed, only 2% were of non-European ancestry – and that number was rounded up. In this sample, the classification 'non-European' encompassed African American, Asian, Hispanic, and Native American archaeologists. Franklin (1997) asked Zeder how many of the respondents were African American, and she responded one to two.

When I compared Zeder's findings with the DART results, I found that the DART results, although personally disturbing for me, were consistent with the ethnic and gender make-up of the archaeological profession. Cordell (1993) quotes Alfred Kidder (1949), one of the founding fathers of American archaeology, as saying that there are two types of archaeologist – 'the hairy-chested and the hairy-chinned.' For most people, this stereotype rings true. This is partly because, until recently, the contributions of women to the discipline were overlooked, and because 'the structure of archaeology as a discipline has not been welcoming to women' (Nelson 1997: 48). The same can be said of Indigenous archaeologists.

Franklin (1997) states that almost all American archaeologists are white and their public image of being the sole arbiters and interpreters of the past has had dire consequences for descendant communities, including African Americans. The immediate response is to encourage more minority participation in anthropology and archaeology. However, it is important to consider the cultural factors influencing the decision on a career in archaeology. Many highly educated African Americans are choosing higher profile careers than archaeology, including medicine, law, and business (Franklin 1997). Perhaps 'archaeology might hold more appeal for black Americans if they knew of its potential as a powerful tool for uncovering black histories' (Franklin 1997: 800). However, black Americans cannot understand the powerful potential archaeology holds for transforming black history and the black experience if archaeologists do not effectively communicate their findings with the very people they impact the most.

As a mixed-race female, who would be considered a black American by most people, I know what a challenge it is for minority scholars to find their place in archaeology, but I also know that great strides are being made, and that the numbers can only go up from here. Research shows that good mentoring has an effect on whether or not women (and I would add people of color) drop out of school at critical points in their careers (M. Nelson and S. Nelson 1994). This is certainly true in my case. At every stage of my education, I was blessed with excellent mentors (white men, I should mention) who took an active interest in me and my career and guided me every step of the way. They were crucial in my decision to stay in archaeology. We as archaeologists need to understand the stereotypes associated with archaeology and combat them in the practicing of our profession – whether in the field or in the classroom.

CONCLUSIONS

The growing popularity of museums, television documentaries, and movies such as *Raiders of the Lost Ark*, contributes to an image of archaeology that is white, male, and focused on the hunt for treasure. The Lara Croft movies and video games help to combat the myth that all archaeologists are men, but they still reinforce the notion that archaeology is an exotic passion of the elite. These images are common in the minds of both students and the general public. The Draw-an-Archaeologist Test is a great tool for eliciting students' conceptions about archaeology, and the feedback from this activity will help determine the archaeological knowledge that students are bringing to the classroom. Often, students come into the classroom with misconceptions about what archaeologists do, and the DART provides a starting place to address those misconceptions in a creative and nonthreatening manner. The method and theory behind the DART is straightforward and simplistic in its nature, but it is an effective tool for teaching archaeology and for combating the dangerous stereotypes that pervade our culture and perhaps discourage participation in our discipline.

REFERENCES AND FURTHER READING

Baxter, J (2002) 'Popular images and popular stereotypes: Images of archaeologists in popular and documentary film', *The SAA Archaeological Record* 2(4), 16–17

Boylan, C, Hill, D, Wallace, A and Wheeler, A (1992) 'Beyond stereotypes', *Science Education* 76(5), 465–476

Chambers, D (1983) 'Stereotypic images of the scientist: The draw-a-scientist test', *Science Education* 67(2), 255–265

Cordell, L (1993) 'Women archaeologists in the Southwest', in Parezo, N (ed), *Hidden Scholars: Women Anthropologists and the Native American Southwest*, Albuquerque: University of New Mexico Press

Dixon, S (2000) 'Archaeologists do what? Students' initial conceptions of archaeology', unpublished paper presented at the annual American Anthropological Association meetings, 15–19 November, San Francisco, CA

Dixon, S (2001a) 'Don't share the dirt', unpublished paper presented at the Annual Society for American Archaeology meetings, 18–22 April, New Orleans, LA

Dixon, S (2001b) 'When I think of archaeology, I *have* to think of Indiana Jones', unpublished paper presented at the annual National Association for Research in Science Teaching meetings, 25–28 March, St. Louis, MO

Franklin, M (1997) 'Why are there so few black American archaeologists?' *Antiquity* 71, 799–801

Goodenough, F (1926) *Measurement of Intelligence by Drawings*, Yonkers-on-the-Hudson, NY: World Book Co.

Judge, C (1988) 'Archaeology and grade school children', *South Carolina Antiquities* 20(1&2), 49–59

Kelly, G (1997) 'Research traditions in comparative context: A philosophical challenge to radical constructivism', *Science Education* 81(3), 355–375

Kidder, A (1949) 'Introduction', in Amsden, C (ed), *Prehistoric Southwesterners from Basket-Maker to Pueblo*, Los Angeles: Southwest Museum

Mason, C, Kahle, J and Gardner, A (1991) 'Draw-a-Scientist test: Future implications', *School Science and Mathematics* 91(5), 193–198

Mead, M and Métraux, R (1957) 'Image of the scientist among high-school students', *Science* 126, 384–390

Nelson, S (1997) *Gender in Archaeology: Analyzing Power and Prestige*, Walnut Creek, CA: AltaMira Press

Nelson, M and Nelson, S (1994) 'Conclusion', in Nelson, M, Nelson, S and Wylie, A (eds), *Equity Issues for Women in Archaeology*, Washington, DC: Archeological Papers of the American Anthropological Association 5

Rahm, J and Charbonneau, P (1997) 'Probing stereotypes through students' drawings of scientists', *American Journal of Physics* 65(8), 774–778

Renoe, S (2003a) 'The draw-an-archaeologist test: A good way to get the ball rolling', *Science Activities* 40(3), 31–36

Renoe, S (2003b) 'Students' conceptions of archaeology: Fact or fiction?' *The SAA Archaeological Record* 3(5), 21–23

Schibeci, R (1986) 'Images of science and scientists and science education', *Science Education* 70(2), 139–149

Strike, K (1983) 'Misconceptions and conceptual change: Philosophical reflections on the research program', in Helm, H and Novak, J (eds), *Proceedings of the International Seminar on Misconceptions in Science and Mathematics*, vol. 1, Ithaca, NY: Cornell University, Department of Education

Strike, K and Posner, G (1982) 'Conceptual change and science teaching', *European Journal of Science Education* 4(3), 231–240

Strike, K and Posner, G (1985) 'A conceptual change view of learning and understanding', in West, L and Pines, L (eds), *Cognitive Structure and Conceptual Change*, New York: Academic Press

Strike, K and Posner, G (1992) 'A revisionist theory of conceptual change', in Duschl, R and Hamilton, R (eds), *Philosophy of Science, Cognitive Psychology, and Educational Theory and Practice*, Albany, NY: State University of New York Press

Zeder, M (1997) *The American Archaeologist: A Profile*, Walnut Creek, CA: AltaMira Press

Using the Fictional Tale as a Learning Tool

Caryn M. Berg

The past is inspirational. It inspires novels, movies, poetry, as well as many aspects of popular culture. Archaeological information is often used to create pictures of the past (Murphy 2002). 'People like to romanticise archaeology – and archaeologists' (Stuart 2000: 3). While this romantic notion may be present, many archaeologists are in conflict with themselves regarding the limitations of the archaeological record. We are not able to provide holistic interpretations of the past. Rather, we only have access to fragments of past behavior. This often leads us to embrace an interpretive or contextual approach (Hodder 1991a, 1991c) that uses the present to create the past (Hodder 1991b). In so doing, many archaeologists reach for multiple meanings of the past based on their own reflective inquiry (Kohl 1993: 13). The creators of fictional tales about the past often do the same, although oftentimes such stories lack much of the archaeological evidence as a basis. Such stories also lack the generalizations that are so common in archaeological textbooks; fictional tales tend to focus on the individuals – this is what makes these tales more interesting to the public than archaeological publications.

The assignment I discuss in this chapter was conceived from the realization that, while archaeologists recognize the importance of the public to our discipline, most of us have no idea how to communicate with the public. Our research generally tends to excite us, but we often have a difficult time conveying this excitement in our journal articles and books. While fiction is certainly not the only means for engaging the public in archaeology, it is certainly a popular medium – one that will reach an extremely varied audience. For this assignment, upper-division and graduate students were asked to write a fictional short story based on data from published archaeological knowledge about a particular region or time period. It was my hope that students would learn to present archaeological data in new ways that might be more appealing beyond the discipline. I also hoped that students would recognize some of the advantages and difficulties with 'personalizing' the past in stories about individuals.

This assignment has been useful in two courses to date. The first time I used it was in a course called 'Popular Archaeology' that examined archaeological data, as well as popular films, fictionalized accounts, and other means of popularizing the past to explore the role and place of narrative and imagination in the constructions of the past. The assigned texts for that course were Kenneth Feder's (1999) *Frauds, Myths, and Mysteries*, Kevin Anderson's (1997) novel *Ruins*, and *The Visitant* by Kathleen O'Neal Gear and W. Michael Gear (2000). I used this assignment again in a course called 'History of the Southwest Through Fiction', in which we examined several fictionalized accounts of life in the (primarily) pre-contact Southwest, many written by anthropologists. We used these novels as a way to probe into not only what we think we know about this topic, from archaeological evidence and from ethnoarchaeological and anthropological research, but also how these data and lines of evidence were used by the authors. The primary readings for this course included David E. Stuart's (2000) *Anasazi America: 17 Centuries on the Road from Center Place*, *The Last Matriarch* by Sharman Apt Russell, Kathleen and W. Michael Gear's *People of the Silence* (2000) and *The Visitant* (2000), *Sing Down the Moon* by Scott O'Dell (1976), and Tony Hillerman's (1989) *Talking God*. In both courses, this was the final major assignment at the end of the term. At this point, we had discussed archaeological interpretation, the role of narrative in archaeology, as well as the use of literary license in fictionalized accounts.

PREPARING THE EXERCISE

The materials for this exercise are:

- An outline of the assignment for the students
- If available, an example of a short story written by students in past classes
- Any aids that may be needed by the students in order to present their story to the class.

APPROXIMATE LENGTH OF EXERCISE

The requirements on the assignment outline suggest that four to seven pages (1,200–2,100 words) is an appropriate length of story. 'Storytelling' will take at least two two-hour sessions, depending on the size of the class.

THE EXERCISE

This project brings together the archaeological evidence/interpretation of a specific time period/culture group, and the popularization or personalization of the archaeological evidence.

In the 'Popular Archaeology' class, the students were asked to choose an archaeologically identified culture group, area, and/or time period. In the 'History of the Southwest Through Fiction' class, students were asked to choose one of the archaeologically or historically identified time periods in the northern (Ancestral Puebloan/Anasazi) Southwest.

In the first part of the assignment, students are required to head to the library and check out some articles or books on the topic they have chosen. While the Internet is an amazing resource, I made a firm statement that students were not to use Internet sources such as web pages to get information on these topics; they were, however, welcome to use articles found at reputable sites such as CNN (www.cnn.com), MSNBC (www.msnbc.msn.com), and other similar sites. While web pages are often useful for pictures and general information, many of the sites appear to be as fictitious as the novels, and the point of this exercise is to learn to turn factual archaeological data into a narrative.

The assignment then requires that this newly acquired information is used to write a concise (2–3 page) summary describing the (general) archaeological interpretations of the time period the student has chosen to study in depth. The students are given general guidelines to summarize subsistence, architecture, location of settlements, social system, group size, and so on. Because this aspect of the assignment is more like a formal paper or report, this summary requires a 'References cited' section that contains all the references that the student actually used to write this summary. Despite the fact that this assignment is supposed to have a fun aspect to it, the use of style guides relevant to the discipline (Society for American Archaeology or American Anthropological Association) is required.

In the next part of the assignment, the students are asked to write a 'day or two in the life' that places themselves within that culture/time period in a 'nonobjective' way. In order to successfully do this part of the assignment, the students are told to choose one or two people to discuss (for example, for the Ancestral Puebloans, they may choose to discuss a child and a parent; or place themselves in the role of a farmer or a potter, etc).

Because the goal of this assignment is to humanize the archaeological data by telling a story about the past, there are minimum requirements that the story should fulfill. Although a fictitious person, the subject should be one who might have existed. To be successful in that regard the student must employ concepts, terms, and historical facts raised in class, in the readings, and through additional research. A successful paper must be well organized and demonstrate creativity. Each story should describe what life is like; this should include a description of the tools and skills that are needed for the main character to successfully perform the activities in which they are involved. There should be a discussion about the daily routine; for example, are there any day-to-day concerns, activities, habits, and so on.

The students are reminded that they probably have an extended family to help feed, and that they may need to help maintain trade contacts, a social and political hierarchy, and a religion or ideology. They should discuss how free time is spent. The days described should be typical and relatively uneventful; no wars, volcanoes, plagues, UFOs, or other similar occurrences are permitted. Other hints given to the students are to avoid clichés. Not all men before agriculture were wrestling sabre-toothed tigers or hitting their enemies on the head with clubs. Not all women stayed at home all day cooking. 'Although the novel is an interesting medium for conveying information about the prehistoric past, it can be seen that they frequently rely on stereotypes, and they also encourage us to understand the past by seeking out the familiar and the safe, the same rather than the other' (Murphy 2002: 63). A subtle and complex description of the past is therefore preferred over a trite, formulaic description. The story should be written in the active voice ('I believed', not 'it was believed'), in either first person ('I, me') or third person ('she, he'). This part of the final project should be at least four to seven pages long (typed, double spaced, one-inch margins, and 12-point font).

As a part of the assignment, each of the students is asked to present their data/story in a 10- to 15-minute presentation. This presentation should include a very brief summary of the archaeological data followed by a telling of the story. Very little structure is provided with regard to this – the students are asked to be creative in their storytelling and to choose a style that suits them best. The students were graded primarily on the quality of the archaeological summary (including the references used), the quality (in terms of thoughtfulness, not necessarily literary ability) of their story or critical evaluation, and on their grammar and spelling.

REFLECTIONS ON THE EXERCISE

This exercise was much more successful in a class devoted entirely to the archaeology of one place. Because the 'Popular Archaeology' class was more general, the students had a difficult time focusing their research on time periods or places with which they had little or no familiarity.

One of the complaints in the past was that narrowing the information into a two- to three-page narrative on what can potentially be a broad archaeological topic or time period is a daunting task. To alleviate the stress the students were feeling with regard to this, I tried to develop some more specific guidelines. In the future, I would modify this exercise to include these specific guidelines and give the students a specific list of topics that needs to be covered in their background discussion and ask them to write one paragraph on each: subsistence, settlement, social organization, and similarly important aspects of human behavior. Once these guidelines were present, the students were much more successful in providing background information on their chosen topic.

In the future, I will also include a discussion about respect in the handouts for the assignment and in the verbal explanations of the assignment. While it has not been a common occurrence, some students have not shown their characters the respect deserved by the people we study. Students have chosen to give characters names such as Beavis, Butthead, Cartman, and other similar names that have no place in a story about the past. Students have used the excuse that they have no idea what names in the past might have been. I have countered with the argument that they could draw names from living descendants or even choose names that are descriptive (such as Brown Eyes or Tall One) rather than select names of questionable cartoon characters created in the modern era. These occurrences have led to me to the conclusion that I will need to be more specific in the future about respect and its place in creating narratives about the past.

The telling of the story is by far the best part of this exercise. It allows the students to hear other stories and to observe the variety of ways in which we can humanize the past while retaining archaeological integrity. The storytelling has resulted in some amazing creativity – acting out the stories, telling the stories through drawn story boards, gathering the class in a circle and reading the story like a 'story hour'. The students have noted that it gives them a greater sense of the humans who lived in the past and 'makes all those facts and data tables more interesting'. Specific comments from the students about the class and the exercise in general ran the gamut. One student noted that this is 'a very interesting way to approach learning history – very effective'. Another noted that 'you had to really focus on factual subject matter and recognize how fiction can blur true history'. The general consensus was that the assignment itself was a different kind of exercise and fun to do, and that it was a lively and fun class.

DISCUSSION

Murphy (2002: 63) asks 'can we really imagine a past that is so different from our own experiences of living and being in the world?' It is difficult to truly imagine that past through articles and texts written by archaeologists for other archaeologists. Science writing provides a significant amount of detail supported by tables, graphs, statistics, and references, but such writing provides very little detail about the humans who created this past. The details that interest people about the past are often lacking in the scientific writing for which we are trained. This assignment teaches students to imagine a past that is different from their own experiences, but also asks them to draw on their own experiences as humans to provide emotional depth to their characters and perhaps to the people of the past, in general. The students also learn that there are multiple ways of interpreting the information derived through archaeological research and that each story may have an equally valid place in history. We have multiple ways of viewing the present; why should our views of the past be any different? Ultimately, the students leave the class and this assignment with a greater understanding of the knowledge that is conveyed through traditional archaeological reporting, as well as a greater sense of the humanity of the past and the present. The assignment also helped students to see how difficult it is to write engaging fiction that does not compromise the archaeological facts. Many of them created compelling stories that captivated their audience and realized that these stories could be interesting and educational. Others struggled with writing the story itself but realized that it is possible to write about archaeological data in an interesting way that will engage rather than exclude the public from the research. This class, coupled with the assignment, certainly illustrates the power of fiction in shaping public perception and the importance of learning to write for the public without compromising archaeological science.

REFERENCES AND FURTHER READING

Anderson, KJ (1997) *Ruins*, New York: Harper Books

Bandelier, A (1971) *The Delight Makers: A Novel of Prehistoric Pueblo Indians*, San Diego: Harvest Books

Feder, K (1999) *Frauds, Myths, and Mysteries*, Third edition, Mountain View: Mayfield Publishing

Gear, K O'Neal and Gear, WM (1997) *People of the Silence*, New York: Tor Books

Gear, K O'Neal, and Gear, WM (2000) *The Visitant*, New York: Tor Books

Hillerman, T (1989 [1991]) *Talking God*, New York: Harper & Row

Hodder, I (1991a) *Reading the Past: Current Approaches to Interpretation in Archaeology*, Second edition, Cambridge: Cambridge University Press

Hodder, I (1991b) 'Postprocessual archaeology and the current debate', in Preucel, RW (ed), *Processual and Postprocessual Archaeologies: Multiple Ways of Knowing the Past*, Center for Archaeological Investigations Occasional Paper No. 10, Carbondale: Southern Illinois University

Hodder, I (1991c) 'Interpretive archaeology and its role', *American Antiquity* 56: 7–18

Kohl, PL (1993) 'Limits to a post-processual archaeology (or, The dangers of a new scholasticism)', in Yoffee, N and Sherratt, A (eds), *Archaeological Theory: Who Sets the Agenda?* Cambridge: Cambridge University Press

Murphy, J (2002) 'A novel prehistory', in Russell, M (ed), *Digging Holes in Popular Culture: Archaeology and Science Fiction*, Oxford: Oxbow Books

O'Dell, S (1976 [1999]) *Sing Down the Moon*, New York: Laurel Leaf

Russell, SA (2000) *The Last Matriarch*, Albuquerque: University of New Mexico Press

Stuart, DE (2000) *Anasazi America: 17 Centuries on the Road from Center Place*, Albuquerque: University of New Mexico Press

Telling Stories About the Past: Archaeology and Museum Interpretation

Jane Lydon

CONTEXT OF THE EXERCISE

This exercise formed part of a subject called 'Archaeology in the Real World', designed to examine how ideas about the past are formed using archaeological evidence, and used in public discourse – by religious groups, nation-builders, and many other communities across the globe. It was designed to teach students how to:

- *define* basic archaeological concepts and approaches;
- *understand* the range of ways that archaeological knowledge is used in our society;
- *identify* different interests that shape interpretations of the past;
- *design* interpretive strategies for heritage places and materials;
- *evaluate* the authority of different arguments made about the past.

The final month of the subject focused upon public interpretation of the past and especially museological approaches to archaeology. The exercise was designed to encourage students to think about the polysemous, contextual meanings of objects and material culture, particularly when drawn into political arguments. Archaeologists are prone to fetishise material culture, losing sight of the human meanings and actions they stand for; during the 1960s especially they tended to focus upon relationships between the objects themselves (Miller 1994:15). Within the context of public display they have often limited their interpretation of material evidence to technical or objectively 'scientific' accounts.

Australian historian Richard Flanagan once scornfully described the Commandant's Cottage at Port Arthur in Tasmania, Australia's best-known convict site, as 'restored in a most bizarre fashion. Like a dead formaldehyde-stained rat whose flesh is peeled and held back by surgical instruments to reveal its internal organs, the building has been clinically and scientifically vivisected' (1990: 35–37). He argued that the building, as artifact, had displaced consideration of the people who worked and suffered within it. While Flanagan's critique is overstated, and indeed many members of the public are fascinated by archaeological method, it is also crucial to think about communicating the larger, cultural implications of material evidence, and to make those results relevant and interesting in human terms. The purpose of this exercise is to encourage students to think about the multiple, contested stories we might tell about objects.

THE EXERCISE

I brought a range of objects to the class, old and new, conventionally archaeological (such as stone tools and ceramic sherds) and quirky. I selected objects that were easily available to me, would not be damaged by handling, and were already somewhat familiar to the students, either because they had encountered them during archaeology classes already, or because they were in contemporary use. Alternatively, the range of items could be specific to particular temporal periods or cultures: I might easily have selected a range of artifacts from the departmental teaching collection pertaining to the Cypriot bronze age, for example, or from my own research addressing European settlement of Australia. A degree of familiarity with the objects is necessary to allow students to supply them with a cultural context. I arranged these items in four places, and the class (all second- and third-year undergraduate archaeology students) was split into four corresponding groups. They were to nominate a re-porter, and were given half an hour to develop an interpretation for their collection of objects, as if displaying it to a public audience. They could present an argument about their assemblage, tell a story, or present a series of different interpretations – I encouraged them to be creative.

REFLECTIONS ON THE EXERCISE

The students seemed to enjoy this session a lot – some of the objects, such as a 1960s Tupperware cruet, were vaguely familiar to them, others (a homemade leather bellows) completely mystifying, others again provoked laughter (for some reason they found a small vial of perfume labeled 'eternity' especially amusing). They responded to the objects themselves, but also started to develop links between them, and to build these into larger stories about how they might have been used by people. When the students reported back, it was interesting to note that some of them were uncomfortable with speculating about these larger meanings, preferring to develop the most detailed description of individual objects they could (date, material, etc, in approved methodological fashion). This discomfort with the 'big picture' and with conjecture became a focus for discussion, as did the objects and their properties, our reaction to actual 'things' by comparison with reading about them, and so on. One group however treated the objects as evidence for a murder, and presented a Hercule Poirot-like explanation for the crime, complete with denouement!

DISCUSSION

While this exercise did not allow for the extended analysis, research, or synthesis that would normally form part of the interpretative process, we also talked about different approaches they might take toward further investigation of these objects: for example, within structuralist-functionalist (Deetz 1977; Leach 1982), or poststructuralist/postprocessual paradigms (Hodder 2000; Tilley 1999, 2002), or as commodities embodying exchange values (Appadurai 1986). What sort of questions might they ask of these objects within each of these approaches? How might they proceed in order to answer them?

The strength of this exercise, however, was in the students' immediate, embodied engagement with objects as clues to larger meanings and narratives about human life in the past. While workshops teaching students how to examine and record artifacts are common within the archaeological curriculum, such sessions focus upon technical, specialist aspects of analysis. In the process of teaching students how to become archaeologists, they are not always encouraged to think about communicating archaeological meanings to nonspecialist audiences, resulting in a professional community that prefers to write and talk only to itself. Ethically and pragmatically, accessible outcomes are an integral aspect of archaeological research, and it is important to develop skills in 'translating' disciplinary protocols into public stories about the past.

REFERENCES

Appadurai, A (1986) *The Social Life of Things*, Cambridge: Cambridge University Press

Deetz, J (1977) *In Small Things Forgotten: The Archeology of Early American Life*, New York: Doubleday, Anchor Books

Flanagan, R (1990) 'Crowbar history: Panel games and Port Arthur', *The Independent National Monthly* (August), 35–37

Hodder, I (ed) (2000) *Towards Reflexive Method in Archaeology: The Example at Çatalhöyük*, McDonald Institute for Archaeological Research/British Institute of Archaeology at Ankara Monograph No. 28

Leach, E (1982) *Social Anthropology*, London: Fontana

Miller, D (1994) 'Things ain't what they used to be', in Pearce, S (ed), *Interpreting Objects and Collections*, London: Routledge, Leicester Readers in Museum Studies

Pearce, S (ed) (1994) *Interpreting Objects and Collections*, London: Routledge, Leicester Readers in Museum Studies

Tilley, C (1999) *Metaphor and Material Culture*, Oxford: Blackwell

Tilley, C (2002) 'Metaphor, materiality and interpretation', in Buchli, V (ed), *The Material Culture Reader*, Oxford: Berg

Scenarios for Archaeologists:
A Teaching Tool

Mitch Allen

The imposing Flinders Petrie VI, your department chair, has commanded you to prepare an exit examination in archaeology for all students graduating from the department. 'Make it tough', he intones. The exam should draw on pedagogical techniques from both Piaget and Howard Gardner. It should give equal due to your chair's ancestors, to Binford, and to Hodder. It should be able to assess students' knowledge of techniques as varied as shovel testing and the use of GPS equipment, and ascertain that they know the importance of Chaco, Cahokia, and Copan. How would you construct this examination? What format would you use? What parts of the discipline would you cover?

Gotcha thinking? If not, please flip to the next article in this collection. If so, consider the use of scenario techniques as a method of eliciting and assessing student knowledge in your archaeology course. Scenarios offer a fun alternative to traditional testing methods, invoking creativity and occasionally humor into the process for you (who invents the scenario) and for the student in responding to it. Properly constructed, scenarios force the student to pull from the material taught in the course and critically analyze it in crafting an active response.

Your dissertation excavation project took place in a remote area of northern Mexico, an area for which there are no dated sites. Being located in high desert, preservation was excellent. Most of the architecture on this site was made of mud bricks, and they used bristlecone pine for the roofing materials. An identifiable obsidian source was nearby, and obsidian tools and debris were abundant on the site as well as being a common trade item with the Maya to the south, where they are often found in precisely dated burials. There are lots of ceramics on this site, too, as well as the remains of charred logs in some of the firepits you excavated. One of those firepits was lined with clay, burned into brick by the heat of the fire and untouched since its last burning. Finally, and most surprisingly, a stele (standing stone) inscribed with Mayan writing was found buried under the floor in the corner of the building. Looks like a royal inscription with a Maya calendrical date. You need to date this site. Name at least *four* techniques you would use. What materials can be dated with these techniques? Which results would you trust the most and why?

Scenarios should be carefully constructed to provide enough 'hints' that students can demonstrate their knowledge from simple inference. If they don't know the material, they'll miss the hint. For example, in the scenario above outlining dating techniques that could be used at a site in Mexico, there are a host of clues for the student. The unprepared one will miss some or all of them, the average student will pick up the obvious ones, the superb student will (we hope) be able to add some of the complexities that multiple dating methods provide, like the possibility that various methods won't produce consistent dates, that multiple samples of carbon can give more robust answers, that bristlecone wood can be used in multiple ways for dating, that the inscription might be in a secondary context (Fagan 2001; Renfrew and Bahn 2004).

Scenarios can serve a second purpose as well, to highlight controversial issues, ethical questions, or best practices in the field.

They're replacing ancient O'Connor Hall on campus with a new state-of-the-art cinema/coffee house complex. You're the archaeologist on the spot assigned to oversee the work. On the first day, the bulldozers lay bare the foundations of what was clearly the long-missing original mission church, where we know the bones of the famous California missionary Junipero Serra were buried. But they also turn up other human bones, Ohlone Indian burial goods, locally produced flints, and other items indicating you've found an Indian burial ground. Tribal representatives show up the next day. So do the fathers from the Jesuit order, interested in excavating the church so they can build a proper memorial to Father Serra. So does the head of the cineplex construction crew, concerned that he needs to meet his deadline or lose the bonuses promised by the university (ie all of the following year's student fees). And then, of course, your job at the university may depend on properly handling the problem. So what do you tell everyone in the high-level meeting you call? What practical, political, legal, and ethical issues are likely to be brought up by the tribal representatives, the Jesuit fathers, the contractor, your archaeological crew; and how do you, an archaeologist, respond to them?

Students responding to this scenario will need to know about historic preservation laws, archaeologists' relations to Indigenous peoples, and the politics of archaeology. But they also need to be able to synthesize that knowledge and present a practical solution to an intractable situation. In short, they will demonstrate to you their ability to critically assess a complex problem using material learned in your course. An open book test? It doesn't matter in this case – the answers won't be in the book.

FROM SCENARIOS TO SCREENPLAYS

But why stop here? With your creative juices flowing, you now have the capability of creating entire archaeological worlds for your students to interpret. At a time when more than a few archaeologists are looking to become novelists or poets (eg Nelson 2004; Praetzellis 2003), how better to channel your energies into the perfect imaginary site description for your students to analyze as their final examination (see Burke and Smith, Chapter 2 this volume). You can create sites without ceramics being jumbled by looters and burrowing moles, where stratigraphic sections are always horizontal, and where buildings exist without generations of later modifications. One of mine begins:

> The grant deadline for renewing your NSF funding is 10 pm Monday night. But if you don't turn in your excavation report from your 6 years of work on Manobowano, they won't even consider a new application. So you have to get the excavation report done now, make some sense out of the mounds of data you've collected. Fortunately, your research assistant, Igor, has summarized all the most important data into a handy brief for you (so why didn't he just write the report?). You've promised NSF you would give them new information on this previously unknown Pacific island culture. The grant officer is particularly interested in 1) dating; 2) the early environment; 3) gender relations; 4) economic system, including food procurement, preparation, and consumption; 5) social structure, including evidence of inequality; 6) symbolic and religious practices; 7) internal and external trade patterns. Since you have identified three separate periods, you will have to look at evidence of change across those periods. Let's just hope you can read Igor's notes.

The scenario proceeds to describe in about 2,000 words Manobowano, a hypothetical Polynesian archipelago, including invented historical records, ethnoarchaeological data, ethnobotanical remains, survey results, and finds located in the various excavated layers of the sites of Ma and Pa. A chart of fish and animal bones located at various levels of one site allows the student to conduct a simple seriation and posit changes in diet that might have accompanied changes in social structure or environmental conditions. A rudimentary map allows students to make statements about settlement pattern. What a site! If only there really was such a place, Igor and I would have written a definitive site report. As it was, we ended up with two dozen site reports to grade that week. A similar fanciful reconstruction of a lowland Mesoamerican site was created for the following year's class. The scenarios I have built have all been fictional ones in the interests of controlling the complexity of the data, but it would be equally valid to build one from real data, such as from your own most recent field project.

While these scenarios have been used mostly as assessment tools in my classroom, they can be used in other classroom contexts – as a starting point for a class discussion or debate, as an oral or written assignment to grapple with complex issues, as a unifying point for collaborative work. And, while the scenarios I have developed have all been paper and pencil ones, the possibilities of virtual scenarios on the web are limited only by your computer skill and the size of the university server.

PROS AND CONS

The advantages of using scenarios are self-evident:

1. Rather than requesting answers, you're asking for synthesis, analysis, and interpretation – higher-order thinking skills.
2. Your creativity is an invitation for the students to be creative. Your playfulness gives them license to playfully respond.
3. No student is ever without something to say, be it sophisticated or simplistic. Their ability to provide opinions and analyses, as well as reciting the facts, empowers them.
4. They offer a simulation of the archaeological endeavor, showing its ambiguities, controversies, and multiple points of view, not unlike the way archaeology operates in the real world.
5. It is more fun to create than a test that begins with 'Which of the following statements is false?'

But creating a scenario is not for the faint-hearted or overly busy:

1. It requires more work to prepare and evaluate than a multiple choice test. A lot more.

2. It has to be good. The only thing that would annoy a student more than a poorly written test is one that is trying to be clever or humorous and is poorly written. A lame scenario, an obscure scenario, an uninteresting scenario, is not likely to have the desired effect on student motivation. Ideally, the scenario should be pre-tested before being given to a class.

3. Cues need to be unambiguous, linked to course material, yet not overly obvious.

4. Evaluating student responses is less clear-cut than in other forms of assessment. How do you weigh creativity? Writing skill? Comprehensiveness? Wrong but interesting guesses? The instructor must decide how to value these other factors as well as the student's mastery of the course material.

OTHER USES OF SCENARIOS

Scenarios are not a new idea. They are regularly used in training in business settings and are cousins to the case study method, the preferred strategy for instruction in both business schools and law schools. They seem to have found a particular niche for teaching professional ethics in business (www.aacsb.edu/resource_centers/Ethicsedu/), accounting (Rao *et al* 2000), psychiatry (American Psychiatric Association 2001), engineering (www.onlineethics.org/reseth/modscen.html), and a host of other fields (www.ethicsweb.ca).

A version of this approach, vignette analysis (Rossi 1979), is a common research technique used in structured interviews in social science, though not often used in archaeology. In one of the few archaeological examples of which I am aware, Joe Watkins (2001) used a set of scenarios in assessing how professional archaeologists would respond to several slightly varying situations concerning the disposition of human remains found in an excavation. Through analyzing the responses to these vignettes, he discovered that land ownership was the most important determining factor of archaeologists' behavior in ambiguous situations.

Scenarios are already used by archaeologists and other anthropologists in teaching. One syllabus, prepared by Elizabeth Kryder-Reid on Museum Methods, in the MATRIX project (www.indiana.edu/~arch/saa/matrix/) to improve college-level instruction in archaeology, includes a set of scenarios for budding museum professionals, including the following:

A local collector who has been a strong supporter of the museum has asked you to look at an item she recently purchased from a private dealer. She wants you to give your opinion on the painting's condition. First, should you look at the piece? Assuming you do, in the course of your examination you discover evidence that suggests that the painting was not really done by the artist attributed by the dealer. What do you do now?

Several scenarios concerning archaeology are available from the National Center for Case Study Teaching in Science (http://ublib.buffalo.edu/libraries/projects/cases). The American Anthropological Association also uses this method to help raise awareness of ethical issues in the field (www.aaanet.org/committees/ethics/ethical_currents.htm). The hosting websites encourage instructors to use these scenarios in classes.

The idea of inventing whole sites or assemblages is also not new. Tom Patterson's (2005) workbook contains a dozen exercises on seriation, stratigraphy, chronology and other topics for the student based on descriptions of several corpuses of data. And electronic simulations such as *Adventures in Fugawiland* (Price and Gebauer, 2002) or *Virtual Dig* (Dibble and McPherron, 2003) allow students to electronically wallow in archaeological sites and are popular enough teaching tools to have gone through multiple editions.

YOUR FINAL EXAM

It's the last week of the semester. Anthro 301 has been the class from hell. Six students fell asleep during your talk on the importance of snail track analysis in archaeology. You know those two tattooed kids in the fourth row hate you. Others have complained to the department chair about your habit of eating Cheetos while delivering your lectures. Your contract for next year became far from certain after that unfortunate incident. Your future at Everyday U rests on your ability to produce a challenging but interesting final exam that will raise your student evaluation scores ...

REFERENCES

American Psychiatric Association (2001) *Ethics Primer of the American Psychiatric Association*, Arlington, VA: American Psychiatric Publishing, Inc.
Association to Advance Collegiate Schools of Business (2005) Ethics Education Resource Center, Available on-line at www.aacsb.edu/resource_centers/Ethicsedu/, accessed 26 March 2005

Dibble, H and McPherron, S (2003) *Virtual Dig: A Simulated Archaeological Excavation of a Middle Paleolithic Site in France*, 2nd Edition, New York: McGraw-Hill

EthicsWeb.ca (2005) Applied Ethics Resources on WWW, Available on-line at www.ethicsweb.ca, accessed 26 March 2005

Fagan, B (2001) *In The Beginning: An Introduction to Archaeology*, Tenth Edition, Upper Saddle River, NJ: Prentice-Hall

Kryder-Reid, E (2005) 'Museum methods course outline', MATRIX (Making Archaeological Teaching Relevant in the XXII Century) Project, Available on-line at www.indiana.edu/~arch/saa/matrix/, accessed 19 March 2005

National Center for Case Study Teaching in Science, University of Buffalo (2005) Case Collection, Available on-line at http://ublib.buffalo.edu/libraries/projects/cases, accessed 26 March 2005

Nelson, SM (2004) *Jade Dragon*, Littleton, CO: RKLog Press

Online Ethics Center for Engineering and Science, Case Western Reserve University (2005) Scenarios for Ethics Modules on the Responsible Conduct of Research, Available on-line at www.onlineethics.org/reseth/modscen.html, accessed 26 March 2005

Patterson, T (2005) *The Theory and Practice of Archaeology: A Workbook*, 3rd Edition, Upper Saddle River, NJ: Prentice-Hall

Praetzellis, A (2003) *Dug to Death: A Tale of Archaeological Method and Mayhem*, Walnut Creek, CA: AltaMira Press

Price, T and Gebauer, A (2002) *Adventures in Fugawiland: A Computerized Simulation in Archaeology*, 3rd Edition, New York: McGraw-Hill

Rao, H, Daneshfar, A and Golen, S (2000) 'The use of ethics vignettes in the accounting classroom', *Arizona Business Education Association Journal* 19, 25–28

Renfrew, C and Bahn, P (2004) *Archaeology: Theories, Methods, and Practice*, 4th edition, London: Thames & Hudson

Rossi, PH (1979) 'Vignette analysis: Uncovering the normative structure of complex judgements', in Merton, RK, Coleman, JS and Rossi, PH (eds), *Qualitative and Quantitative Social Research: Papers in Honor of Paul Lazarsfeld*, New York: Macmillan

Watkins, J (2001) *Indigenous Archaeology: American Indian Values and Scientific Practice*, Walnut Creek, CA: AltaMira Press

Watkins, J (ed) (2005) Ethical Currents Case Studies, American Anthropological Association, Available on-line at www.aaanet.org/committees/ethics/ethical_currents.htm, accessed 26 March 2005

Part VI

Critical Reflection

The Scrapbook Exercise: Teaching Archaeology of Death as Critical Thinking

Patricia E. Rubertone

I recently overheard a colleague comment that no one teaches archaeology of death anymore. Courses in the archaeology of death were obsolete. In the US, they were vestiges of a pre-NAGPRA (Native American Graves Protection and Repatriation Act of 1990) curriculum informed by assumptions that graves and other mortuary sites were merely scientific data, and that archaeologists had exclusive authority over their study and interpretation. Such courses bore the stigma of failing to represent diverse interests, of ignoring questions of relevance in the contemporary world, and, in some cases, of distorting and sensationalizing the past by emphasizing the opulence of royal tombs, the intricacies of burial rituals, and the vagaries of preservation. Furthermore, from many students' perspectives, an entire course on the archaeology of death seemed excessively morbid, if not downright depressing.

Are these criticisms necessarily valid? I hope not, because I have taught an upper-level undergraduate course, 'Archaeology of Death', since the mid-1980s. It continues to be one of the most challenging and stimulating courses in my teaching repertoire. But increasing concerns about the status of undergraduate teaching at research universities and about undergraduate archaeology curricula in general (eg Bender and Smith 2000; Pyburn 2003) persuaded me to address the critics and argue for the sustainability of 'Archaeology of Death' in the 21st century (Rubertone 2003). Indeed, such a course can be relevant today, while also being responsive to the needs of students and the concerns of those whose pasts are being studied. Furthermore, it might teach important lessons about being human – ones that might even help to imagine and build a better world.

In this chapter, I begin by giving my reasons for teaching a course on the archaeology of death, then explore the challenges the course presents and review the pedagogical techniques I use to engage students.

Among the alternatives to lectures as usual is a scrapbook exercise designed to encourage critical thinking that I discuss and evaluate using examples and student 'voices' from past assignments.

COURSE RELEVANCE

I developed 'Archaeology of Death' because of my involvement in the study of a 17th-century Narragansett Indian burial ground threatened by development, a study that began in 1983 and grew into a long-term commitment (Rubertone 2001). Initially, I saw the course as a way for students to learn about the principles of mortuary analysis and interpretation, and how these might be applied in exploring questions about social issues like population dynamics, health and disease, and inequalities in past societies. However, I realized that the course could accomplish other educational goals as well. Among these were questions about the excavation and treatment of mortuary sites and their contents, different views of the past, and preservation regulations and real-world problem solving that I faced in the context of my partnerships with a descendant community and a historic preservation office.

But the overriding reason for teaching 'Archaeology of Death' was (and is) that death is a fact of life, and an unavoidable subject for anthropologists studying humans both past and present. The topic provides unique insights into the human condition and its institutions by shedding light on such themes as the origins of religion, the nature of society, and the structure of ritual. While undeniably universal and democratic, death is also culturally and historically constructed, as anthropological knowledge has suggested from richly detailed studies of specific cultural practices in the contexts of daily life and over the long term. Clearly, archaeology has been critically important to illuminating these contextual histories.

TEACHING CHALLENGES

The challenges in teaching 'Archaeology of Death' today are daunting. The vast literature serves as compelling testimony to archaeology's longstanding involvement in the excavation and analysis of mortuary remains that can be traced to the beginnings of the discipline as a systematic set of practices, and the willingness of later generations of archaeologists to rely on them to test the interpretive possibilities (and indeed limits) of archaeological evidence (eg Binford 1971; Hodder 1984; O'Shea 1984; Saxe 1970). Since the 1960s, this literature has been greatly enriched by the addition of historical archaeological studies of above-ground mortuary remains using noninvasive techniques and textually anchored approaches; and more recently, by archaeological inquiries into monuments and commemorative processes in contemporary societies (eg Dethlefsen and Deetz 1966; Ingersoll and Nickell 1978; Parker Pearson 1982; Tarlow 1999). While there is enough material for several courses, 'Archaeology of Death' surveys the scope of research.

Because there is no single textbook that covers the full range of archaeological interpretations of mortuary remains and also engages the complex issues surrounding their excavation, study, and repatriation, the course readings draw from a selection of books, edited volumes, and journals. For instance, the assigned readings have included historical and cross-cultural overviews, such as Philippe Ariès's *Western Attitudes Toward Death: From the Middle Ages to the Present* (1974) and Peter Metcalf and Richard Huntington's *Celebrations of Death: The Anthropology of Mortuary Ritual* (1991). Along with these books, I also assign at least one or two in-depth case studies like Elizabeth Wayland Barber's *The Mummies of Ürümchi* (1999), Robert Blakely's *The King Site: Continuity and Contact in Sixteenth Century Georgia* (1988), or Tamara Bray and Thomas Killion's *Reckoning with the Dead: The Larsen Bay Repatriation and the Smithsonian Institution* (1994). In addition, I supplement book-length readings with articles and book chapters focusing on applications of recent theoretical and technical advances to emphasize that the study of the archaeology of death does not rest on any single monolithic approach.

However, the 'how-tos' of teaching the material are formidable. Can the course be organized so that it does not just convey a history of research? Can it be presented as something other than a forum for archaeologists' rights to excavate and study ancestral graves regardless of the human costs? Is there a way to teach the course without simply indicting archaeology and dismissing mortuary archaeology altogether? These challenges – together with concerns about meeting the needs of new cohorts of students (mostly nonarchaeologists and nonanthropology majors), balancing 'fact-based learning' and 'ways of knowing', and using archaeology as an arena for teaching critical thinking – have called for pedagogical innovations instead of lectures as usual.

EXERCISES IN CRITICAL THINKING: THE SCRAPBOOK PROJECT

Some of the material covered in the course such as rates of bodily decay, good vs. bad mummification techniques, what cremation does to bones, and Victorian mourning customs is suited to 'fact-based-learning'. I attempt to ensure that students gain this knowledge by asking some objective questions on exams, and by playing a classroom version of the game show 'Jeopardy!' in the hope that even learning facts about death can be – yes, fun. The 'game', which asks for answers in the form of questions (and here rewards correct responses with chocolate) helps students to focus on the important points of lectures and readings and serves as a good review for exams.

But besides (and more important than) making sure that students learn facts, the course seeks to provide opportunities for the critical assessment of theoretical positions, the evidence supporting archaeological interpretations, and issues concerning archaeology's wider discourses. Lectures, films, and discussions are aimed at encouraging critical thinking, but these pedagogical approaches alone cannot accomplish it. As educators concerned about teaching archaeology in the new millennium, especially in ways that communicate the discipline's relevance to a broad student constituency, we need to think seriously about how archaeology can help them to achieve this type of thinking.

Although critical thinking has become a buzzword that distinguishes courses emphasizing thinking abilities over mastery of content and transferable skills over arcane knowledge, the concept is neither easily defined nor easily communicated to students. Surely, textbooks abound with definitions, but these are largely written by and for specialists in the fields of education and philosophy, not archaeology. Yet archaeology is an ideal arena for teaching critical thinking (Conkey 2003). The partialities of the evidence and the reliance on inferences in the interpretive process place a premium on recognizing problems, marshalling pertinent information, and appraising evidence and assumptions. On the other hand, because material remains often supplement and interrogate historical documents, archaeology can uncover bias and prejudice, illuminate alternatives, and raise difficult questions not previously imagined (Brumfiel 2003). Thus, archaeology can help students develop the self-confidence to question arguments and assertions, rather than just learning brain-numbing typologies or abstract theories.

In 'Archaeology of Death', I have experimented with different exercises aimed specifically at teaching critical thinking. One project focused on the reconstruction of the past using data from a fictitious cemetery. Students were asked to analyze and interpret patterns relating to age, gender, status, and ethnicity among burials by relying only on the background information, site plan, and list of grave goods that I supplied. Details about the fictitious cemetery offered variations on familiar archaeological subjects and names that had students guessing about the sites, characters, and even research agendas. Some of the burial data was intentionally ambiguous so that students would have to think carefully about what kinds of interpretations they could make and their archaeological credibility, and ultimately, about what kinds of societies they wanted to reconstruct. The exercise encouraged critical thinking by asking students to recognize similarities, detect subtle differences, and judge ambiguity. Furthermore, because students were expected to make observations tied to evidence and furnish support for their reasoning, it provided them with a better understanding of the interpretive process in archaeology than could be gained from readings or lectures alone.

The other learning device aimed at critical thinking, and the one I want to discuss in more detail, is a scrapbook project. The exercise raises questions about representation, and about which pasts are represented and how. More important, it encourages students to think about how topics discussed in the classroom are relevant in today's world. For this assignment, I ask students to examine narrative as well as visual representations of the archaeology of death in the popular media (eg newspapers, magazines) and to compare these reports to the scholarly literature assigned as course readings.

The semester-long project requires students to assemble a scrapbook of articles that they should begin compiling on the first day of classes and complete near the end of the course. The finished scrapbooks are expected to have articles arranged by theme and include a brief interpretive essay of two to three pages in length. By insisting that students organize their scrapbooks thematically, the chance that the assignment will merely be an exercise in collecting devoid of compelling examples is greatly reduced. Additionally, by requiring an interpretive essay, students have the opportunity to express their opinions on topics in the news germane to the archaeology of death, articulate differences in content and emphasis between popular and scholarly writing, and comment on how issues about death and burial are reported for past and present societies.

Given these objectives and requirements, I evaluate the exercise on three criteria: format (organization, style of presentation), scope (number of articles, media consulted), and analysis (identification of themes and assumptions, clarity of ideas). Under titles such as 'Death Media', 'Death Files', 'The Deathly Times', and 'The Be-Buried Gazette', students have produced exquisitely crafted, visually striking, and provocative scrapbooks filled with articles collected from a wide variety of sources and insights that have far exceeded my expectations for what the exercise could achieve pedagogically.

In terms of media consulted, many students culled articles from magazines widely known for their stories and photographs of archaeological discoveries, adventure, and ancient and exotic cultures such as *National Geographic*, *Archaeology*, and *Smithsonian*. They also looked at well-known, weekly news magazines like *Newsweek*, *Time*, and *US News & World Report*, but also *Farmer's Weekly* and *The New Statesman*. However, daily newspapers – *The Providence Journal-Bulletin*, *The Boston Globe*, *The New York Times*, *The Chicago Tribune*, *The Los Angeles Times*, *The Albuquerque Journal*, *The Christian Science Monitor*, and the ever-ubiquitous *USA Today* – comprised the bulk of the printed news media consulted. One student added to this list with articles from Indian Country taken from *The Navajo Times* and *Indian Country Today*. In addition, many used online news services. However, one student, who initially relied only on specialized search engines, decided that newspapers with wide circulation such as *The New York Times* and *The Boston Globe* would be more informative sources of public perceptions and became a voracious newspaper junkie for the duration of the semester.

As might be expected, the range of topics covered in the scrapbooks reflects current events and science news, but some subjects – namely mummies, ritual sacrifice, burial origins, and repatriation – have appeared consistently since I first assigned the exercise several years ago. Taking their cue from the news, students have included numerous reports about deaths in the War in Iraq and before that, the mass casualties of 11 September 2001 in their scrapbooks. Additionally, they have amassed articles about abuses in cadaver programs and crematoria, and about the neglect and overcrowding of cemeteries. Others collated reports on the memorialization of the dead from World War II and the Vietnam War, and of sites of tragedy and violence such as places associated with the Holocaust or highway fatalities. While death is considered a topic to be avoided in contemporary society (eg Ariès 1974; Mitford 1963), students had no difficulty identifying articles on the subject. Despite widespread theorizing about death avoidance, they noticed that death dominated the news.

Many students noted that the popular media reports on unusual burial customs, such as bodies immersed in peat bogs or frozen in ice. They viewed the media's attention to 'oddities, shocks, and mysteries' and its fascination with 'all things Egyptian' (ie pyramids and mummies) as a noticeable departure from the scholarly literature's focus on the mundane. In addition, many felt that the media's treatment of these topics emphasized differences between the past and the present by calling attention to aspects of the past that might seem alien to contemporary people. Some students took a harder line and accused the media of making implicit or explicit value judgments about 'how far we had come', particularly in reporting on evidence for ritual sacrifice found in Maya *cenotes* and for cannibalism among members of the Donner Party, a group of 19th-century American pioneers stranded in California's Sierra Nevada Mountains during a blizzard.

In contrast, others remarked that popular writing focused on aspects of the past that seemed familiar and evoked a common humanity. For example, funerary practices involving body adornment, the careful treatment of the corpse, and even the interment of pets seemed to appeal to common-sense notions that people in the past behaved much in the same way as people today. Moreover, they implied that the media's reporting often made these practices seem natural for human beings when in fact they are not so at all. Some students cited the media's suggestions that bejewelled corpses and buried cats transcend time and particular cultural logics and experiences as a major shortcoming.

Overall, students observed that popular accounts were short on detail and, to paraphrase one astute analyst, 'like a spicy dish that had to be toned down to suit a less sophisticated palate'. They surmised that, by omitting lengthy description and neglecting the finer points of methodology, authors writing for general audiences were much less likely to acknowledge the uncertainty of an interpretation compared to archaeologists writing for scholarly audiences. For many students, these contrasts between popular and scholarly writing revealed greater scepticism about science among scholars than they would have been able to detect from reading only the assigned literature.

Students' perceptions about the broader relevance of issues discussed in the course were insightful. Many were drawn to the obituaries written about the people who died in the events of 11 September that appeared in *The New York Times* every day from 15 September to 31 December 2001, and continued to be printed in the Sunday edition into the following August. Unlike most obituaries that list basic facts of an individual's life and accomplishments, these told stories. They were personal and intimate accounts about day-to-day routines, habits, quirks, joys, disappointments, and plans for the future that poignantly underscored that individual lives are not scripted. These moving obituaries led students to question the dehumanized and impersonalized reports about ancient people in headline-worthy archaeological news and in most scholarly writing. For some students, these obituaries provoked comments about the relevance of the categories typically used by archaeologists in describing human remains and the material aspects of death. They felt that these imposed categories obscured the visibility of certain age groups, genders, and classes and their particular lived experiences much in the same way as ordinary obituaries.

Many students were drawn to the media's reporting of mass deaths from suicide bombings, war, and natural disasters. Although they confront these statistics every day, the issues discussed in the course led them to think about these deaths less abstractly. They raised questions about how families were able to retrieve the remains of the dead for burial (under conditions that often placed their own lives at risk); how they were able to follow through on prescribed ritual practices; and how they were able to deal with loss, especially of those who died prematurely and perhaps unnecessarily. Using stories and photographs of the flag-draped coffins of US servicemen, the residents of Fallujah burying the dead in a makeshift cemetery in a sports stadium, and communities in Arizona grieving for Lori Piestewa, a young mother, and Pat Tillman, a former NFL football star, both killed in combat in Iraq, they asked critical questions about indifference and about the impacts of death in human terms.

Most, if not all, students concluded that the media's reporting on repatriation issues tugged at emotions; and that its accounts of vandalism and mistreatment of the dead chronicled outrage. In general, they perceived the media's handling of the reburial controversy to be more sympathetic and 'humanistic' than many pieces on the topic written by and for scholars. For one student, photographs of Haida tribal members at Chicago's Field Museum preparing to repatriate remains of their ancestors and a passer-by walking hurriedly past the front entrance to the Burke Museum at the University of Washington, the court-ordered repository for the Ancient One (aka Kennewick Man), illuminated the vastly different concerns and levels of awareness in American society about the complicated issues surrounding the repatriation of Indigenous remains and funerary objects. Although articles on the Kennewick case were numerous and appeared in practically all scrapbooks, students found reports on many other repatriation cases in the news. They raised questions about why some claims for the repatriation of ancestral remains proceed with few objections, whereas others are hotly contested. While many students surmised that the majority of disputes over Indigenous burials highlighted continuing confrontations between long-time adversaries, others offered considerably more nuanced views that they supported with articles about successful repatriation efforts and widespread incidents of desecration involving the remains and cemeteries of non-Indigenous peoples.

Finally, a number of students included articles on commemorative processes in their scrapbooks. For example, some collected articles on the World War II Memorial in Washington, DC, that discussed the monument's aesthetic qualities as public art. Other students compiled articles on the burial of eight Confederate soldiers whose remains were recovered from the *H. L. Hunley*, a Civil War submarine, nearly 140 years after the crew had perished; and the reburial of more than 400 enslaved Africans at New York City's African Burial Ground Memorial Site in 2003. The students' comments recognized that monuments, and more specifically monument building, were part of the process relating to interring and memorializing the dead. However, these events also suggested to them that remembrance and commemorative acts could occur without tangible monuments, as was indeed the case for World War II veterans who were remembered in stories, films, and songs long before any monument was raised to them in the US capital. Likewise, they noted that elaborate funeral rites for the crew of the *Hunley* and reburial ceremonies for enslaved Africans, exhumed from their graves because of construction for a federal office building, were both conducted without a public monument being in place.

These various examples illustrate how the scrapbook exercise enables students to discover firsthand that issues discussed in the classroom are important in the real world. They also demonstrate the ways in which the project challenges students' preconditioned imaginations about the past and how it should be portrayed. Moreover, by raising their awareness that various publics have stakes in the past, the exercise facilitates discussions of controversial issues about archaeological ethics, human rights, and indeed, repatriation that are too complex and too important to be oversimplified in ways that do not engage students to think critically and seriously about them. The realization that there are different interests to be represented and contingencies to be considered helps ease the awkwardness and silences which often stifle discussion because of self-conscious efforts to be correct and inclusive, especially when some students enrolled in the course may be members of descendant communities whose very histories and ancestors are being argued over.

Although there are no easy formulas for ensuring meaningful dialogue or achieving a common ground, exercises in critical thinking like the scrapbook project help students become aware of alternatives and recognize that these alternatives may be rooted in experiences independent of intellectual endorsements. Thus, scrapbook projects could also be appropriate assignments for exploring other issues that interest (and may very much matter to) archaeologists and different publics, such as human evolution, war and violence, gender, indigenous arrivals and first peoples, and the protection and ownership of archaeological resources and monuments.

SOME FINAL THOUGHTS

With death so much in the news, it should come as no surprise that there are more courses on the subject than ever before. More to the point, many of these courses are now being offered in disciplines other than anthropology that are responding to demands for explorations into death and dying, protocols about notifying survivors, and guidelines for grief counseling. Although there has been some recent ambivalence about the place of archaeology of death in anthropology curricula, there are profound reasons why such courses continue to be relevant and, indeed, distinctly different from courses on death taught by colleagues in other disciplines. However, the pressing question we face as archaeologists is how we can teach such courses differently than we have been – that is, better, more inclusively, and more creatively – given our unique comparative and long-term perspective, and our role as suppliers and interpreters of material remains of death and burial and, increasingly, as collaborators with descendant communities. The challenge is to impart to students archaeology's lessons about death and life, individual experiences and communities, and emotion and commemoration, while at the same time also giving attention to the practices of archaeological research and pedagogical innovations. With these possibilities in mind, I propose that 'scrapping' is not only fun, but can also serve as a valuable exercise in critical thinking that contributes to penetrating the indifference and emotional density that often creates barriers to understanding how people comprehend death across cultures, space, and time, as well as the 'difference' and 'diversity' of other experiences.

REFERENCES AND FURTHER READING

Ariès, P (1974) *Western Attitudes Toward Death: From the Middle Ages to the Present*, (trans Ranum, P), Baltimore: Johns Hopkins University Press

Barber, EW (1999) *The Mummies of Ürümchi*, New York: W.W. Norton and Company

Bender, S and Smith, G (eds) (2000) *Teaching Archaeology in the 21st Century*, Washington, DC: Society for American Archaeology

Binford, L (1971) 'Mortuary practices: their study and potential', in Brown, J (ed), 'Approaches to the social dimensions of mortuary practices', *Memoirs for the Society for American Archaeology* 25, 6–29

Blakely, R (ed) (1988) *The King Site: Continuity and Change in Sixteenth Century Georgia*, Athens: University of Georgia Press

Bray, T and Killion, T (eds) (1994) *Reckoning with the Dead: The Larsen Bay Repatriation and the Smithsonian Institution*, Washington: Smithsonian Institution Press

Brumfiel, E (2003) 'It's a material world: history, artifacts, and anthropology', *Annual Review of Anthropology* 32, 205–223

Conkey, M (2003) 'Teaching gendered alternatives: archaeology as critical thinking', paper presented at the 5th World Archaeological Congress, Washington, DC

Dethlefsen, E and Deetz, J (1966) 'Death's heads, cherubs, and willow trees: experimental archaeology in colonial cemeteries', *American Antiquity* 31, 5–27

Hodder, I (1984) 'Burials, houses, women, and men in the European Neolithic', in Miller, D and Tilley, C (eds), *Ideology, Power, and Prehistory*, Cambridge: Cambridge University Press

Ingersoll, D and Nickell, J (1978) 'The most important monument: the tomb of the unknown soldier', in Ingersoll, D and Bronitsky, G (eds), *Mirror and Metaphor: Material and Social Construction of Reality*, Lanham, MD: University Press of America

Metcalf, P and Huntington, R (eds) (1991) *Celebrations of Death: The Anthropology of Mortuary Ritual*, 2nd edition, Cambridge: Cambridge University Press

Mitford, J (1963) *The American Way of Death*, New York: Simon and Schuster

O'Shea, J (1984) *Mortuary Variability: An Archaeological Investigation*, Orlando, FL: Academic Press

Parker Pearson, M (1982) 'Mortuary practices, society, and ideology: an ethnoarchaeological study', in Hodder, I (ed), *Symbolic and Structural Archaeology*, Cambridge: Cambridge University Press

Pyburn, KA (2003) 'M.A.T.R.I.X. project. Making archaeology teaching relevant in the XXI century', Available on-line at: www.indiana.edu/~arch/saa/matrix, accessed 14 March 2005

Rubertone, P (2003) 'Teaching anthropology in the 21st century: a case for "archaeology of death"', *Anthropology News* 44(9), 19–20

Rubertone, P (2001) *Grave Undertakings: An Archaeology of Roger Williams and the Narragansett Indians*, Washington: Smithsonian Institution Press

Saxe, A (1970) 'Social dimensions of mortuary practices', unpublished PhD thesis, Department of Anthropology, University of Michigan, Ann Arbor

Tarlow, S (1999) *Bereavement and Commemoration: An Archaeology of Mortality*, Oxford, UK: Blackwell

Brain Candy

K. Anne Pyburn

The more years I put into teaching, the more ways I find to have fun. One of the greatest tragedies of modern life is that people do not grow up in families that have long philosophical discussions with no television to distract them. I know that sounds silly, but arguing about the meaning of a public event or analyzing your day or doing a deep critique of a sitcom can really be great fun. I find it sad that people don't learn to have fun with ideas, because that is really one of life's greatest pleasures. If you don't know that, you don't really know how to have fun.

So my mission is to get my students to leave behind the idea that thinking and learning is strictly a drudge and to engage in some types of intellectual play that will make university life more attractive, and also possibly more useful. I play tricks on them in my classes to jar them out of complacency and give them the idea that not only can they think for themselves, it's worthwhile to do that all the time.

I guess I should say that I do not teach archaeology to undergraduates to make them into college professors, or even into archaeologists. I think they need certain practical skills before they can choose a career, so I use archaeology to teach about thinking and analysis and ideas in general. I think archaeology is a kind of brain candy – people love it and come to the field with their minds open for something interesting and fun. I have colleagues who think it's their duty to mash all the entertainment out of their classes, but that seems unnecessary to me. Why not let students enjoy it if they learn just as much?

SCIENCE AND AUTHORITY: ARE YOU REALLY SERIOUS ABOUT TEACHING CRITICAL THINKING?

For ethical reasons I think the claims about the past that archaeologists make should be verifiable. I realize that more than one interpretation can be appropriate, but there has to be some way to decide between stories when heritage, property rights, and identity are at stake, so I want my students to be aware of the value (and limitations) of the scientific method. Empiricism is a reasoning process that is used to varying degrees by everybody in all cultures (Pyburn 1999), so instead of focusing on how to make a verifiable inference (Keyes 2002), I start my freshmen classes by showing students how cowed they are by authority. I do this to show them that everybody is influenced by their social context so they will pay more attention to this source of bias in their lives and in their studies.

I got this idea from Jay Shelton, who teaches high school physical science at Santa Fe Prep in New Mexico. I make a pendulum for each pair of students out of a nail and a string and tell them this is their chance to witness a mysterious process for themselves. 'For reasons I cannot really explain', I say ominously, 'it makes a difference whether you hold the pendulum over a man's hand or a woman's hand. Over one it swings in a circle, and over the other it swings back and forth in a line'. I split them into two groups and send them outside to try it for themselves. Then I go outside while they are starting and tell the first group that they will see that it makes a circle over a woman's hand; while they are fooling with this I go around and tell the other group the opposite: it makes a circle over a man's hand.

When they are all done and come back into class, I have them raise their hands to indicate what they found. This works really well with a large class; both groups will have found what they expected to find (and the opposite finding) – to a statistically significant degree. Then I tell them what I did to them – lied – and ask them what happened. It is partly caused by the fact that I didn't define the terms *line* and *circle*, since of course the pendulum usually makes an ellipse, but the real reason it works is that they believed me when I told them it worked. Then I ask them how many of them were really, in their hearts, skeptical of what they found and *all* of them raise their hands. So then I say 'See, you should trust yourself. You are plenty smart enough to see through tricks, so you should give credit to your own good sense'. Then I write the first rule of the class on the blackboard 'DO NOT TRUST DR. PYBURN', and they all laugh.

Someone asked me once if the students get mad at me for tricking them. They don't, and I think it's because I am not trying to show them they are stupid, but that they are smart. It actually seems to make them happy.

TAKING SIDES: USING PEER PRESSURE TO RAISE PERFORMANCE STANDARDS

I usually do not have much trouble getting students to come to class, and I think it is because I am comfortable with the fact that archaeology is and has always been political. The only way to deny this is to be dishonest. Whether you are sorting potsherds or interfering with the last resting place of someone else's relatives or trying to answer questions about the past posed by tribal elders, you are working with a set of assumptions that have a historical context and fit into someone's political agenda, possibly just your own, but not necessarily. Consequently I never shy away from political issues in my classes, since I maintain that evenhandedness comes from being honest about perspectives and agendas, not pretending that there are people called scientists who have none. I always shy away from teaching only one point of view, but I make it clear that I am as biased as anybody else and try to focus on giving students credit for thinking critically and originally. The reason people want to come to class is that young people are very politically excitable and engaged, and talking about ethics and beliefs is very important to them (Juli 2002), but they have little opportunity to express themselves on these 'taboo' subjects in their 'apolitical' classes. Mine is political and I let them talk about it; in fact, I *make* them talk about it.

The best way to get a good conversation about ethics and politics going is to give students background information in an interesting way and then get them to use what they have learned to take sides in a debate. One of my favorite ways to set up a debate about repatriation is to begin with a group project in which I get students to make a map of the tiny cemetery on campus. The first step is to show them how archaeologists turn information into data; here are the instructions I give them:

Cemetery Field Trip

I will guide you to the cemetery on campus and help you get organized and started on your map and analysis. You will make a map on a piece of graph paper that I will provide. You will use your own pace to represent one square on the map – absolute size is irrelevant – all you will need to record is the relative distance between things.

1. Make a map of the cemetery: divide your group into four separate task groups, and decide on a stone numbering system *before you begin*.

- Task group 1: Map the perimeter of the cemetery, then map the stones, giving each a number (your instructor will help you make a pace map; it works better if one person does most of the pacing, since people of very different leg lengths can make the map too skewed).
- Task group 2: Collect the names and dates on the stones.
- Task group 3: Collect the dimensions of the stones (use your hands as units of dimension).
- Task group 4: Describe the shape and any designs on the stone, note the typeface of the lettering, which stones are the same.

2. Put all your data (or as much as possible) onto the map. Look for patterns in the distribution of your data. From your map answer the following question: What factors determine the size, shape, positioning, and style of these stones?

3. Make a list of all group members; specify what each person did. (Whichever task group finishes their task first can make this list.)

4. Hand in your map, your data summaries, your participant list, and a one-paragraph conclusion answering question 2, above. Use the course website to get the rest of your group to comment on the conclusion so that what you turn in is really a group product. You have two weeks to turn in this completed assignment.

5. Email your professor an evaluation of the participation of each member in your group. If someone didn't do their share, tell me; if someone did extra, tell me.

During this experience they ask me all sorts of questions: Should our map include broken stones? Should our map estimate the original size of the stones? What if the stones are of different types of material? I refuse to answer any such questions, I tell them it is their map, they know what questions they are trying to answer, they will have to make these decisions for themselves.[1]

I do not use tape measures or transits or even have them figure out the true length of their pace. My reason is that experience has shown me that these tools turn the exercise into a focus on the measurements and not on what the measurements show. People will spend an entire class figuring out their pace and hours measuring the width of a broken stone. Simple tools – feet and hands – place the emphasis on what I really want them to learn. It's a thinking technique, not a measuring skill.

Step 5 is designed to make the group grade as fair as possible. I do not let these comments completely determine grades, but I do some-times contact people who have been singled out as unhelpful or disrup-tive. What I find is that people are very honest about their own contribution – if Johnny fails to come to the group meeting to put the map together, his group will tell me – but so will Johnny! Very rarely do personal disagreements show up, and when they do they are easy to spot.

This exercise leads naturally into the class debates, one of which goes like this:

> GROUP ONE: Divide into four groups. One group is descended from the people in the graveyards on campus. The second group is a group of scientists researching tuberculosis and its spread among the 19th-century residents of Bloomington. The third group is a group of his-toric preservationists whose mission is to preserve the historic grounds of the Indiana Campus. The final group is made up of a sorority and a fraternity each of which want to build a new chapter house on the site of one of the cemeteries. Divide yourselves into two groups, one for and one against. People from any one of the four groups above could be on both sides of the fence about whether excavation should be allowed. Check out: http://archaeology.about.com/cs/asia/a/nara.htm and http://archaeology.about.com/bldevelop.htm for help with ideas for argu-ments. Prepare a good debate.

This is a great way to teach students about repatriation, since they are not just thinking about other people's ancestors, but about their own. I find that because they fear being embarrassed in front of their peers (Silberman 1996: 5–6), they need very little pushing to spend plenty of energy researching the perspective they have been given, both online and in the library. The quality of the debates has been outstanding. I also find that debates give me a very good idea whether my students are learning what I am teaching, or something else entirely, and it is always more heartening to evaluate learning under conditions in which everyone is trying to do their best (see Angelo and Cross 1993: 343–361 for more on this).

ALL TOGETHER NOW: MORE LEARNING, LESS GRADING, GOOD FUN

I once ended a class with a group final. It happened to be a very excellent class but it was a large one and I was worried about how I was going to grade 100 essay exams, as I was leaving for the field immediately after my last lecture. I decided to see if they could collaborate and it worked like a charm. (This strategy is similar to the one described in Novak *et al* 1999: 17, called 'collaborative recitation'.)

I gave them a set of essay questions one week before the exam – one for each 10 students, and told them to be prepared to answer all of them in essay form with citations. I formed them into study groups of 10 (I had actually already done this earlier in the semester) and suggested that each group member be assigned a question to answer, but that it would be a good idea for them to review each other's answers. I got a lot of reports on how avidly people were studying – I told them they could avoid a written exam if they passed the oral exam as a class.

On exam day I gave each group one question and 5 minutes to put an answer together. A spokesperson (usually the person who had been responsible for that question in that particular group) presented the answer aloud to the class. The answer was evaluated on citations (20 points), lecture references (20 points), creativity (20 points), completeness (20 points), and accuracy (20 points). Since the whole class was dependent on each answer (only two could be missed orally to prevent the evil written exam), I allowed each group to help another group one time. The class did two rounds, that is, each group had to answer two questions drawn out of the hat.

The answers were amazing! I swear one of them was publishable! The class got into a sort of camaraderie over the situation and as soon as I awarded points, they cheered each other madly. In only one case was there a wrong answer; that particular group had not checked up on each other's answers and it came down to the answer given by one woman who misunderstood the question. After a brief bit of squirming, another group immediately used up their chance to help and gave the correct answer. The cheering must have disrupted other people's classes a mile away.

A friend of mine, a pedagogical expert named Ed Neal, got me started on teaching for fun. He told me how odd it strikes him that his colleagues often complain so bitterly about how stupid and lazy their students are and how hard it is to get them to come to class. Ed says this makes him think of Medgar Evers' saying, 'There's nothing wrong with the prison system, we just need a better class of prisoners'. Students are students; they don't know how to reach us, it's our job to reach them.

And more than teaching them facts or making them clones of ourselves, we need to give them the joy of learning, because that will not only make them good archaeologists, it will make them good people.

NOTE

1. The number one complaint US employers have about graduating students is their inability to perform in teams. All my students get experience working in teams; needless to say, no archaeologist can succeed without teamwork skills.

REFERENCES

Angelo, TA and Cross, KP (1993) *Classroom Assessment Techniques: A Handbook for Teachers*, San Francisco: Jossey-Bass

Juli, H (2002) 'The illegal antiquities trade, looting and archaeological ethics', in Rice, PC and McCurdy, D (eds), *Strategies in Teaching Anthropology*, Upper Saddle River, NJ: Prentice-Hall

Keyes, G (2002) '"TSM cube": illustrating the scientific method', in Rice, PC and McCurdy, D (eds), *Strategies in Teaching Anthropology*, Upper Saddle River, NJ: Prentice-Hall

Novak, GM, Patterson, ET, Gavrin, AD and Christian, W (1999) *Just-in-Time Teaching: Blending Active Learning with WEB Technology*, Upper Saddle River, NJ: Prentice-Hall

Pyburn, KA (1999) 'Native American religion versus archaeological science: a pernicious dichotomy revisited', *Science and Engineering Ethics* 5: 355–366

Silberman, M (1996) *Active learning: 101 Strategies to Teach Any Subject*, Boston: Allyn and Bacon

Index

About the Contributors

Mitch Allen is an archaeologist who has taught at Santa Clara University and Mills College. He is also publisher of Left Coast Press, Inc., which produces texts and scholarly and professional books in archaeology. He was also founder and publisher of AltaMira Press, another archaeological publisher, from 1995–2005.

Caryn M. Berg received her PhD in Anthropology from the University of Colorado, Boulder, and is currently teaching at the University of Denver. Her research interests include the transitions to agriculture and sedentism in the American Southwest, technological change (with a particular focus on flaked stone technology), public archaeology, and curriculum development. Recent publications include entries on the Navajo, Kennewick Man, the Culture Area Approach, Ancestral Puebloans, and the Subdivisions of Anthropology for the *Encyclopedia of Anthropology* (Sage Publications, 2005) and 'Selling Archaeology: Interpretations in Public Archaeology' (*Public Archaeology Review*, 1999).

Bradley F. Bowman is currently the Director of the Museum of Archaeology and Material Culture in Cedar Crest, New Mexico. Bradley has conducted archaeological research in Texas and New Mexico, as a contract archaeologist specializing in bioarchaeology. This work has produced numerous contract reports and articles published in journals, including *Plains Anthropologist* and *The Bulletin of the Texas Archaeological Society*. Museum volunteers, under his direction, are presently involved in educational programs at the Museum and a long-term research project in western New Mexico.

Heather Burke lectures in the Department of Archaeology at Flinders University, Adelaide, South Australia, specializing in historical archaeology, theory and method, and the representation of the past. Prior to moving to Flinders, she worked as a consultant archaeologist in various parts of Australia. Her current research interests center on the archaeology of contact and the colonial process. Her most recent publication is *The Archaeologist's Field Handbook*, co-authored with Claire Smith (Allen and Unwin 2004).

John Carman has recently been appointed as Birmingham University Research Fellow in Heritage Valuation. He specializes in archaeological heritage management, from which his interest in the history of archaeology particularly derives, and in archaeological approaches to warfare, especially studying historic battlefields as cultural landscapes. Previous publications include the books *Valuing Ancient Things: Archaeology and Law* (1996), *Archaeology and Heritage: An Introduction* (2002), *Against Cultural Property: Archaeology, Heritage and Ownership* (2005), and *Bloody Meadows: Investigating Cultural Landscapes of Battle* (with Patricia Carman, 2006). He has also edited *Managing Archaeology* (with Malcolm Cooper, Anthony Firth, and David Wheatley, 1995), *Material Harm: Archaeological Studies of War and Violence* (1997), and *Ancient Warfare: Archaeological Approaches* (with Anthony Harding, 1999). Other research interests include the social archaeology of archaeological practice and archaeological theory.

Glenna Dean is the State Archaeologist of New Mexico and works for the Historic Preservation Division, Department of Cultural Affairs, in Santa Fe. Holding graduate degrees in archaeology and botany, she specializes in archaeobotany, the study of people's interactions with plants as revealed in charred seeds, broken plant parts, pollen grains, basketry, sandals, and other textiles made of plant fiber. Her duties as State Archaeologist balance the review of work by professional archaeologists, coordination with law enforcement agencies on archaeological looting, and fostering understanding of archaeological goals and preservation among lay-public audiences. She has published technical articles in *American Antiquity* (2004), *North American Archaeologist* (1986), *Journal of Ethnobiology* (1993), *Proceedings of the American Association of Stratigraphic Palynology* (1998), and the volumes *The Illustrated Library of the Earth: Deserts* (Weldon Owen, 1994) and *Tobacco: Sacred Smoke, Silent Killer* (University of Oklahoma Press, 2000). Articles written for the general public have appeared in *The Chihuahuan Desert Discovery* (1984), *Handwoven* (1997), and *Spin-Off* (2000, 2003, 2005) magazines.

Michael Diplock is a graduate of the Department of Archaeology at Flinders University, Adelaide, South Australia. His main focus is rock art, although he is also interested in pedagogy, with a focus on contemporary Indigenous systems of knowledge and learning, in addition to early human cognitive development.

A. Gwynn Henderson received her PhD from the University of Kentucky and currently is staff archaeologist and education coordinator for the Kentucky Archaeological Survey. Her interests lie in researching the Late Prehistoric and Contact Period farming cultures of the middle Ohio River Valley, working with educators, and writing for the public. Her most recent publications include articles in *The Encyclopedia of Prehistory, Volume 6: North America* (2001) with David Pollack; *Southeastern Archaeology* (2002) with David Pollack and Christopher T. Begley; the National Trust for Historic Preservation's *Forum Journal* (2004) with Linda S. Levstik; *DIG Magazine* (2004) with W. Stephen McBride; *Ohio Archaeology: An Illustrated Chronicle of Ohio's Ancient American Indian Cultures*, (2005); and the *International Review of History Education, Volume 4* (2005) with Linda S. Levstik and Jennifer S. Schlarb.

Gail Higginbottom is the Sites and Monuments Records Manager for the Glamorgan Gwent Archaeological Trust in Wales and currently participates in a national initiative to enhance local SMRs. She has worked at universities in Australia and the United Kingdom, including the University of Newcastle-upon-Tyne where she taught theory and prehistoric archaeology. Her own research focuses upon the connection between monuments, landscape, and belief systems and her published papers include 'Orientations of the dolmens of west-central France' (with Michael Hoskin, 2002) and 'Incorporating the natural environment: investigating landscape and monument as sacred space' (with Andrew Smith, Ken Simpson and Roger Clay, 2001). Gail works with GIS and quantitative analyses, as well as more interpretative approaches. Her current work focuses upon notions of time in prehistory.

Morag Kersel is a doctoral candidate at the University of Cambridge studying the legal trade in antiquities in the Middle East. She was a consulting archaeologist with the Cultural Heritage Office, United States Department of State, from 2000 to 2003. She is a co-editor of the Antiquities Market section of the *Journal of Field Archaeology* and a co-editor of *Archaeology, Cultural Heritage, and the Trade in Antiquities* (University of Florida Press, 2006).

Melinda Leach is an Associate Professor and Chair of the Department of Anthropology at the University of North Dakota. She has conducted archaeological field research for the last 30 years in the American desert West (California, Nevada, New Mexico, and Texas). Her research and teaching interests include gender in prehistory, human evolutionary ecology, foragers, textiles, and lithic production systems. She also explores issues of student learning and assessment in higher education. Some of her publications include 'Great Basin Peoples' (2001, *Encyclopaedia of the Ancient World*, Salem Press); 'In Search of Gender in Great Basin Prehistory' (1999, in C. Beck [editor] *Models for the Millennium: Great Basin Anthropology Today*, University of Utah Press); and 'Reflection and Integration: Program Assessment through an Anthropology Senior Capstone Seminar' (2005).

Jane Lydon is a Postdoctoral Fellow at the Centre for Australian Indigenous Studies at Monash University, and has worked as a historical archaeologist on numerous sites and projects around Australia. Between 2000 and 2002 she developed and coordinated a new heritage management program at La Trobe University, and with Tracy Ireland, has edited a book collection titled *Object Lessons: Archaeology and Heritage in Australia*, which explores how Australian society uses the past and its material remains (2005, Australian Scholarly Publishing). Her publications include a study of Chinese-European interaction in Sydney, published as *Many Inventions: The Chinese in the Rocks 1890–1930* (1999, Monash Publications in History), and a book about colonial photography on Aboriginal missions, emphasizing the role of Indigenous people, titled *Eye Contact: Photographing Indigenous Australians* (2005, Duke University Press). She is currently working in collaboration with the Indigenous community on an interdisciplinary project at Ebenezer Mission, northwestern Victoria.

Sarah E. Miller serves as staff archaeologist for the Kentucky Archaeological Survey. She supervises excavations at Ashland, the Henry Clay Estate in Lexington, Kentucky, where over 1,000 students visit each year to participate in the ongoing dig. In addition to archaeology education, she is interested in applied archaeology (projects that promote social change within communities), cemetery studies, conservation of artifacts, and site protection. Papers presented and in preparation include 'The south will rise or be razed, again!: A community's perspective on the benefits of archaeology', 'Warning, recent finds may cause scales to grow all over your body!: The blessings and the curses of the Picadome Time Capsule Project', and 'Keeping on the sunny side: Evaluating the educational potential of disturbed sites in the bluegrass'.

Clive Orton is Professor of Quantitative Archaeology at University College London Institute of Archaeology. His main research interests are in archaeological method, from research design through data acquisition and analysis to interpretation, all of which he sees as inextricably linked with statistics and quantitative methods. These interests have been pursued in various aspects of archaeology, in particular ceramic studies, sampling and surveys in fieldwork and museums, and 'everyday' uses of statistical approaches to refine archaeological arguments. He has written part or all of *Spatial Analysis in Archaeology* (1976), *Mathematics in Archaeology* (1980), *Pottery in Archaeology* (1993), and *Sampling in Archaeology* (2000) and is collaborating in an INTAS-funded project involved in the excavations of medieval Novgorod in Russia. This project is about to come to fruition in a series of four volumes, one of which – *The Pottery from Medieval Novgorod and Its Region* (2006) – he has edited, with contributions from several Russian authors.

K. Anne Pyburn is Professor of Anthropology and Gender Studies at Indiana University, Bloomington, director of the MATRIX Project (http://www.indiana.edu/%7Earch/saa/matrix/homepage.html), principal investigator for the Chau Hiix Project (http://www.indiana.edu/~overseas/flyers/chauhiix.html), and co-editor (with Nick Shepherd) of *Archaeologies: The Journal of the World Archaeological Congress* (http://www.altamirapress.com/RLA/journals/Archaeologies/index.shtml). She writes about ancient women (*Ungendering Civilization*, Routledge, 2002), the Ancient Maya ('The hydrology of Chau Hiix', 2003, *Ancient Mesoamerica* 14), archaeological ethics ('We have never been postmodern', in *Maya Archaeology at the Millennium*, Routledge 2003), teaching ('What are we really teaching in archaeological field schools?' in *Ethical Issues in Archaeology,* AltaMira, 2003), and community engagement ('Archaeology for a new millennium: The rules of engagement' in *Archaeologists and Local Communities: Partners in Exploring the Past*, Society for American Archaeology, 2003).

Susan Renoe received bachelors and masters degrees in anthropology from the University of Missouri-Columbia and masters and doctoral degrees in education from the University of California-Santa Barbara. Her dissertation research was an ethnographic study of an introductory archaeology course that focused on two things: how archaeology was presented to students through the various media of the course and how that version of archaeology was re-presented by students through their written texts. Her current research interests include public archaeology, archaeology education, and increasing minority participation in science.

Susan is currently the Assistant Director of the Office of Undergraduate Research at the University of Missouri-Columbia.

Patricia E. Rubertone is an Associate Professor in the Department of Anthropology at Brown University, Providence, Rhode Island. Her research combines archaeology, history, and anthropology to study questions of colonialism, landscape and memory, and cultural diversity. She has conducted archaeological fieldwork in New England, where she has collaborated with the Narragansett Indians, and in the American Southwest and Morocco. Among her publications are *Grave Undertakings: An Archaeology of Roger Williams and the Narragansett Indians* (Smithsonian Institution Press, 2001) and 'The historical archaeology of Native Americans' in *Annual Review of Anthropology* (2000). She is currently exploring tensions between commemoration and myths of Indigenous extinction through an archaeological study of Native American monuments.

Claire Smith is an Associate Professor in the Department of Archaeology at Flinders University, Adelaide, South Australia. She specializes in rock art, gender, and Indigenous archaeology and has conducted fieldwork with Indigenous communities in Australia, Asia, and North America. Her current research interests lie in decolonizing archaeology and she is president of the World Archaeological Congress. Her recent publications include *Country, Kin and Culture: Survival of an Aboriginal Community* (Wakefield Press, 2004), *The Archaeologist's Field Handbook* (with Heather Burke, Allen and Unwin, 2004) and the edited volume, *Indigenous Archaeologies: Decolonizing Theory and Practice* (with H. Martin Wobst, Routledge, 2005).

Having completed her honors degree in psychology, **Abigail Stein** trained as a primary school teacher and has taught in many countries including England, Uganda, and Portugal. She currently teaches in Adelaide, and is interested in teaching with remote Aboriginal communities in central Australia.

M. Jay Stottman is a staff archaeologist at the Kentucky Archaeological Survey, a PhD student at the University of Kentucky, and a part-time lecturer at the University of Louisville. His interests lie in urban, historical, and public/educational archaeology. He co-developed the award-winning 'Building Blocks of History' educational program at Riverside, the Farnsley-Moremen Landing in Louisville, Kentucky, that features archaeological excavation field trips for nearly 5,000 children a year. He has taken an interest in applied archaeology and is editing a volume on archaeology activism. His most recent publications include an article in *Historical Archaeology* titled 'Out of Sight, Out of Mind, Privy Architecture and the Perception of Sanitation' (2000), the public booklet *Bringing the Past into the Future: The Reconstruction of the Detached Kitchen at Riverside* with Patti Linn (Kentucky Archaeological Survey, 2003), and 'Consumer market access in Louisville's 19th century commercial district' in *Ohio Valley Historical Archaeology* (2001).

H. Martin Wobst is interested in the theory of archaeology, the theory of method, Indigenous archaeologies, and the materialities of U.S. society and of societies that are contrastive to it. In the Palaeolithic, he was a Palaeolithic archaeologist, but today, he is more interested in how archaeology helps to construct the present, and how material culture, such as toilets, helps to constitute individuals and social groups. He is currently Professor at the University of Amherst at Massachusetts. His most recent publication is the edited volume *Indigenous Archaeologies: Decolonizing Theory and Practice* (with Claire Smith, Routledge, 2005).

Larry J. Zimmerman is Professor of Anthropology and Museum Studies and Public Scholar of Native American Representation at Indiana University-Purdue University Indianapolis and the Eiteljorg Museum. His research interests include North American archaeology and Indigenous relations to archaeology.